Tourism and Modernity in China

An important feature of China's rapid modernization has been the rise of a consumer society in the cities. Retail, entertainment, leisure and tourism industries have developed quickly to help service the ever expanding consumer demands of China's new cosmopolitans. However, big changes are also taking place in rural areas as consumption patterns continue to grow and diversify.

Tourism and Modernity in China explores how the experience of modernization is revealed in its newly constructed tourist landscapes. It argues that in China's burgeoning ethnic tourist villages and theme parks can be seen all the contradictions, debasement, and liberating potentials of Chinese modernity. Tim Oakes uses the province of Guizhou to examine the Chinese tourist industry as an example of the state's modernization policies and how local people have engaged with these changes.

This book offers some important new perspectives on the experience of modernity in China. In particular it reveals the dynamic responses of ethnic minorities as they encounter the forces of state-sponsored modernization in the form of tourism development.

Tim Oakes is an Assistant Professor of Geography at the University of Colorado at Boulder, USA.

Routledge Studies on China in Transition
Series Editor: David S.G. Goodman

Tourism and Modernity in China

Tim Oakes

London and New York

First published 1998
by Routledge
11 New Fetter Lane, London EC4P 4EE

Simultaneously published in the USA and Canada
by Routledge
29 West 35th Street, New York, NY 10001

© 1998 Tim Oakes

Typeset in Times by Routledge
Printed and bound in Great Britain by TJ International, Padstow, Cornwall

British Library Cataloguing in Publication Data
A catalogue record for this book is available from the British Library

Library of Congress Cataloguing in Publication Data
A catalogue record for this book has been requested

ISBN 0–415–18850–4

Contents

Illustrations

Tables

Figures

Series Editor's preface

In the late 1970s, as China's reform era opened, the Communist Party of China committed itself to first doubling and then redoubling the aggregate size of the economy of the People's Republic of China by the end of the millennium. At the time, and into the early and mid-1980s, it was a prospect greeted as a desirable aspiration by most academic observers of China, but as little more. Many economists in particular pointed out the difficulties in the project and the near-impossibility of its achievement. In the event the target was attained with almost five years to spare, some time in 1995.

The rapid growth of China's economy is a useful starting point for this series, intellectually as well as chronologically. It is not only that China has developed so spectacularly and so quickly, nor that in the process its experience has proved some economists to be too cautious. Rather, its importance is to demonstrate the need for explanatory theories of social and economic change to adapt and change as they encompass the processes underway in China, and not to assume that previous assumptions about either China or social change in general are immutable.

China in Transition aims to participate in these intellectual developments through its focus on social, political, economic, and culture change in the China of the 1990s and beyond. Its aim is to draw on new, often cross-disciplinary, research from scholars in East Asia, Australasia, North America, and Europe, as well as that based in the more traditional disciplines. In the process the series will not only interpret the consequences of reform in China, but will also monitor and reflect the changes of the future.

The manipulation of Chinese culture is by no means a new phenomenon, but with the decentralization and the drive for economic development that has been at the heart of the reform era, the encouragement of local identities and cultures has taken on new dimensions. This impact of the reform era is particularly acute in the tourism industry, largely undeveloped before the 1980s. Tourism not only thrives on the construction of new and "different" cultures and identities, but to some extent needs to ensure the perception of an exotic culture gap between the tourists and the sites of their adventures.

In the Southwest China province of Guizhou – distant from the epicentre of the economic boom of the 1980s and politically distinct not least because of its high proportion of non-Han Chinese minority groups – tourism has become regarded as an essential part of its comparative advantage in the province's response to the imperatives of economic reform. As Timothy Oakes highlights, this has resulted in a series of paradoxes that go a long way to explaining the tensions and ambiguities inherent in the project of modernity. These tensions and ambiguities are particularly acute in an environment such as Guizhou, where modernity interacts with an acute multiculturalism. One, and in many ways the most obvious paradox, is that modernity is being brought to the province by stressing tradition, no matter that the traditions in question may have all but disappeared from contemporary practice or may even be complete (re)constructions. However, another – and to some considerable extent more important – paradox, is that the process of construction of local identities is not after all so easily controlled. It is often far from clear precisely whose identity is being articulated, by whom and for whom. Tourism in Guizhou is not only a state-sponsored process of national integration and cultural development, but also a discourse that can be appropriated by locals, including those who are the object of tourism.

David S.G. Goodman
Institute for International Studies, UTS
February 1998

Preface

Many of the ideas in this book came to me during 14 months of travel in China in 1987 and 1988. At that time, I was pursuing an extravagantly far-fetched project of examining the symbolic transformations of the Long March as an ever-changing metaphor for China's revolution. My idea was to travel the actual Long March route while interviewing people about the meaning of this singularly expressive event of the communist revolution in the context of the post-Mao reforms. Most people I talked to were understandably baffled about my intent, although they always had plenty to say about the changes they had lived through. Yet, beyond the ostensibly academic concerns of the project itself, it was a journey of many great discoveries, both about China and about myself. It was during the course of this journey, for example, that I abandoned my initial desires to study Chinese literature, and instead embarked on a pursuit of ideas that brought me to cultural geography. More importantly, though, was the fact that I found it increasingly difficult to distinguish myself, as an aspiring scholar, from the many other "back-packing" travelers I encountered in the far flung hinterlands of China's interior. I grew increasingly fascinated by these connoisseurs of authenticity who vigilantly searched for the last vestiges of some mythical pre-contact China. Committed followers of the sublime, they traded with each other in the currency of pure experience, swapping stories of peasant families stayed-with, and villages-found, where each of them was sure that he or she had been "the first foreigner" to penetrate the virgin terrain of one of the last travel frontiers on earth. My simultaneous attraction to their quest, and discomfort at the ease with which they wrote-off places and people "done," became the driving curiosity behind this book. I entered this research, then, with the explicit purpose of recovering a dynamic human dimension to the people who so often served as the "raw material" for the exotic fantasies of Western travelers.

That initial journey through China would not have been possible without the generous support of the Thomas J. Watson Foundation. The Watson Fellows program not only supported my travel, but allowed me the freedom to allow the journey to unfold in its own unpredictable ways. Financial support for fieldwork in 1993–4 was provided by the National Science Foundation and the United States Information Agency. The USIA grant was administered by the Committee on Scholarly Communication with China, whose organizational assistance contributed much to the successful completion of my fieldwork. I am grateful for the help I received from many people in China, only a few of whom can be listed here. Professors Guo Laixi of the Chinese Academy of Sciences and Chen Yongxiao of Guizhou Normal University sponsored my research and offered valuable advice and suggestions. An Yulun assisted with translation and interpretation. Zhu Guihua, Liu Xiuluan, and Dui Jianfeng provided vital information about and contacts within Guizhou's tourism industry. Fieldwork in Qiandongnan would have been nearly impossible without the enthusiastic cooperation of Pan Xinxiong. Liao Rujun, Wang Shengxian, Lu Genming, Jun Mingyu, Pan Yuzhen, Feng Jinguo, and Chen Yuhui all provided valuable assistance in Qiandongnan.

I am grateful to Wing Shing Tang for his help in Hong Kong, and for his comments and suggestions regarding this project. I would also like to acknowledge my colleagues in the "Guizhou school" of Chinese cultural studies: Siu Woo Cheung and Louisa Schein. Their work was instrumental as I began to develop the project in its early stages. Louisa was also very helpful during the first month of fieldwork in 1993; her work remains an inspiration to me.

In Seattle, I would like to thank my dissertation supervisory committee collectively for their trust and support: Kam Wing Chan, Lucy Jarosz, Stevan Harrell, Victoria Lawson, William Beyers, and Ann Anagnost. Many thanks also to James Bell, Patricia Price, Rachel Silvey, Linda Becker, and Doug Mercer. I would like to thank my parents for giving me such support and for helping me cultivate my curious mind. And finally, ten thousand "thank yous" to Julie – for everything.

Portions of this book have previously appeared in published form. Grateful appreciation is acknowledged to the University of Hawaii Press for the reproduction of some material in Chapter 5, originally appearing in *Tourism, Ethnicity, and the State in Asian and Pacific Societies* (M. Picard and R. Wood, eds, 1997). Lyrics by Joe Jackson, from the 1986 album *Big World*, are reproduced with permission, courtesy of Pokazuka Ltd.

T.S.O.
Boulder, Colorado
October 1997

Introduction

"What are *you* doing here?" The American woman suddenly lowered the shiny black Nikon from her eye, having just trained its peering lens directly upon me, and stared at me directly, her view now unmediated by the camera's authenticating frame. She asked again, "Who *are* you?" There was a mixture of surprise, incredulity, and downright anger on her now fully revealed face. To say our encounter, here at the gateway to a Miao village deep in the misty folded mountains of southwestern China, was laden with irony would be an understatement. Not only was this American tourist meeting another American among the women and men welcoming her to their village with an elaborate ceremony of music, wine, and song, but I was myself dressed – like the rest of the welcomers – in elaborate Miao festival costume. Add to this the fact that it was a *woman's* costume that I wore as I offered the American tourist a bull's horn full of potent rice wine, and the true richness of this ironic encounter becomes even clearer. The dissonance between the humor of my role playing and the woman's shock and anger at the immediate and complete bursting of her carefully honed bubble of authenticity speaks volumes about the forces at work in the ethnic tourist encounter.

What was most revealing to me about the encounter, however, was not the privileged "back-stage" perspective that my dressing up as a Miao woman had afforded. No, that perspective could too easily translate into bemused contempt for the hapless tourist as she sought out an exotic fantasy in the village where I had now been living for a month. I knew better than that. I was no "insider" by any means, and could not hold my own fantasies of "belonging" against this woman in order to valorize myself as some kind of elite adventurer, exiled among the natives. Rather, what was revealing was the knee-slapping jocularity that surrounded the event. The villagers were having far more fun putting me on display for the tourists than I was having in offending this woman's touristic sensibilities. It had been their idea, and it was their show, and I was their latest, most exotic prop for a ritual that had been repeated thousands of times for countless tour groups over the past decade and a half.

I recalled how the morning had unfolded. Shaman Chen, the village tourism director, had announced over breakfast that an American tour group was coming to the village. This filled him with considerable glee. "Your people are coming," he would say, giving me a playful nudge, "you must be very happy!" Word quickly spread throughout the village that the day's scheduled reception was to be for an American group, and soon there was a discernible buzz of excitement at the prospect of entertaining people from the same place as myself. This was a special occasion, deserving something more than the standard reception routine. Some of the older women in the village, Shaman Chen's wife among them, hit upon the idea of dressing me up in festival costume. Implicitly, this meant *women's* costume, since the most striking ornamentation was always reserved for women's clothing; women were always dressed up as beautifully wrapped prizes in a festival tradition that primarily served as a social stage for courtship rituals between young men and women from different villages.

I had already been apprehensive about meeting the Americans. I knew that they would be a discriminating group of elite tourists, experts in authenticity. They would be unhappy with the village, I expected. Its standardized reception program, its persistent and aggressive hawking of souvenirs, the Mickey Mouse and Hello Kitty T-shirts worn by the girls under their festival jackets, these would disappoint the Americans. They would not be fooled by the village and its "staged authenticity." Not that their Chinese tourist counterparts were themselves fooled when they visited the village. They knew they were getting a performance too. The difference was that Chinese tourists *expected* a performance and generally had a fun time during their visits, drinking wine, dancing with the natives, and themselves dressing up in costume. The Americans and Europeans came looking for the "real." Their travel became an exquisitely strategized quest of debunking the tourist traps thrown at them and somehow maneuvering behind the veil to discover the real China. The village where I was staying would simply be written off as another obstacle in that ultimate quest. My presence there would only confirm this. More troubling, even, was that I knew I would be expected to tell them how to find the *real* villages, now that this one had clearly been spoiled.

I protested that the Americans wouldn't appreciate seeing me dressed up as a Miao woman. "Nonsense," sputtered Shaman Chen's wife with a dismissive wave of her tiny hand, "you'll look *beautiful!*"

"But I'll feel embarrassed," I insisted.

This only unleashed a chorus of cackles from the women who had gathered around, ready to do their work on me, just as they prepared their own daughters for a festival. My discomfort only encouraged them. Indeed, my embarrassment would be their prize, a briefly savored moment of the white man emulating *them*, rather than the other way around, as was normally the case in a region ever desperate for any kind of modernity.

As the scheduled arrival time neared, Shaman Chen began his usual routine of administering the reception program and making sure everyone

Figure I.1 Japanese tourist at the village of Langde

Figure I.2 Beijing tourist "going ethnic" at Shidong's *Zimeifan* festival

was in place. He carried a big battery-powered megaphone and bellowed commands that echoed across the narrow valley. Older men put on long home-spun robes and gathered along the entrance path. Each carried a *mangtong*, a pipe-shaped bamboo horn that produced the deep sound of a distant foghorn, a sound not so much heard as felt. A group of younger men gathered near the village gate bearing *lushengs*, multi-piped horns reminiscent of bagpipes or a concert of Andean flutes. Women were setting up tables along the entrance path; each table was equipped with a clay pot of rice wine and several small cups. The women wore brilliant blue jackets decorated with silver ornaments, tall silver headdresses, and long dark blue skirts.

The Americans soon pulled up in a sleek Japanese van, accompanied by an unctuous entourage of tour guides from the various hierarchies of China's International Travel Service: the state guide who accompanied the group for the duration of their trip through China, the guide from the provincial capital, and a pair of guides from the prefectural capital thirty miles down the river. The local guides knew the routine and began herding the group into a line to march up the entrance path toward the village gate. More eager to start taking pictures of the spectacle laid out before them than join the performance itself, the Americans proved difficult cattle to round up. But finally they began the obligatory march through the gauntlet of women proffering "road block wine" (*lanlujiu*) while being serenaded from above by the orchestra of *mangtong* and *lusheng*. I was positioned with the last group of wine-bearing women, in front of the village gate. We offered not the small cups of wine encountered along the path below, but whole bull horns full of the stuff, and it was perhaps this final intoxicating hurdle more than anything that put the Nikon-toting American over the edge when she suddenly registered my presence. It was, perhaps, too much for her to take – a theme-park style performance (when all she really wanted was to see the *real* village going about its daily tasks as if she wasn't there), enforced drinking of multiple cups of rice liquor (it wasn't even *noon* yet), and now this white man mocking her with his costume and annoying greeting, "Welcome to the village!"

Not one of the Americans took my picture. The local guides, however, thought this great fun, and posed with me for multiple pictures, a few of which later appeared in various provincial and prefectural newspapers. Their delight at this new, exotic addition to the village's welcoming routine resonated with that of the villagers, who savored with relish each encounter between myself and the tourists as they hurried past, trying to avoid this final and most daunting drinking obligation in which all the racial and gendered norms driving their tourist experience were playfully tossed to the wind. Although this cross-dressing charade had purportedly been conjured for the entertainment of my own "native people" (that is, the Americans), it was clear that I had been put on display for the villagers themselves. This subversion of the dominant ethnic tourist experience – where the native is

Figure I.3 On display at Shidong's *Zimeifan* festival

Figure I.4 Preparing to meet tourists at Langde

put on display for the tourist to gaze upon and fantasize about – marks a local subjectivity that subtly disturbs our assumptions about the colonizing powers of tourism in the Fourth World.

What was going on here was more than the straightforward procedure of Western tourists descending upon some impoverished, tradition-bound village, injecting their money and modern ideas for better or worse. This was not simply the buying and selling of a tourist experience, a project that entails significant consequences for the future cultural practices and expressions of identity among locals. These familiar processes were occurring to be sure, but what I witnessed was also an elaborate staging of desire and the purposeful manipulation of contradictions. Far from the reproduction of a "traditional" village welcoming ceremony, the village's tourist reception program was a ritualized encounter with modernity itself. It was not until I myself was enlisted to play a role in this ritual that I began to understand that the welcoming ceremony was not just the tired replaying of an old tradition now trivialized by touristic commercialism. It was also a staging of modernity, in which all the contradictions of a new political and economic order were served up for interpretation, understanding, and ultimately, reclamation by the villagers themselves.

To make such a claim requires a considerable amount of ground-laying. Ultimately, this book offers an argument about modernity in which rural

Figure I.5 Singapore tourists drinking *lanlujiu* ("road-block wine") at the village of Changlinggang

Chinese villagers in a far-flung and impoverished place can be considered as modern subjects. That argument requires an approach to modernity that finds the construction of new subjectivities not only possible within the often alienating experience of Chinese modernization, but also imaginable beyond the "streets of the city" where modernity is so often thought to be located. At first glance, the geographical setting for this book, China's southwestern province of Guizhou – a place neither well known for its tourism nor thought to be, by any means, modern – seems to contradict the very spirit of a book about modernity in China. Why not address the meaning of modernity in China's hyperventilating cities where a host of new studies have been discovering a new world of Chinese modernism "on the street"?[1] And if tourism is the subject, why not go to the Great Wall, the gardens of Suzhou, or the fairytale landscape of Guilin's karst pillars? These places see millions of tourists each year, while Guizhou's tourist villages receive only a small handful. But it is precisely because of Guizhou's poverty and peripherality that I chose to explore my argument there. For modernity is not a geographically defined "thing" that exists here but not there. It is not a "goal" to be reached through progressive state interventions of "modern-ization." Modernity, I will argue, is a tense and paradoxical *process* through which people produce, confront, and negotiate a particular kind of socio-economic change. As such, it is experienced just as profoundly in a Guizhou village as on the streets of Shanghai.

Yet despite this claim about the nature of modernity, one which I will elaborate further below and throughout the chapters that follow, people in Guizhou clearly *think* of modernity as a very specific objective, an objective that they have not yet reached. Two meanings of modernity thus pervade my analysis. One is what I've termed the "false modern" – that is, the utopian, teleological modernity of nineteenth- and twentieth-century historicism, of the nation-state, and of the institutions of rationalism and scientific objec-tivity. It is this sense of modernity that people in Guizhou believe they are pursuing, and the industrialized West remains their most significant model for that pursuit. The other meaning might be termed an "authentic modern," though not "authentic" in terms of some discernible modern "essence," but rather in terms of a process-oriented approach to modernity, one in which human subjectivity is ambivalently but irrevocably engaged in a struggle over the trajectory of socio-economic change. While the people of Guizhou may not think they have achieved modernity, their desire to "be modern" is in fact an expression of "authentic" modern sensibilities and a recognition of the struggle they find themselves engaged in: how to derive a better, more liberated life from the forces of change swirling around them.[2]

Guizhou is a province steeped in desire. The enticements of consumption, the convenience of technology, and the freedom to be more than a strug-gling farmer – these things weigh heavily on the minds of the rural population. Even in the cities, the stigma of "backwardness" remains a preoccupation among urbanites who have little more to do with their money than visit karaoke bars or watch videos that only reinforce how much better people have it in Hong Kong, Taiwan, or Los Angeles. But, as Chapter 3 will argue, "backwardness" is less an inherent condition than a product of broader forces. It is these forces – structural processes that have conspired to produce in Guizhou a chronic condition of political and economic dependency since the province's founding in the fifteenth century – that, ironically, have established the condition of modernity in Guizhou. For they help create an atmosphere of desire – desire for affluence, for freedom – even as they effectively assert the continuing inaccessibility of these things. The struggle between desire and imprisonment is what defines the modern condition in Guizhou.

Imprisonment is perhaps an awkward metaphor to use here. Certainly life in Guizhou has imprisoning qualities. Locals refer to Guizhou as *men*, enclosed, covered with a tight lid, sealed off, depressed. Even the climate seems to evoke this feeling, with a heavy blanket of clouds perpetually hiding away each isolated valley and basin. Like the character *men* itself, Guizhou is a stifled heart. But the region can also be conceived as a frontier, a place of escape beyond the confines of civilization. This kind of positive spin on Guizhou's geography would be of little consolation to those desperately seeking alignment with China's core or with the industrialized West, but it does speak to both the historical process of Guizhou's development as well as the contemporary marketability of tourism there. Guizhou is an exotic place of exile, of escape – just the sort of place metropolitan tourists are looking for in their quest for a "real" experience.

"Internal colony" is how a number of scholars have characterized Guizhou (Spencer 1940; Goodman 1983). The province straddles a rugged plateau of eroded limestone mixed with rumpled folds of clastic mountains. Guizhou is a topographical maze that for centuries proved resilient against the encroachment of imperial Chinese culture as it seeped its way into the valleys and alluvial plains of southern China. It remained, instead, a region of rebellious natives, hostile chieftains, and exiled officials. Indeed, exile seems to be Guizhou's most consistent claim to fame. The famous "Young Marshall" Zhang Xueliang cooled his heels in Guizhou after staging a mutiny against Chiang Kai Shek during the war with the communists. The entire Communist Party Politburo, for that matter, conducted one of its most important meetings ever while "exiled" during the Long March in Guizhou. It was at that meeting, in Zunyi, that Mao Zedong emerged as the undisputed leader of the Party.

But Guizhou's claim as a space of exile or escape is for the most part an infamous one, the stigma of a province that has been unfit to be included in China's classical core cultures. Rather, Guizhou is regarded – even today – as a region of abject poverty, uncivilized minority tribes, and general dreariness. Over one-third of the population consists of some 33 officially recognized "minority nationalities" (*shaoshu minzu*). Only Yunnan and Xinjiang are home to more minority groups in China. Of Guizhou's 33 groups, the Miao, Bouyei, Dong, and Tujia are the most numerous. In a province already desperately short of good-quality arable land, minority groups tend to dominate in the regions where poverty is greatest. This can largely be attributed to the quality of their land holdings – which is generally poor due to thin, acid soils distributed on rocky slopes – and their relative isolation due to lack of infrastructure throughout the mountainous terrain. Even most county towns in the province are difficult to reach on the few narrow winding roads that have been built.

Historically, Guizhou was indeed something of a refuge for many of these groups. As Chinese culture and civilization gradually spread southward, the southerners who predated the Chinese were either assimilated into the Chinese cultural stew (becoming "cooked" as it was called), or they resisted (remaining "raw"). Those who resisted tended to concentrate in relatively inaccessible regions, such as Guizhou, where eking out a difficult living in a harsh environment would be the price of staying out of the imperial orbit. One popular myth of the origins of the Miao, for example, tells of a people who once lived in lowland prosperity but were forced to flee as the Chinese began to crowd them out. Going into exile, they lost their culture (their written language) as they crossed a deep river, thus explaining their contemporary lack of a written language. In Guizhou, the imperial government practiced an indirect form of administration that empowered native chieftains to rule over the local population as long as they supplied the obligatory taxes and tributes to the imperial court. The long process of dismantling this system during the late-imperial era – local chieftains were thought to be too powerful and oftentimes abusive – precipitated dozens of major rebellions in Guizhou during the eighteenth and nineteenth centuries. This only fueled the popular consensus that Guizhou remained a region dominated by "raw" people who shunned civilization and would prefer to live in poverty and darkness.

Mountains have long been regarded a curse by the poor people who must live on them. For affluent metropolitans, however, mountains have come to be appreciated for their aesthetic qualities. Visually stunning, the same mountain ridges that wall in impoverished communities allow metropolitan elites to escape their crowded, materialistic worlds for brief periods of physical and spiritual recuperation. Guizhou's mountains are not so much spectacular and imposing, as they are wild and bizarre. The predominance of limestone – and the relatively high rainfall – has yielded a porous landscape of immense caverns, subterranean rivers, waterfalls, deep gorges, and forests of gnarled rock formations. In an effort to finally cast off its "backward" status, the province began to embrace tourism enthusiastically in the early 1990s as a means of capital accumulation ideally suited to the very conditions that render Guizhou so poor: its captivating and cruel topography. In fact, provincial leadership indicts not only geography as the primary culprit for "backwardness", but the large proportion of minorities as well. These people, it has been claimed, lack sufficiently developed "culture" to achieve modernity, and thus represent something of a drag on the province overall. And so, tourism becomes doubly appropriate: tourists come to see fantastic scenery and get to experience some exotic native peoples as an added bonus. In the process, the minorities will become modernized, the landscape tamed, and Guizhou will finally become modern.[3]

The village in which I was staying was one of several dozen in the province that were being promoted for the development of ethnic tourism. It had received grants from the province in order to improve the village environment and make preparations for receiving tourists. As an officially recognized tourist village, it was essentially part of a larger state-sponsored modernization and development project. But while the state saw commercialized villages becoming well connected to broader markets as a specific goal of ethnic tourism development, the overall vision of modernity, as an objective, was clearly being defined on the state's terms. Ethnic groups were thus promoted as colorful and exotic components of Guizhou's overall marketability. On the one hand, solving their intransigent backwardness would allow the province to get on with the business of "becoming modern." But on the other hand, the prosperity of ethnic groups *per se* was not the core of the modernization agenda as much as attracting external capital investments for large-scale projects that would benefit the provincial economy overall. The role of ethnic tourism, then, was best summed up by *enticement*. Minority groups would be served up as the bait for profit-hungry outsiders who would quench the modern desires of Guizhou's elite with lucrative business contracts.

This easily could have been a book, then, about yet one more level of exploitation visited upon Guizhou's ethnic peoples. Indeed, the story of this new addition to the multifaceted experience of colonialism in Guizhou is woven throughout the chapters that follow. Tourism has, in many ways, been an alienating experience for the people whose "backwardness" it targets. But my purpose has not been to write a book about the tourism industry's exploitations *per se*, but to write about the experience of modernity in China. The state's version of that experience – for instance, the building of dams and bridges, the establishment of joint-venture enterprises, the securing of leisure resorts for the wealthy – offer us an accounting of the consumable victuals of a "false modernity," a modernity of spectacle, ostentatiousness and Olympian feats. This version of modernity was something villagers *lacked*, and that lack would make them marketable to tourists – the purveyors of a spectacular modernity desired by the state.

Yet while villagers clearly saw themselves as lacking modernity in many significant ways, they also asserted a modern subjectivity in their ability to stage the tourist experience, self-consciously play prescribed roles for tourists, and even irreverently turn those roles into acts of humor and subversion. They had succeeded as a tourist village not because they were more traditional, but because they were good at *playing* tradition. More than this, though, the tourism experience for the villagers had become an opportunity to stage the modern desires of both the tourists and the villagers alike. The contradiction between the tourist desire for authenticity and the village desire for modernity was managed in the elaborate staging of tradition, consumption, and commerce that welcomed tourists to the village. Tourists themselves legitimated the modern desires of villagers – not so much through their purchase of a performance and its associated souvenirs and photo opportunities, but simply through their presence and participation in the village's staging ritual. The tourists became, very briefly, exotic objects for the villagers to consume in their own way, a consumption that was made stunningly obvious when they dressed me up as a Miao woman to receive a group of American tourists.

In what way, then, can this be said to represent an "authentic" modern subjectivity on the part of the villagers? This book is largely devoted to answering that question. In the chapters that follow, the complex issues underlying that question will be unpacked and examined in detail. Chapter 1 discusses the relationship between tourism and modernity. It argues that tourism is a particularly meaningful metaphor for the experience of modernity in that it displays both modernity's relentlessly objectifying processes as well as its promise of new and liberating subjectivities for those participating in either side of the tourism encounter. The chapter seeks to establish the idea that tourism is not just a profoundly modern phenomenon, as MacCannell (1989) and Horne (1984) have argued, but that it offers an especially appropriate illustration of the paradoxical struggles between the objectifications of "false modernity" and the promise of an "authentic" modern subjectivity that is potentially liberating. The experience of modernity, here, is conceived as an on-going struggle for meaning within, along with a desire for repair of, the fragmentation, dislocation, and alienation that accompanies modernization. The idea of the "false modern" emerges as the seductive promise of a resolution to that struggle for meaning and desire for repair. Its primary agents are the nation-state and capital, and one of its principal vehicles is tourism, in which places saturated with tradition and authenticity are constructed and consumed. As such, tourism is marked by what I refer to as the "misplaced search for authenticity." That this search is misplaced, and that it represents a "false" conception of modernity, leads to the primary issue underlying Chapter 1: that "authenticity" and "tradition" are themselves modern sensibilities, and that modernity is not the careening, progressive counterpoint to these ideals, but is rather the tension-filled project of building a sense of identity – that is, a truly liberating subjectivity – in a chronically unstable and ever changing world. This approach to modernity is then explored in relation to China and the struggles over the meaning of Chinese modernity, and is used in interpreting the tourist landscapes being built as China's modernization and development ensues.

In Chapter 2 we examine theoretical approaches to tourism and place. Place becomes a pivotal concept in exploring the possibility for tourist

landscapes to be read and experienced as expressions of "authentic" modernity even as they are built to satisfy the quick-fix nostalgia of the false
modern in its voracious consumption of tradition and authenticity. The
chapter argues that the nation-state and capital are not the sole agents in
building a tourist landscape that capitalizes on public ambivalence towards
modernity. Rather, those upon whose bodies the tourist gaze falls strive
themselves to mediate the construction of that landscape in order to maintain their own subjectivity, to make their experience of modernization one
that is meaningful and potentially liberating. It is by directly manipulating
tourism's falsifications, for instance, that Guizhou villagers struggle to maintain their own authenticity, rather than through their resistance to or escape
from tourism's essentializing abstractions and objectifications. Indeed, I
argue that only by facing these dislocating falsifications can an "authentic"
modern subjectivity be attempted at all.

Chapter 3 seeks to situate the tourism experience in Guizhou within a
broader historical and geographical context, establishing the particular
conditions through which modernization in Guizhou has been experienced,
as well as the ways desires for modernity have been acted upon. The chapter
provides not simply a background to Guizhou tourism, but offers an argument about the power relations that have infused Guizhou's development
and modernization. The struggles over modernity in Guizhou take place on
a terrain in which power is distributed extremely unevenly. The context of
these struggles is thus not simply an historical geography of modernization
in Guizhou, but of Guizhou's *colonization*, first by the Chinese state, and
more recently by Chinese capital. The process of internal colonization has
left a distinctive mark on the kind of modernization experienced in
Guizhou, and on the imaginings of modernity among its people. The
chapter, then, examines the history and geography of Guizhou's colonization and explores the consequences of this for the kind of modernity
pursued in Guizhou in the 1990s.

Chapter 4 provides an analysis of the tourism industry in Guizhou and its
attendant cultural productions. While not denying the colonizing nature of
tourism in Guizhou, the chapter argues that the alienating potential of
tourism as a modern project is perhaps most significantly found in its
powers of representation rather than its logic of accumulation. Villagers are
not just integrated into the broader labor and commodity markets of the
state, but are more importantly expected to become willing performers of
"folk tradition" in terms that are deemed acceptable to the needs of the
abstract nation. This "tradition" is the modern product of a dominant state
and the forces of capital, each of which profits from its production in
different, though often complementary, ways. But precisely because tourism
is an industry driven by the powers of representation, it is also susceptible to
divergent interpretations and subversive reworkings of its dominant tropes.
It is in this context that we approach the case studies laid out in Chapter 5.
Four different village tourism experiences are examined, with each revealing

the kinds of subjective appropriation inherent in a more complex reading of modernity as a paradoxical process of establishing meaning in an ever shifting world. The chapter seeks to reveal, finally, that the village tourist encounter is one in which "authentic" modern subjectivities are being worked out by villagers themselves.

It remains, then, to provide a brief background to the approach to modernity that underlies this book. The discriminating between a "false" and "authentic" modernity that supports much of my analysis demands, in other words, a more committed defense before we proceed with the body of the book. That a "false" conception of modernity can be distinguished at all derives primarily from the general impression that modernity has been experiencing a severe crisis, its advocates increasingly reduced to conservative nationalists and apologists for capitalist development. Successive generations of intellectuals have been abandoning modernity *en masse* in favor of an ambiguous and tenuously defined post-modernity. Yet the very lack of clarity offered by the mixed bag of post-modern claims seems to speak to their prematurity. We do not as yet live in a post-modern world. Indeed, in China the obsession with achieving modernity remains paramount. As Anthony Giddens (1990: 163) argues, "we are currently living in a period of high modernity." It is in this age of what he terms modernity's "radicalization" that we may begin to speak of a "false" modernity, as well as imagine its "authentic" counterpoint.

The radicalization of modernity is characterized by Giddens as a period of its heightened reflexivity, or "modernity coming to understand itself." Inherent in the concept of modernity, for Giddens, is a fundamental quality of reflexivity, in which "social practices are constantly examined and reformed in the light of incoming information about those very practices, thus constitutively altering their character" (p. 38). Thus, it is not simply modernity's insatiable appetite for the new that drives it forward, but its "wholesale reflexivity" – a quality that proves fundamentally destabilizing to all fixed values and ideals. Far from providing a degree of scientific certitude, then, knowledge is continuously being revised through unrelenting reflection, criticism, and reconstruction. Much of modernity's chaotic experience emerges from the fact that "we can never be sure that any given element of that knowledge will not be revised" (p. 39). As Karl Popper put it, "all science rests upon shifting sand" (Popper 1962: 34). To experience modernity is to be faced with an seemingly infinite gauntlet of contradictions, and the pressure to resolve these, once and for all, is enormous.

Modernity "understanding itself" is precisely a realization that it is the contradictions, not their resolution, that lie at the heart of the modern project.

> Modernity turns out to be enigmatic at its core, and there seems no way in which this enigma can be "overcome." We are left with questions where once there appeared to be answers, and I shall argue subsequently

that it is not only philosophers who realize this. A general awareness of the phenomenon filters into anxieties which press in on everyone.

(Giddens 1990: 40)

This, then, helps us understand modernity in all its true complexity – as a condition of paradox, contradiction and basic anxiety that desperately demands, and yet simultaneously denies, constructions of meaning and identity to provide some stability on the "shifting sands" of reflexivity. The condition of anxiety which presses in on everyone, however, can yield not simply the on-going effort to construct a sense of identity – an effort I will discuss below as a practice of modern subjectivity – but also the uncritical acceptance of ready-made identities and social roles. These might include, for example, a patriotic national identity based on the institutions of the nation-state, or an occupational identity based on one's self-disciplining for the purpose of enabling the extraction of surplus value from one's labor power. These represent one's willing submission to the seductive promise of stability and resolution in the modern world. But this is a false promise that yields a narrow and imprisoning conception of modernity. It is, however, a false promise that for most of the nineteenth and twentieth centuries has proved so successful as to have become equated with modernity itself. The promise of a rational utopia as the teleological outcome of modernity has left a legacy in which the whole idea of modernity has been largely abandoned for a poorly defined alternative that can only be articulated as "something after modernity."

In its classical European form, of course, modernity emerged as the "light of reason," a product of the Enlightenment and its radical critique of the church as the purveyor of the absolute and arbitrary word of God (see Touraine 1995: 9–32). Fundamental to the idea of modernity was the principle of reason, and through reason the overpowering wholeness of a spiritually governed world could be broken down and reconstructed according to "natural" laws. Reason, in these terms, was a rebellious and highly critical idea. Nature came to replace the church as the origin and foundation of truths, and these truths applied not only to the so-called physical world "out there," but to the intellectual and moral world of humans. To be a rational person was to be "united with nature" in the most complete sense of the term, and to be modern meant to be engaged in rational activity that reflected the universal truths of nature. The pursuit of rationality, though, also meant an increasing differentiation of the realms of social life, for all activities and behavior needed to be judged upon the internal absolutes of reason rather than according to their relation to other activities. In this way, one's family activities could be separated from one's work activities, religion could be separated from politics, science separated from faith. This process of differentiation also entailed what Giddens (1990: 21–9) refers to as a "disembedding" of social activities from their broader historical-geographical contexts. For Giddens, disembedding means the removal of social relations from their immediate temporal-spatial present; modern people relate to each other across vast stretches of time and space – distances enabled by science and technology, and contemplated through reason – and this requires specific kinds of institutions that help us become "reembedded" at any given time and place. But disembedding requires that time and space be wrenched apart from each other and standardized as distinct and "empty" categories of science. Thus the very fabric of human existence – time and space – become subject to rationalization in order to complete the social differentiation necessary to operate in accordance to "natural law."

That modernity is very much based on the principle of reason, then, is undeniable. However, as Touraine argues, problems arise when rationality is marshaled in the pursuit of a modern society where reason becomes a set of laws governing the social body. Modernity's qualities of reflexivity make possible the imaginings of ever-more rational ways to unify humans with the world – even as its disembedding qualities take us farther and farther from such a unity. Modernization, then, becomes the set of procedures mustered in pursuit of what essentially becomes the ideology of rationality. It translates the principles of rationalism into political and social objectives (Touraine 1995: 61). Its rallying call is progress, which is articulated as the removal of obstacles to reason in our political and social lives. Insofar as progress entails an eventual end-point in which instrumental rationality finally triumphs in a brave new world of utopian reason, modernization is supported by historicism, the idea that we are moving ahead along a discernible trajectory of ever-increasing rationality.

While time becomes rationalized into historicism, space is reconfigured as the nation – the geographical embodiment of a rationally ordered society. The state emerges as the dominant purveyor of modernization through its mobilization of political power in support of social and economic progress within a demarcated container of space: the nation-state. Within this space, then, the process of rationalization means that local traditions and loyalties must be subordinated to the state, just as individuals must be subordinated to the society. At the same time, the "imagined community" (Anderson 1983) of the nation is offered as a new source of identity and stability to compensate for the disruptions of modernization's relentless removal of the "obstacles to reason" (Touraine 1995: 65). These disruptions are primarily achieved via the logic of capital accumulation as it seeks out ever more rational means of appropriating surplus labor power. It is in these terms – that is, in the service of the nation-state and of capital – that rationalism loses its critical edge and rebellious spirit. Indeed, it merely becomes an even more thorough instrument of oppression than the word of God it sought to displace.

Rationalization is a noble word when it introduces the scientific and critical spirit in to domains hitherto dominated by traditional authorities and the arbitrary decisions of the mighty; it becomes a fearful word when it designates Taylorism and other managerial methods which destroy the craft autonomy of workers and forces them to submit to rates of production and orders that claim to be scientific. They are of course no more than ways of maximizing profits and they pay no heed to the physiological, psychological and social realities of human labour.

(Touraine 1995: 91)

Similarly, the rationality of the nation too easily degenerates into a destructive nationalism manipulated by a modernizing, authoritarian state and its construction of an essential folk culture towards which all identities within the nation must converge. It is the increasingly inescapable realization of these dilemmas that has brought modernity to a crisis, raised the flag of a post-modern sea change among critical theorists, and made it possible to propose a more "authentic" alternative.

Nietzsche perhaps came closest to understanding the falsities underlying modernity as it came to be increasingly linked to an oppressive rationality in the service of the state and of capital (Berman 1992: 40). Modernity as such led only to nihilism and to the exhaustion of the soul. Its alienating qualities produced a deep nostalgia for Being, for immutability. As MacCannell and others have noted, nostalgia has become one of the driving elements behind what Urry (1990) refers to as the "tourist gaze." This particularly significant consequence of "false modernity" will be taken up more thoroughly in Chapter 1. But Nietzsche's attack on the utilitarian individualism of rationality, and his longing for a holism to overcome the disembeddedness of modernity too easily translates into a nostalgia manipulated by narrowminded nationalists and their destructive visions: thus Heidegger's Nietzsche-inspired alliance with Nazism. Nietzsche's critique of modernity is a fundamental starting point to imagining an authentic alternative, but we must ultimately look beyond it.

For Touraine (1995: 201–32), that alternative lies in recovering the idea of the Subject as too-often forgotten balance to the principle of reason that has predominantly characterized modernity. The crisis of false modernity, its teleological historicism in the name of progress, its oppressive rationalism, and the sheer coldness of what Weber called its disenchantment with the world, has made necessary the recovery of its buried rebelliousness and critical edge. This is particularly important given that subjectivity and identity have been regarded as largely irrelevant in much late twentieth-century social theory (Lash and Friedman 1992: 3). Modernity's critics have revealed the true depth of this crisis, but too often they have simultaneously denied the possibility of achieving any kind of authentic subjectivity within the experience of modernity. Nor can this perspective be limited to social theorists, such as Lyotard, conventionally allied with post-modernism. The critics of the Frankfurt School, for instance, saw in twentieth-century modernity the complete obliteration of any vestiges of unity between humans and the world. The Enlightenment's liberating project of reason was, for Horkheimer, ultimately perverted in Nazi Germany and its mass-produced culture of destructive nationalism. In condemning industrialism and the triumph of instrumental reason, however, the Frankfurt School effectively denied the possibility that human subjectivity could be conceived autonomously from the functionalist hegemony of advanced capitalism and its paranoid state. Gramsci, too, conceived of cultural hegemony as the product of a dominant political economy that infused subject positions from within, making an autonomous modern subject extremely difficult, though not completely impossible, to imagine. Alternative subjectivities were, for Gramsci, at once resistant to, and a product of, the social relations of dominance and subordination that characterized "Fordist" capitalism in the twentieth century.

But perhaps the most thorough critique of the possibility for an autonomous modern Subject has come from Foucault. Like Gramsci, Foucault realized that fundamental to the triumph of instrumental rationality was the hegemonic quality of its power. The modern power of the state and the capitalist class was not a unidirectional force of straightforward subjugation and disciplining in the interests of false modernity. Rather, power was reproduced through modern subject positions themselves. Rather than simply being concentrated within the institutions of the state and capital, power is everywhere and nowhere. Society is therefore governed not so much through the objectifications of instrumental rationality *per se* as through its normalizing "technologies of power." Modern subjectivity, then, arises within a terrain saturated with power, as a product of "the whole technology of power over the body that the technology of the 'soul' – that of educationalists, psychologists and psychiatrists – fails either to conceal or to compensate, for the simple reason that it is one of its tools" (Foucault 1977: 30). In these terms, then, modern subjectivity – that is "subjectivization" – cannot be imagined as autonomous from the subjection of instrumental reason.

For Touraine, this is not a definition of subjectivity at all. Rather it represents total objectification. Touraine argues, however, that even Foucault, like Gramsci, could not fail to recognize the constant disruptions and protests that forced the state and capital to generate yet another layer of power technology. While many see in Foucault's analytics a deep pessimism regarding the possibilities for any kind of liberating subjectivity, Touraine himself finds in Foucault the seeds of a whole new approach to conceiving a modernity where autonomous subjectivity is, ironically, possible, yet at the same time increasingly difficult to recognize as the same "revolutionary subject" imagined by Marx.[4] Touraine (1995: 170) claims that Foucault himself "comes close to recognizing that there are limits to the controls exercised by mechanisms of normalization, and therefore to recognizing the constant presence of a protesting or rebellious Subject." Foucault's technologies of power must principally be recognized as objectifying forces which generate a subjectivity that is at once rebellious and appropriating. Foucault thus might be credited for clearing the way to a radical new understanding of the paradoxical qualities of modern subjectivity. His work makes it necessary to recognize that the struggle for meaning and identity cannot but occur *within* the landscape of modern social power relations, and that this makes subjectivity a particularly constrained and contradictory process of negotiation.

Ultimately, though, we must depart Foucault's bracing analytics in order to assert that such a subjectivity might ultimately recover the rebellious and critical edge of modernist thought. Modernist subjectivity, as characterized by Berman, does not simply reproduce the normalizations of power, but maintains a wary tension between rationalism's objectifications and the need to claim for oneself the radical transformations that modernity promises.

> Modernists, as I portray them, are at once at home in this world and at odds with it. They celebrate and identify with the triumphs of modern science, art, technology, economics, politics: with all the activities that enable mankind to do what the Bible said only God could do: to "make all things new." At the same time, however, they deplore modernization's betrayal of its own human promise. Modernists demand deeper and more radical renewals: modern men and women must become the subjects as well as the objects of modernization; they must learn to change the world that is changing them, and to make it their own.
>
> (Berman 1992: 33)

Similarly, Giddens (1990: 53, 139) likens the experience of modernity to one of "riding the juggernaut." Modernity is not a "carefully controlled and well-driven motor car" but a "runaway engine of enormous power" that is capable of crushing all who resist and stand in its way. The struggle of the modern Subject is not over dismantling the engine itself, but over the steering wheel. Even Marx, for whom modern subjectivity could not even be imagined until the capitalist institutions of instrumental rationality were toppled once and for all, could not help but see modernity as an unfinished project ultimately subject to human control (Giddens 1990: 138). Touraine (1995: 207) summarizes this sentiment in stating that the central ethical principle of modernity is freedom. "Calls to serve progress or reason, or the State which is their secular arm, are less modern than calls for freedom and the right to take responsibility for one's life." This is not to argue that modernity can simply be reduced to individualism, which may be thought of as little more than an ideology of capitalist industrialization. Indeed, the struggle for an authentic modern subjectivity runs counter to the idea of the individual, perhaps the ultimate entrepreneurial agent of instrumental rationality. Rather, Touraine (1995: 202) imagines modern Subjects as a social movement, and as a collective of travelers:

We are all embarked on the adventure of modernity; the question is whether we are galley slaves or passengers with luggage who travel in hope, as well as being aware of the breaks we will have to make. Simmel saw the foreigner as the emblematic figure of modernity. Its emblem today is the emigrant, a traveller full of both memories and hopes who discovers and constructs himself in his daily attempt to connect past and future, a cultural heritage and membership in a socio-professional category.

With the image of the traveler-emigrant now before us, we also return to the world of the tourist. As will be discussed in Chapter 1, the tourist has similarly been conceived as the "emblematic figure of modernity." Yet we must qualify this as well, for two very important reasons. One is that if the modern Subject is a traveler, then what of the places that serve as the traveler's destinations? Are the inhabitants of these places incapable of a modern subjectivity independent of that experienced by their fleeting visitor? Surely they cannot be reduced to an exotic backdrop for the modern exile. Another reason is that travel cannot even be imagined as a modern experience without also recognizing its reliance on the uneven distribution of power. The emigrant, or Simmel's foreigner, cannot be isolated from society – for he may also be a refugee who does not have the luxury of constructing his new "membership in a socio-professional category." Along these lines, Caren Kaplan has argued that the tropes of travel, exile, and emigration – as fundamental expressions of modern subjectivity – must be recognized as having been produced within the historical and geographical contexts of imperialism, colonialism, patriarchy, and uneven development. The tourist-traveler-exile, Kaplan (1996: 57) argues, "cannot be universalized to stand for every subject position in modernity." Modern subjectivity, in other words, cannot be limited to the trope of one taking a journey. The tourist, as MacCannell has conceived her, is striving for meaning and continuity in a fragmented world; she seeks the exotic and authentic in an effort to displace the instrumental rationalism that has come to dominate her life. But her very search is also presaged upon the false modernist belief that tradition and authenticity are modernity's antithesis, not its own creation. Her search for authenticity is misplaced and ultimately fails to escape the teleology of the false modern. Equating the tourist with the modern Subject only reveals what Kaplan calls a middle-class Euro-American cultural myopia. The tourist may be an astute critic of instrumental rationalism, as MacCannell and Horne imply, but he remains a relatively privileged subject in a world of vast discrepancies in power and wealth. The tourist is "a specifically Euro-American construct who marks shifting peripheralities through travel in a world of structured economic asymmetries" (Kaplan 1996: 63).

Kaplan's critique highlights two important issues that present themselves as we prepare to translate these ideas into the Chinese context. One is the need for consistent vigilance against equating modern subjectivity with individualized voluntarism. The modern Subject, here, is not the High modernist identity envisioned by Weber and Habermas, a subjectivity privileging the "cognitive and moral over the aesthetic and the libidinal, the ego over the id, the visual over touch, and discursive over figural communication," as well as "the individual over the community" (Lash and Friedman 1992: 5). The possibility for an authentic modern subjectivity remains profoundly conditioned by the objectifications of Foucault's "technologies of power." It is a subjectivity negotiated, as Berman insists, in *la vie quotidienne*. A second issue highlighted by Kaplan's critique is that an approach to modernity in which autonomous subjectivity figures prominently (though which is not limited to "the tourist") seems necessary if we are to avoid the assumption of a "master text" for modernity that characterizes its increasingly global permutations in terms of the triumph of Western rationalism. As Rofel argues (1992), the project of modernity in China is always being subverted and challenged by unruly subjectivities that defy any broader disciplining regimes of the state and capital. Indeed, as Chapter 1 will argue, the Chinese state itself advocates a modernization paradigm that is explicitly non-Western in ideology, despite all its trappings of instrumental rationality. Modernity in China is thus characterized by shifting meanings that are contingent upon local histories and geographies, and the articulations of these with the state and with global capitalism. Kaplan's work reminds us that while the West may occupy a privileged position in defining the stakes at risk as the modern juggernaut careens ahead, our attention must also turn to the peripheries where modern subjectivity is being articulated in often radically different ways. It is for these reasons that this book focuses not on tourists in Guizhou, but on the Guizhou people themselves. Modernity, for them, remains an unfinished and open-ended project, one that looks quite unlike the modernity of the Euro-American tourist, and yet which is also inextricably tied to the power technologies emanating from the West, from the broader Chinese nation-state, and from the increasingly powerful presence of capital in China. Their struggle for identity is a struggle over the right to claim modernity as their own contradictory and paradoxical experience. As long as villagers can laugh aloud at the consternation of their tourists, they are winning that struggle.

1 Tourism and modernity

Strange how the world got so small;
I turned around and there was nowhere left to go.
So sad, the dream always dies;
Each new arrival closes places in my mind.

But I can dream
Until I go
Of smells that I don't recognize.

And by the river
In Shanghai
The color of the sky
Is something I've never seen.
After the summer rain
Children smile
Curious and kind
And the world is big again.

                    Joe Jackson, "Shanghai Sky"

Hey pal, can I take your picture for the people back home?
They won't believe it when they see this stuff.
Ya see the camera that I got in Hong Kong?
Completely duty free.
This really is a pretty scene,
But could you ask your kid to smile please.
Sorry, what exactly do you mean?
Can you say it in English?
'Cause we're the jet set, get outta our way.
And don't be messin' with the jet set, get outta our way.
'Cause we gotta lot of things to see.

Let's get a Big Mac,
Get it while the dollar's worth a thousand Yen,
It's quite a bargain here.
Next year we'll save some money and we'll hire Big Ben
For our anniversary.
This really is a pretty place,

But I'm happy I don't live here.
Hey, what's the matter with the waiter's face?
Can you say it English?
'Cause we're the jet set, get outta our way.
And don't be messin' with the jet set, get outta our way.
'Cause we gotta lot of things to see.

Joe Jackson, "The Jet Set"

SEARCHING FOR OTHER PLACES

These songs, from Joe Jackson's 1986 album *Big World*, launch us on a journey through modernity's contingencies and contradictions, manifest in the tourist experience. Modernity consumes the world, discovers it, colonizes it, rationalizes and orders it, knows it with science and categories. In the process, modernity brings the promise of freedom even as it profoundly destabilizes, uproots, and displaces those in its wake. The sensibilities of modernity are paradoxical: a wary faith in progress accompanied by a melancholy sense of loss, a need to recover a sense of authenticity and repair the ruptures of modernization even while realizing that such ruptures create whole new landscapes upon which we must live and from which we must derive meaning. The traveler in "Shanghai Sky" expresses these sensibilities; the tourist experience it articulates is a journey of repair, a fleeting discovery of something authentic in Shanghai, even as the journey continues on, inexorably wrapping the world, shrinking it, killing dreams with knowledge. "Shanghai Sky" begins with a melancholy confrontation with the reality of modernity, and seemingly relegates the authentic and unexpected to the world of dreams. Yet, arriving in Shanghai, we see something else happening, in the seemingly mundane recognition of a rain washed summer sky and the smiles of children. The modern traveler will always find the fragments of truth and the shards of hope that also mark the ever-shifting face of modernity. Even for only a fleeting moment, the world is big again, and *this* is what pushes the modern traveler on, not the desire to simply mark off another place "done," colonized and consumed, but to strive for something authentic and immutable within the reality of constant change. To travel is to be ever dissatisfied, and yet we still see something of what the world *could* be.

But Jackson also reminds us of how powerful the debasements of modernity's colonizations can be, and how we can get swept up in them, losing any sense of the deeper truths we may discover in Shanghai. The tourists of "The Jet Set" are ravenous consumers of place and of Big Macs, preying on servile waiters, favorable exchange rates, and the pathetic quaintness of "local color." There is no paradox here, as far as these travelers are concerned. They are not concerned with the death of dreams in a global village. They are scandalized by disorder, by children who won't smile for them and by the inability of "natives" to speak *their* language. For they travel to *order* the world and to make it sensible. They travel in a steam-roller, squishing the world into a flatscape.

For many critics, "The Jet Set" is tourism in a nutshell. And in many cases they're right. Tourism is frequently interpreted as the new colonizing vanguard of modernity (Graburn 1983: 18; Iyer 1988: 6; Turner and Ash 1975). This book is written in order to counter that simplistic conclusion. For the tourism experience also captures something else, a counter force, in which that colonized landscape also becomes something new, invested with new meanings which defy the ordered ideals that underlie the voraciousness of "The Jet Set." Indeed, this is true of the experience of modernity in general, an experience characterized not simply by the rational abstractions of order and development, but more profoundly by the recognition that such abstractions are but one attempt to "fix" the ruptured terrain of modern life. People, however, will always come up with their own methods of repair as they confront the new instabilities of their lives. And so modernity is a contingent and dynamic field of destruction and renewal, of power and resistance, of the constant struggle to define the meaning of one's life in the face of ever new forces which threaten to take that meaning away.

But with this, we are fast entering murky water of touristic modernity. The above points will be made repeatedly throughout this book, but let us now pursue a more careful route toward making sense of them. We will begin with an important claim that underlies the whole approach taken in this book: tourism may be seen as a succinct metaphor for the experience of modernity itself, an experience professing human liberation and enlightenment, but often at the cost of alienation and displacement in a world of rationality, scientific reason, and other touchstones of progress. Dean MacCannell (1989: 1) has written that "our first apprehension of modern civilization . . . emerges in the mind of the tourist." John Urry (1990: 2), likewise, suggests that acting like a tourist, "is one of the defining characteristics of being 'modern.'." Nelson Graburn (1978) has defined tourism as a distinctly modern form of pilgrimage. Malcolm Crick (1989: 333), in claiming that tourism is "essentially a (post-) modern activity," complicates the picture somewhat with his parenthetical uncertainty, but nevertheless finds tourists to be ideal subjects acting out our contemporary cultural consciousness. What is it about modernity that is so intriguingly expressed in the tourist experience? Why has the symbolic and metaphorical richness of tourism been so enthusiastically mined by those of us so eager to represent the modern experience? While tourism itself is an enormously diverse set of activities which defies a single core definition, it is, to a large extent, deeply bound up by two concepts which are, paradoxically, central to the sensibilities of modernity. These are authenticity and tradition.

MacCannell (1989: 3) summarized the relationship between tourism, modernity, and authenticity in the following passage:

For moderns, reality and authenticity are thought to be elsewhere: in other historical periods and other cultures, in purer, simpler lifestyles. In other words, the concerns of moderns for "naturalness," their nostalgia and their search for authenticity are not merely casual and somewhat decadent, though harmless attachments to the souvenirs of destroyed cultures and dead epochs. They are also components of the conquering spirit of modernity – the grounds of its unifying consciousness.

The ideal of authenticity – in which an individual is able to "engage the world with an immediacy and fullness of being" – was, ironically, something conjured by the experience of modernity itself (Berman 1970: 4). Marshall Berman has argued that modernity enables one to imagine the possibility of an authentic life, while paradoxically setting in motion forces that render such authenticity increasingly difficult to achieve. "The modern age was, above all, an age of paradox: an age in which the potentialities for the self-development of men had multiplied to infinity, while the range of their authentic self-expression had shrunk to nothing" (1970: 153). This profoundly troubling realization leads one to both embrace inauthenticity, reducing oneself to what Rousseau called "an image of fashion" – that is, submitting to the institutions of rationality, order, and style that are established to rein in the chaotic freedoms unleashed by modernization – and to seek authenticity in other places and times, where it can be colonized and consumed. To be modern is to not only espouse a "conquering spirit" of progress and constant change, but to embrace a world of instability and inauthenticity. Yet recognizing one's world as such depends fundamentally on the construction of that which is authentic and stable, that is, "traditional." To be modern thus entails a search for the authentic, as a place from which one gains a meaningful perspective on the casualty of progress: self-alienation. For this reason, the trope of exile has had particular currency in representing the experience of modernity, especially among modern Euro-American writers such as Conrad, Hemingway, Joyce, and Mann. As Caren Kaplan (1996: 34, 45) argues, the trope of exile fosters "a culture of nostalgic melancholia" which is expressed through fantasies of escape, whereby the past is exoticized in a distant, often highly sexualized place and culture. Tourism, MacCannell (1989: 9) argues, appropriates and commodifies the experience of exile. Tourism becomes the contemporary embodiment of the exiled modernist's search for authenticity; it is part of the process whereby modernity constructs and appropriates a distant non-modern world, and puts it on display in museum-like fashion, thus defining the boundaries of modernity "by rendering concrete and immediate that which modernity is not."

In her history of tourism, *Going Places*, Maxine Feifer describes concretely this need for "reintegrating a fragmented world." Describing the scene at one of France's most famous tourist sites, Mont St Michel, Feifer comments on how the tourist's gaze has been curiously conditioned to regard even the most mundane events as mystically authentic. In this case, authenticity is found in the famous restaurant of Mere Poulard, whose traditional French omelets are featured in all the guidebooks to this medieval island-castle:

> The event has become mystified by the curious process that tourism brings into play: set up by the travel writer and framed by the camera, other people's ordinary lives are transformed into exotic entertainment, history into myth. There was also something singularly *modern* about it: who but "alienated" twentieth century urbanites would be mystified by somebody whisking eggs (a kind of reversal of the savage astonished by the cigarette lighter)?
>
> (Feifer 1985: 1)

Not only does tourism involve a search for authentic places, but it invests those places with what Umberto Eco (1986) called "hyperreality," in which the ordinary and mundane are elevated to a status where they are "more real" than the reality of modern life itself. MacCannell (1989: 6) notes that in modern society, where most of us are alienated from the products of our work, we make a fetish of the work of others, and that only by doing this can we comprehend work as a meaningful part of our modern lives.

Feifer makes this point in a fictional account of the archetypal modern tourists, "Homer and Mabel," as they take a holiday in Fiji. On their itinerary one day is a visit to a "typical Fijian village." Here they are confronted with reconstructed ordinariness and hyperreality:

> People put on old fashioned clothes that they hadn't worn normally for years and displayed the outmoded traditional crafts of weaving, basket making, grinding nuts. The village represented the coordinated efforts of electricians, payroll clerks, mechanics, florists, PR men, and anthropologists; but Mabel couldn't get over how "real" it seemed, even "realer" than the *real* markets they had just seen. She stared, fascinated, at the nut grinding. "It's really just like what I do for the almond cakes, Homer!" she marveled, and, in fact, it was; but somehow the Fijian way seemed so much "realer".
>
> (Feifer 1985: 243)

The "typical Fijian village," an obvious touristic reproduction, is nevertheless presented to tourists as an "authentic" representation of traditional life in Fiji. Like MacCannell, Jonathan Culler sees tourism as a perpetual quest for the authentic, and has commented on this ironic quality of tourism: "The distinction between the authentic and the inauthentic, the natural and the touristy, is a powerful semiotic operator within tourism" (Culler 1981: 131). But authenticity, of course, is impossible to represent. Thus, the tourist's quest for authenticity is catered to by the *marking* of authenticity.

Authenticity itself, claims Culler, depends on signs that tell us it's authentic. "The existence of reproductions is what makes something original, or authentic, and by surrounding ourselves with markers and reproductions we represent ourselves, as MacCannell astutely argues, the possibility of authentic experiences at other times and in other places" (Culler 1981: 132). But in this we see an inherent contradiction:

> The paradox, the dilemma of authenticity, is that to be experienced as authentic [a place] must be marked as authentic, but when it is marked as authentic it is mediated, a sign of itself, and hence not authentic in the sense of unspoiled. We want what we buy to have a label, "authentic native craftsmanship woven by certified natives using guaranteed original materials and archaic techniques" (rather than, say, "Made in Hong Kong"), but such markers are put there for tourists, to certify touristic objects.
>
> (Culler 1981: 137)

Lately, as Urry (1990: 11) points out, many tourists have come to accept that there is perhaps no such thing as the authentic tourist experience. Feifer recognizes this aspect of tourism as she ascends the Eiffel Tower in Paris, with a copy of Roland Barthe's *The Eiffel Tower and Other Mythologies* as her guidebook. She asks the other tourists on the observation deck, Why do people come to see the Eiffel Tower? What kind of authentic truth is to be gained from it? She finds that, "the answer turns out to be as obvious as Andy Warhol's soup can. 'It's the tourist thing to do.'" (Feifer 1985: 267). Fittingly, in this age of post-modernism, post-structuralism, and post-industrialism, she labels those who make a playful game of the tourist's ritualistic search for the authentic, "post-tourists." For the post-tourist, authentic places are already closed off from view; there is not even the hope for an authentic "Shanghai Sky." This denial of authenticity returns us, however, to Berman's (1970: 155) observation that modern society is "permeated by universal and perpetual discontent." The post-tourists may simply be the latest revelers in the inauthenticity of modern life, having concluded that even tourism cannot bring about the completeness of being that modernity promises yet stubbornly holds out of reach.

Obviously, tourism is far too complex to be simplified into one overall framework, characterized by a search for the authentic place and experience. The complexity of the tourism experience is such that claiming a single conceptual scheme for its analysis does a disservice to our overall understanding (Nash 1984: 504). Nor, as Kaplan (1996: 57) has argued, can the tourist be conceived as some kind of universal modern Subject. Just as the trope of exile and its aestheticizing of displacement and nostalgia easily slips into a *style* that itself becomes dislodged from the historical and geographical forces that violently uproot and destroy placed lives, tourism cannot be separated from its imperialist and colonial roots. In our metaphorical renderings of modernity, the tourist cannot be isolated from the places and people he or she visits. This is particularly important when contemplating the modern experience in China, as a process that must be understood within the specific historical and geographic contexts of China itself. Rather than limit our analysis, then, to the *search* for the authentic, we might instead concentrate on the *construction* of authenticity in tourism, as a project undertaken by a diverse array of subjects. In these terms, we can explore the tourist experience from a broader perspective, as an agent of modernity through which deeper questions of identity, tradition, and continuity are raised and negotiated not simply by tourists, but more importantly by those who have entered the business of "selling experience." Indeed, more than tourists themselves, the providers of the tourist experience may more directly confront that contingent quality of modernity as they participate in the exhibition of their places and lifestyles.

MENDING THE FRACTURED TERRAIN OF MODERNITY

[A]mbivalence characterizes much of what's called modern life, and as modernity gets updated we must keep sightseeing just so we can understand our place in it. Our cultures, our landscapes, our social institutions are continually demolished and rebuilt. Each new moment of modernity promises to heal the wounds it continues to inflict, while at the same time encouraging us to imagine an open future. We tour the disparate surfaces of everyday life as a way of involving ourselves in them, as a way of reintegrating a fragmented world.

(Wilson 1994: 5)

Like MacCannell, Alexander Wilson finds in tourism a behavior that only makes sense in the broader social context of the experience of modernity. What this passage also suggests, however, is that the tourism experience can be viewed as an act of repair. Following from Urry (1995: 145), this act of repair can be interpreted as an aspect of modernity's qualities of reflexivity, a crucial topic that MacCannell ignores. What Urry emphasizes, however, is not the cognitive reflexivity referred to by Giddens (and Habermas), but rather what he calls "aesthetic reflexivity," whereby symbols and images are mobilized around what Raymond Williams would call "structures of feeling." This aspect of modernity, for Urry, yields an "aesthetic cosmopolitanism" in which notions of tradition, taste, distinction, and authenticity are all marshaled to "make sense" of the modern experience. Significantly, "aesthetic cosmopolitanism" depends to a great extent on mobility. Hence Wilson's claim that we tour in order to reintegrate ourselves with a fragmented world. Uprooted and alienated, we convince ourselves that tradition – the organic folk village, and the community street – is where the authentic ideal conjured by modernity's self-reflexive preoccupations can be found. Tradition is the glue that is used as we clumsily build our contingent monuments to immutability in the face of change. But, mending the "disparate surfaces of everyday life," by constructing and consuming places saturated with authenticity, is a process of not just servicing the desires of tourists, but of articulating, in broader terms, the meaning of tradition and identity in the particular places visited themselves. While the providers of the tourism experience may be less concerned than tourists with the kind of authenticity Culler finds so ironic, the ideas of tradition and continuity are certainly of great importance in their construction and maintenance of place-based identity within tourist places. Rather than relying solely on tropes of travel and exile, then, the tourism experience may more broadly express those transient and contingent qualities of modernity as they relate to the places traveled to and exiled within. It is in these places that the modern desires for tradition and continuity take on a particular immediacy for locals, for they must negotiate both the socio-economic changes brought by tourism and the misplaced desires of tourists themselves.

The idea of tradition derives from that disquiet articulated by artists like Baudelaire and Yeats. Discussing Victorian Britain at the height of industrialism, David Lowenthal (1985: 97) characterized the dominant public culture as one in which Victorians knitted together a blanket of tenuous identity from the fragments of their past: "To secure themselves against the evils of rampant change and the dangers posed by the new industrial order, Victorians took refuge in one or another past, pasts not so much preserved as extravagantly re-created in architecture, art, and literature" (1985: 102). Lowenthal (1985: 69) interprets this process as the necessary cultural handling of change. Modernity is paralyzed without an accompanying sense of malleable tradition:

> We cannot function without familiar environments and links with a recognizable past, but we are paralyzed unless we transform or replace inherited relics; even our biological legacy undergoes continual revision. Yet to cope amidst change we also need considerable continuity with the past. The cultural legacy, too, is conservative *and* innovative; survival requires an inheritable culture, but it must be malleable as well as stable.

Lowenthal's claim that change is handled by appealing to a stable yet malleable past leads us to look more closely at the idea of tradition as not simply given (the received past), but as a contemporary social construction. This idea has been labeled the "invention of tradition" by Hobsbawm and Ranger in a collection of essays by historians intrigued by the contrast between "the constant change and innovation of the modern world and the attempt to structure at least some parts of social life within it as unchanging and invariant" (Hobsbawm 1983: 2). In this, invented traditions become the product of a past manipulated and recreated for contemporary reasons;

invented traditions are thus necessarily selective. They are also, according to Raymond Williams (1977: 115), hegemonic. For Williams, tradition is an aspect of contemporary social and cultural organization, reproduced in the interest of a dominant class. But what is perhaps most intriguing about the invention of tradition is not simply that a particular contemporary cultural practice is legitimized by appealing to an invented tradition, but that this tradition is articulated and defined *according to its loss* under the wheels of contemporary change.

Tradition therefore becomes an essential component of the bittersweet sensibilities of modernity. In Europe, modernity engendered a longing for a lost sense of organic wholeness even as it provided the liberating subjectivity from which one could express such decadent nostalgia. Such a sensibility, according to Lukács (1968, 1972), pervaded the tragedies of eighteenth- and nineteenth-century European fiction and drama, in which "the tragedy of the modern world is the simultaneous presence in the individual of a desire to unify the inner and outer worlds in a manner of the classical epic, and the recognition that this is no longer possible, that the cultural conditions which sustain such a unity are gone beyond recall" (Sim 1994: 37). Goethe's *Faust*, for example, trumpets the "spiritual awakening of bourgeois Germany," a time when "the thread of its organic development was snapped," requiring a taking-stock of Germany's historical heritage (Lukács 1968: 161). The drama articulated individual struggles within the context of a great historical shift from organic medieval life to a dislocating modernity (Lange 1968: 2). But even as *Faust* seeks to recover the fragments of some mythical organic German unity, it finds itself played out upon a fractured modern landscape which is incapable of supporting the historical continuity necessary to recover an authentic present. Instead, Faust and Mephistopheles must first invent new and increasingly contingent myths and then build a new landscape (in *Faust II*) which, as it turns out, merely monumentalizes its own inadequacy for the unifying task put before it. For Goethe (1983: 168–9), modernity was simply "Permanence of Change" – a condition of chaos, disorder, and paradox; the only meaningful response was not to seek resolution through the imposition of formal abstractions, but to "invite the anxiety of form in motion" (Fink 1996: 97).

Similarly, Thomas Hardy's Wessex landscapes conveyed a "brooding ambivalence" over the tension between change and immutability (Rabbetts 1989: 4). As Terry Eagleton (1981: 128–30) has suggested, Hardy's fiction is marked by an "ideological disarray," revealing, ultimately, his refusal to resolve the contradiction between two competing visions of literary representation: humanist voluntarism and deterministic alienation. The places of the Wessex landscape offered a terrain upon which these competing visions were struggled over but rarely resolved. Most readers, of course, have read Hardy's Wessex as an authentic counterbalance to placeless modernity; mainstream criticism has claimed "the poet of Wessex" as a pastoralist-humanist. Indeed, Hardy's work was appropriated by early twentieth-century

British nationalists and patriots in the "formation of a pastoral myth of rural England – often recalling a past, more glorious heritage – which is the true 'essential England' of national identity" (Widdowson 1989: 61). Yet it is a strange pastoralism that Hardy offers. For while novels such as *Tess of the D'Urbervilles* (1891) and *The Return of the Native* (1878) ostensibly suggested authentic landscapes of organic continuity – Egdon Heath and the Vale of Blackmoor – their inhabitants are plagued by the "ache of modernism." Those who sought in Hardy a progressive affirmation of humanist resistance to the ills of modernity were repeatedly frustrated by the uncertain subjectivity of characters such as Clym Yeobright, Eustacia Vye, Tess Durbyfield, Jude Fawley, and Sue Bridehead. All of them emerge from landscapes which at first glance appear "eternal and immutable," and yet their stories are of dislocation, alienation, and tragedy.

Hardy's Wessex was, thus, not a stable and enclosed landscape of tradition, but an unstable and ambivalent landscape of modernity, defined less by the organic community than by a tense relationship between that community and its continuous displacement. Raymond Williams (1966: 195–6) wrote that the "real" Hardy country, "is that border country so many of us have been living in: between custom and education, between work and ideas, between love of place and experience of change." Hardy was driven to write about the profoundly uncomfortable state many were living in as agricultural and industrial capitalism intensified in Britain – a place between dwelling and displacement – and found *that* to be the condition of modernity (see Entrikin 1991). Those struggling to maintain a sense of identity and subjectivity within the forces of modernization would have to confront the fact that authenticity could not be drawn out of the past, but would have to be crafted from the paradoxes and contradictions of modernity itself.

But if the best of European realism captured the inherent tension in modernity between progress and loss, the more common aesthetic response to modernization was to either uncritically embrace the ideals of rationalism, progress, and abstract order, or to seek refuge in the "golden age" of a bucolic past. The latter tendency has been subjected to a sustained critique in Williams's *The Country and the City* (1973). In examining the pastoral literature of "rural intellectual radicalism" in Britain, Williams argues that the recovery of a "lost" pastoral tradition is simply a hegemonic fiction which, ironically, legitimizes the alienating abstractions of industrial capitalism itself. Here, tradition is indeed enlisted as part of the "conquering spirit" of modernity.

As the title of Williams's work suggests, however, modernity does not simply conquer time by reinventing history in order to legitimize the present. It colonizes space as well. The invention of tradition in the service of modernity has a distinct geography, as the traveling urban eye casts its aesthetic gaze upon its imagined counterpoint: the countryside of the traditional folk. For Williams, such an urban gaze emerged from the particular "structure of feeling" that accompanied industrialization, and which defined a rural, pastoral landscape in terms of its regretful loss at the hands of progress. The pastoral took on a meaning that privileged the urban dweller's need for some beautiful and morally correct place: "Its most serious element was a renewed intensity of attention to natural beauty, but this is now the nature of observation, of the scientist or the tourist, rather than the working countryman" (Williams 1973: 20). Rural places were transformed by urban viewers from landscapes of work to landscapes of aesthetic appreciation.

The rural places of Williams's own fiction – the Welsh borderlands – were represented as landscapes shaped by local social relations of production, but which were also problematically linked to a broader history and geography. His most well-known novel, *Border Country* (1960) – one of a trilogy of Welsh novels – evokes a sense of place defined by the participation of locals in the processes of change; the valley dwellers of Glynmawr play out their lives as a balancing act between modern integration and pre-modern isolation. The resulting tension in their lives underlies, for Williams, the very process of local cultural production. Regional Welsh culture was not simply the reheated leftovers of a pre-modern tradition spoiled by the ravages of modernity; it was an on-going construction, crafted out of the multiple instances of individuals inhabiting unstable, in-between places and acting on the contradictions of their lives. This was the modern Welsh experience. It was defined by the many problematic and complex connections between individuals and a broader political economy, rather than some fantasy of the organic community making its last stand against the unfeeling steamroller of progress. What was important for Williams, then, was that the landscapes of Wales be represented not as enclosed places being corrupted from without – as in the well-established genre of Welsh literary regionalism, the association with which Williams greatly resisted – but as on-going historical processes of both local and broader social relations. His fiction articulated a tense and wary linkage between local cultural expressions and broader material processes, specifically agricultural and industrial capitalism.

We thus find a fundamental contradiction being played out in these imaginative geographies of modernity and tradition. On the one hand, the experience of modernity encourages a colonizing gaze on the part of the urban-industrial subject, a gaze directed toward both an imagined pre-industrial past and a carefully enframed non-urban present. I would characterize it as the misplaced search for authenticity in an effort to repair the fragmented terrain of modernity; misplaced due to its failure to recognize the ideal of authenticity as a modern product itself (that is, a product of modern reflexivity). This gaze is one of order and abstraction, as well as aesthetics, and a restless need to find authenticity in some other, exotic place. At its worst, it is the tourist gaze of Joe Jackson's "Jet Set." But it also inspires the tourist in "Shanghai Sky," who has traveled far for that fleeting glimpse of the authentic "big world." As will be revealed in Chapter 4, it is a powerful force in the construction and enframing of folk landscapes for metropolitan tourist consumption. On the other hand, those for whom the experience of modernization is an immediate and dislocating force, those objects of the urban tourist's colonizing gaze – the rural folk themselves – struggle to define their authenticity and subjectivity within the experience of modernity, rather than being relegated to the status of quaint anachronisms and objectified victims of modernity. As Berman has so eloquently argued, their struggle is the same struggle we all face, to carve a space of authentic identity between dwelling and displacement, between the imprisonments of tradition and the oppressiveness of the new order. It is a struggle that has been poignantly felt in twentieth-century China. The case studies offered in this book are meant to provide an account of just such a struggle being played out in the mountains of southwest China.

But the case studies don't merely offer an account of the local struggles to overcome modernity's alienating logic. More important, we see these struggles going on under the objectifying gaze of metropolitan tourists. This complicates the picture greatly. For the tourist gaze attempts to construct a landscape of aesthetic beauty and exotic experience, a landscape that offers little to support a dynamic subjectivity for those who must live within it. If locals are to indeed live authentic lives, then they must build them out of the social situations in which they live, social situations significantly conditioned by the tourism experience. Thus the struggle for authenticity – that is, a truly modern subjectivity – is doubly difficult. The villagers of Guizhou who have become tourist attractions must confront not simply the gaze of metropolitans, but of the modern nation-state itself. This is because the misplaced search for authenticity is not simply felt on an individual level, but has been significantly institutionalized by the forces of nationalism and state building, representing a whole "structure of feeling" that conditions village lives. Indeed, tourism is in many ways a project of nationalism; repairing the fragmented terrain of modernity is not simply a process of tourist consumption, but, more importantly, serves to legitimize the space of the nation as a timeless, essential geography. The following section is thus devoted to elaborating the role of the nation-state in the construction of imaginative geographies of modernity and tradition.

PLACING THE RURAL FOLK IN THE MODERN NATION

Hobsbawm (1983: 13) mentions "one specific interest for 'invented traditions'" that should always be singled out: "They are highly relevant to that comparatively recent historical innovation, the 'nation,' with its associated phenomena: nationalism, the nation-state, national symbols, histories, and the rest." Echoing the same theme, Benedict Anderson (1983: 28) has said that, "It is the magic of nationalism to turn change into destiny." Working from these perspectives, the nation may be viewed as a hegemonic ideology advocated by a dominant class and founded upon the invention of a particular selected tradition which, generally, is conceived as having been or just about to be lost. It goes without saying that in such a definition, the nation is conceived as a specific response to the experience of modernity, a response based on the idea that out of the displacements of modernity could be fashioned, systematically, a new, highly rationalized and centralized territorial space. As Knox and Agnew (1994: 199) have suggested, the emergence of nation-states cannot be separated from the basic material processes of European modernization: "Nation-states were constructed in order to clothe, and enclose, the developing political economy of industrial capitalism." In Europe, Enlightenment thought and the growth of capitalism presented a profound set of changes, generating a collective sense of loss which became the fertile ground for the construction of a scaffolding defining in unambiguous terms that which was, in Baudelaire's words, "eternal and immutable." The nation was offered as a ready-made identity, a standardized medium to which everyone was to subscribe. Convincing people they *should* subscribe was, of course, a major cultural project. Derived from his work in Southeast Asia, Anderson's argument is that print media was the cultural workhorse of the hegemony of nationalism. Ultimately, the cultural project of nationalism was one for which tourism would be particularly suited as well.

The tourist industry, in its representations of authentic pasts and places, constructs a contemporary mythology in alignment with the dominant ideology of nationalism. The Great Exhibition of 1851 in Britain, for example, was an enormously successful tourist attraction, drawing six million visitors in the less than half a year it was open. With unprecedented extravaganza the Great Exhibition glorified material progress, and helped turn technology into a grounding myth of British national identity (Horne 1992: 165–71). Prince Albert's tribute to the wonders of modern British technology perhaps marks the beginning of tourism's nation-building project. When tourism and nationalism collaborate, the result has been a selective and sanitized representation of reality; any contradictory and confusing parts of that reality must be banished if they do not contribute to the nationalistic ideology, which depends fundamentally on an imagined sense of common identity, solidarity, and community. In the following passage on the development of an "open air museum" at the British tourist site of Ironbridge, Donald Horne discusses how tourism colludes with nationalist ideology to create a cozy past which did not exist but upon which a common sense of happy solidarity may be built. The goal of this kind of tourism is collective nostalgia of tradition, the hegemonic glue that holds "imagined communities" together.

At Ironbridge, something very sickly got into them when they made such a mess of the Blists Hill Open Air Museum that is part of the complex, although not in the gorge itself. Blists Hill was a mining village with three blast furnaces and a brickworks. There are relics of these noisy and noisome activities, but a "model village" has been set up, containing quaint structures from other parts of the country—a butcher's, a baker's, a candlestick maker's (literally) and other shops reminiscent of cottagey calendar illustrations. Instead of flames shooting up and illuminating the village twice a day when the furnaces were tapped, there are now cozy fires in the grates of nice little cottages, with cats dozing in front of some of them. One doesn't want the Ironbridge authorities to simulate a satanic industrial village, but they might be expected not to "re-create" what didn't exist. It is as if all this industrial activity had been performed not by 400 or 500 employees living in an industrial settlement, but by the worthy shopkeepers and their cats.

(Horne 1992: 188)

Tourism not only fuels collective nostalgia, but also helps construct a landscape in which the "essence" of a nation is represented. John Sears (1989: 3) has noted that, "tourism played a powerful role in America's invention of itself as a culture," and that, "tourist attractions enabled the members of an emerging mass society to participate in a common national experience." Horne (1992: 269) adds that during the nineteenth century,

In paying homage to the attractions of Niagara Falls, or "doing" the Hudson Valley in a steamboat, or going on a guided tour of Mammoth Cave, Kentucky, or, later in the century, in standing in reverence before the sequoias in the Mariposa Grove or the grandeur of Yosemite, some tourists referred to themselves specifically as "pilgrims." The tourist landscapes of Europe were created as part of the romantic imagination that invented nations: the Swiss spirit was to be found in the Alps, the Scottish in the Highlands, the Norwegian in mountains and fjords, the Hungarian in the Great Hungarian Plain, and so forth.

Here, a final component of tourism's iconographic landscapes of national essence must be added: it must be populated by "the people," the invented folk who embody the cultural spirit of the nation. More than any other element of the touristic nation-building project, the folk are not only the mythic embodiment of national culture, but represent a way of life that has been lost, or is at least on its death bed, and is thus worthy of preservation and museumification. The first open air folk museum was founded by Artur Hazelius in Skansen, Sweden, just outside Stockholm, in the 1890s (Horne 1992: 199). Soon, folk museums were being built throughout Europe, marking clearly the spread of urban industrialism's colonizing gaze upon the mythologized landscape of tradition. As Pred's work (Pred and Watts 1992: 136) demonstrates, Stockholm in the late nineteenth century was experiencing rapid industrialization and capital over-accumulation, its urban landscape truly melting into air as the "rural idyllic qualities of many parts of the city disappeared in wave upon wave of creative destruction." In its attempts to maintain control over space as modernization rendered the landscape increasingly contingent and unstable, the bourgeoisie imposed on Stockholm a rationalization of previously chaotic streets, normalization of the general population through public health and welfare campaigns, and regulation of public spaces and public behavior. This established an urban space based on ideals of modern science and progress, in which all that was morally decadent, unhealthy, and dangerous about the old order was exposed to the healthy breeze of circulation and flushed out (see Berman 1982: 147–55; and Rabinow 1989: 73–81).

The Stockholm bourgeoisie's attempts at spatial hegemony were supported by the paradoxical foundation of a collective sense of loss and nostalgia for the "imagined community" of tradition and of the nation. Maintaining a representation of space based on the ideals of modern science and progress entailed the construction of a sense of national tradition, the glue needed to hold the fragmented and unstable landscape of modernity together. The ordering of urban space went hand in hand with an organic mythology of national romanticism and solidarity. This, in turn, depended upon the invention of a shared past and common cultural heritage and territory:

> The rural "past" was not merely to invoke the once-existing past but was now to signify "the good old days," an age of unity to be recaptured, a time when life in agricultural villages "was simple and harmonious," an epoch free of speedy technological change, an era when the everyday was uncomplicated, straightforward, and frictionless, a period when people "knew their place" and relations between high and low were marked by paternal care and attention on the one side and contentedness on the other.
>
> (Pred and Watts 1992: 146–7)

This, in short, is the misplaced search for authenticity discussed in the previous section. It was only a matter of time before an entrepreneur like Hazelius would recognize the confused metropolitan idealism of authenticity as a profitable route toward capital accumulation. Since his time, nations have again and again turned toward a mythologized rural folk as the embodiment of national essence. Soon, this essentializing gaze could be found in the Asia-Pacific arena, with the construction of the Polynesian Cultural Center in Hawaii, the Korean Folk Village in South Korea, and the "Beautiful Indonesia" in Miniature Park (known as Mini) near Jakarta. "When the first Korean Folk Village was put together in 1974 at Yongin, 41 kilometers south of Seoul, the buildings and the items within were assembled for the same reason that Hazelius invented the idea of Skansen 83 years before – industrialization meant the end of an old order. It was time to put what remained into museums" (Horne 1992: 200).

Promotional literature in Korea made clear the role of invented folk custom for modern nationalism:

> The Korean Folk Village near Soul is a peek [sic] at a past that's still living and breathing ... That's why Koreans like to visit the folk village too, for an authentic glimpse of how their ancestors lived: the customs and designs, the artifacts and pastimes of each province rounded up and set down on a single 245-acre size only 50 minutes from the capital city.
>
> (Cited in Wood 1984: 367)

In Indonesia, at Mini's ceremonial opening, the minister of religious affairs was moved to prayer: "Dear God, our Lord, with the intention to build up our people's and nation's love for the fatherland do we build this 'Beautiful Indonesia' in Miniature Park" (cited in Pemberton 1994: 244).

Nationalism, however, is not a static concept, nor are its collective myths everywhere the same. Nations and nationalism has been continually reproduced according to very specific historical and geographic contexts. There are at least two significant issues which condition both the experience of modernity and the relationship between tourism and nationalism in East Asia. These are (multi)nationalism and the discourse of (East–West) difference. Whereas in the post-industrial West the tourist landscape has been complicated by the rise of multiculturalism, in which alternative representations of "the people" have only relatively recently asserted themselves (only, perhaps, to be swallowed up by touristic capitalist commodification and appropriated as simply a more up-to-date version of the nation), the experience of regional ethnic and cultural differences has been a much more fundamental problematic of nation building in East and Southeast Asia. In addition, Asian nationalism has been complicated by the postcolonial discourse of difference, in which "the people" must be defined not only as bearers of an all-encompassing national essence – a resource of tradition from which all national subjects can construct a common identity – but also as a distinctly "non-Western" people whose indigenous traditions are capable of providing the glue for an "alternative" non-Western modernity.

In Indonesia, the nation-building tourist project is based not on one essential landscape and cultural tradition, but on many landscapes of cultural and regional diversity, all of which are supposed to add up to a whole greater than the sum of its parts: the Indonesian nation. But in order for this kind of ideology to work, each "regional culture" must be represented in much the same fashion as a single "national culture" was represented in industrializing Europe. Regional cultures must be invented as selective traditions of essential (and unique) folk quaintness. Writing about tourism and culture in Bali, Michel Picard (1993: 92) describes how nationalism, regional diversity, and tourism are worked together in Indonesia:

Now, as one *kebudayaan daerah* [regional culture] among others, Balinese culture is considered not for what it means to the Balinese people but for what it can contribute to the Indonesian "national culture" (*kebudayaan nasional*). Regional cultures are seen as a "resource" (*sumber*), providing "cultural elements" (*unsur-unsur kebudayaan*) to the development of the Indonesian national culture in the making, just as the participants in these cultures are Indonesians in the making. These cultural elements – regarded as the "peaks" of each regional culture – are expected to provide "nuances of color" (*aneka warna*) to the national culture. This conception of Indonesian culture(s), inscribed into the national motto "Unity in Diversity" (*Bhinneka Tunggal Ika*), is best exemplified in such creations as the "Beautiful Indonesia in Miniature Park" (*Tamen Mini Indonesia Indah*), an outdoor museum erected in Jakarta in the early 1970s, where each of the twenty-seven provinces is represented by a "traditional house" (*rumah adat*). The point here is that the locus of "tradition" has become the province, in effect creating a provincial *abat*.

Tourism in Indonesia has selectively weeded out whatever elements of local culture detract from the myth of a harmoniously (multi)national Indonesian identity. Balinese culture, Picard (1993: 93) argues, is "sieved through the filter of national ideology and sorted out." The parts which contribute to the construction of an imagined multicultural community get salvaged and preserved, "whereas those deemed too primitive or emphasizing local ethnic identity should be eradicated."

This "filtering" of regional ethnic and cultural essences has become a common theme for state-sponsored tourism development throughout Southeast Asia. As part of an effort to establish an integrated trading bloc capable of competing globally, the Association of South-East Asian Nations (ASEAN) has promoted a model of national economic development (inspired largely by the economic success of Taiwan, South Korea, Hong Kong, and Singapore) emphasizing a highly centralized state apparatus, export-oriented industrialization, encouragement of foreign investment, and a significant commitment to socio-cultural rationalization and stability. ASEAN specifically promotes cultural tourism as part of this overall modernization strategy (Hitchcock *et al.* 1993). Tourism has long been an important source of income in certain Southeast Asian settings, such as the beaches of Bali and the sex-tourism districts of Bangkok and Pattaya, but the ASEAN approach has added an important dimension to developing tourism throughout the region: the socio-cultural transformation of (multi)national states into integrated nations with a common sense of identity. What distinguishes this "Southeast Asian model" of tourism development is its emphasis on cultural, as much as economic, transformation.

Initially, state support of tourism development among ASEAN countries came about as part of structural adjustment efforts to offset declining foreign exchange earnings in other sectors. In Malaysia, declining tin and rubber prices had depressed the economy, fueling social and political chaos which led to the implementation of the New Economic Policy (NEP) in 1970. During the 1980s, Indonesia experienced significant losses as petroleum prices fell, leading to new policies aimed at attracting transnational capital, and opening up other parts of the country besides Bali to foreign tourists. In Thailand, active tourism development followed the departure of the US military after the Vietnam War in the early 1970s. A state-sanctioned tourism industry, it was reasoned, would provide a convenient alternative source of livelihood for the tens of thousands of prostitutes who had been servicing American GIs. In each of these cases, tourism was clearly envisioned as a force to be marshaled by the state in bringing about economic integration and regional development. But national governments also found that tourism could be effectively deployed not simply in attracting foreign exchange, but in promoting a vision of national unity built upon a selectively sanitized representation of multicultural diversity.

In Malaysia, the NEP was implemented largely as a result of racial tensions inherent in the unequal economic opportunities among the country's three major races: Malay, Chinese, and Indian. "The NEP's main objective was to promote national unity through both the eradication of poverty, irrespective of race, and the restructuring of Malaysian society, to eliminate the identification of race with economic function and geographical location" (Oppermann 1992: 227). The policy thus called for a regional redistribution of wealth and increased integration for the country's more remote states. Tourism development was an early priority in the NEP, leading to the formation of the Tourism Development Corporation in 1972. The luring of foreign exchange in the form of international tourists subsequently encouraged an emphasis on Malaysia's exoticism and benign charm. This has led to an overall approach within the state tourism industry which downplays any culturally divisive aspects of Malaysian society, particularly of the violent kind that erupted during the late-1960s before the NEP was implemented. Thus, Islam is virtually absent from marketed images of Malaysian tourism, despite the fact that most of the Malays are Muslims (Wood 1984: 365). Instead, diverse cuisines, festivals, handicrafts, and the harmless and meaningless touristic amenities of "charm and friendliness" are all promoted as exemplars of "Malaysian culture." As summarized by Victor King (1993: 109), the task of tourism development in Malaysia has partly been to "engender a local awareness of cultural matters and national identity and heritage, and to enhance national pride and commitments." It has thus been aimed as much at domestic tourists as foreigners.

Tourism development has played a similar role in Indonesia, where the nation-building project faces an even greater array of cultural and ethnic diversity. As exemplified in Mini, the ethnic divisions which threaten to obstruct the construction of a nation-state with a common sense of cultural identity and civic pride have been refashioned as benign regional distinctions. In this sense, regional cultures have been represented at Mini not as systems of meaning and values, but as collections of arts and performances, features which the state regards as healthy and not detrimental to (multi)nationalism. Building Mini was a high priority for the state, despite widespread opposition that questioned the use of scarce public funds for a theme park, protested the eviction and inadequate compensation of residents to make way for its construction, and challenged the images of Indonesia which the park would present.[1] Wood (1984: 367) notes that as protests mounted, President Suharto, in a 1972 speech, "threatened to use his most draconian executive powers against any continuing opposition to the Mini." Benedict Anderson adds that in the same speech, Suharto "went on to reveal that the project was intended to make Indonesia known to tourists and to raise national consciousness" (cited in Wood 1984: 367). The state's commitment to building Mini has been paralleled by its approach to encouraging the healthy development of regional cultures as a foundation for political and economic integration as well as "national consciousness."

As Picard (1993: 92) argues, this approach has been especially successful in Bali. Emphasizing tourism development based on a healthily sanitized cultural diversity has opened up a space for a relatively autonomous local identity within national integration. For this reason, local Balinese authorities were inclined to support the central state's emphasis on Bali as a means of generating foreign exchange (most of which would flow to Jakarta), since Balinese culture would be officially promoted and preserved in the process. Extolled by central and local officials as the agent of a cultural renaissance in Bali, Picard argues that tourism has simply become part of the island's cultural landscape, and that Bali's is increasingly a "touristic culture." As such, it can be likened to a local resource developed, exploited, and mined by the central state, part of a set of raw materials used to build a mosaic of multicultural unity. Bali's is a modernized, integrated, *regional* (as opposed to ethnic) culture, an integral component to the nation.

The emerging picture of this "Southeast Asian model" of tourism development, then, includes a number of important features. Throughout the countries of ASEAN, centralized states are directly involved in all aspects of tourism promotion and development. Tourism is regarded as an integral component of a development strategy that will result in a modernized national culture with a civic sense of commitment and a common sense of identity. These features are all apparent in China, which has perhaps been looking closely at the experience of its ASEAN neighbors as it formulates its tourism development plans. In particular, in regions such as Guizhou and Yunnan, which share Southeast Asia's patterns of regional ethnic diversity, the promotion of tourism as a means of achieving (multi)national modernization has clearly been a central feature of tourism development efforts.

Yet it is not just (multi)nationalism that marks the distinctive nature of tourism development throughout East and Southeast Asia. More important, perhaps, is the discourse of difference, of Asia's "alternative" path toward modernity, and the important role of tourism in building this path. Asian nationalism seeks to overcome more than local or regional ethnic differences; European nationalism has always sought to do this. What is important in the Asian context is that elites have sought to build the modern nation as an explicitly non-Western space of alternative modernity.

Economic success in East and, until recently, Southeast Asia, has perhaps been the most significant factor enabling the imagining of an "Asian alternative" to Western modernity. Economists, business leaders, and policy officials throughout the West, for example, have long touted the success of the so-called Asian "tigers": South Korea, Taiwan, Hong Kong, and Singapore. Japan, of course, has long been regarded a modernization success story, but has also been commonly represented simply as another "Western" industrial power inconveniently located. With the rise of the "tigers," however, a new discourse of East Asian economic success developed. The rise of East Asia heralded not simply an "economic miracle," but marked the rise of a new center in the global political economy, the core of a new Pacific Century, and a paradigm shift in the morphology of capitalism (for example, Naisbitt 1995). Thus, in an unprecedented way, the rise of East Asia was offered as a challenge to the hegemony of modernity defined in purely Western terms; "capitalism with Asian characteristics," it has been claimed, offers a path of modernization with largely non-Western roots.

This "Asian Way" can primarily be attributed to the lucrative deployment of the subcontracting mode of capitalism, exploiting in successive waves new labor markets conveniently disciplined by largely authoritarian regimes. There are plenty of explanations being offered to account for why this has happened. For Global Systems theorists and many industrial geographers, East Asia's success has come about due to the increasing sophistication of communication technologies, the globalization of currency markets, the development of new manufacturing technology enabling the deskilling of assembly labor, and the deregulation of East Asian labor markets and liberalization of trade policies. This package of changes has been referred to as the "new international division of labor" (Frobel *et al.* 1980), but can more generally be associated with what is variously called "post-Fordism," "late-capitalism," or "flexible accumulation" (Harvey 1989; Jameson 1984), in which capital has become highly mobile and transitory, requiring firms to rapidly adjust production processes through geographically dispersed subcontracting arrangements.

Yet most observers have sought to attach more socio-cultural significance to East Asia's rise than the above explanation offers. That the "Asian way" is simply a predictable outcome of capitalism's inexorable logic of accumulation, or, even worse, a purely technological phenomenon, is at best simplistic. Many have seen in East Asia the opportunity to legitimize the various competing development paradigms vying for influence over the course of Third World modernization. The most significant example here is the debate over socialism vs capitalism as the appropriate state-sponsored approach to modernization. Yet, with the end of the Vietnam War, the Chinese reforms of Deng Xiaoping, and the fall of the Soviet Union, the terms of the debate have shifted to alternative approaches within capitalism itself. Thus, advocates of neo-liberal policies of structural adjustment and deregulation see in the East Asian "miracle" a case for *laissez-faire* economics. Likewise, their detractors point to the strong role of the state in East Asian economies in advocating a kind of neo-Keynsian answer to the challenge hyper-mobile capital represents to nation-state sovereignty (see Berger 1996).

Among a triumphant capitalist elite, however, the most compelling explanation for the "Asian way" looks beyond political and economic factors. For those well-versed in the "Rimspeak" (Cumings 1993) of the new "Pacific Century," East Asia's alternative modernity is best explained in cultural terms, in the region's common roots in Confucianism. This culturalist explanation centers on the idea that East Asia's modernization is being built upon a moral economy based on so-called "Confucian values" in which society accepts authoritarian, paternal state control in exchange for the guarantee of collective welfare and stability. Beyond this, however, "Confucianism" has come to encapsulate an increasingly standardized litany of values that supposedly add up to a more "humane" capitalism. As summed up in a 1994 *Economist* article (May 28), these include: "the family, education, high savings, hard work, home ownership, and clean living." Exactly what distinguishes these values as Confucian, as opposed to, say, Weber's Protestant work ethic, remains unclear (Dirlik 1997: 313; Ong 1997: 189). Nevertheless, the deliberate wrapping of such values in the timeless mystique of a common Asian tradition represents clearly an appropriation of capitalism in the service of a new non-Western center. As Aihwa Ong (1997) points out, this triumphalist discourse of Confucianism as the core of the "Asian way" is being articulated most clearly by an international business elite of ethnic Chinese, who see themselves as citizens of a "Greater China."

Ong argues that the unlikely marriage of Confucianism to the subcontracting mode of capitalism in Asia is a contradiction brought about, in part, by what she terms "self-orientalization" (see also Dirlik 1997: 323). While East Asian modernity remains significantly conditioned by indigenous ideas, Western representations of Asian culture, ironically, are also being recapitulated to mark an oppositional alternative to the West itself. The reconstruction of Confucianism, in other words, is as much a product of Western orientalist concepts about the essential features of East Asian culture as it is an indigenous innovation. These essential features focus on interpersonal networks of *guanxi* relations among firms (as opposed to legalistic contractual relations) and on the primacy of "Confucian values" of benevolent paternalism at all levels of society (as opposed to liberal-humanist individualism and democracy) (Hu 1997). Such dualisms have long been the staple of modern Western binary discourses through which the West has defined itself (Said 1979). It is thus profoundly ironic that they have been repackaged by the business and political elite of "Greater China" as they continue to negotiate their own position of power *vis-à-vis* Western capitalist domination. For Ong (1997: 195), then, "alternative modernity" denotes "not so much the difference in content from Western [modernities] as the new self-confident political reenvisioning of futures that challenge the fundamental assumption of inevitable Western domination."

The most provocative rhetoric of this "new self-confident" alternative modernity has been coming from Singapore and, somewhat surprisingly, Malaysia. In Singapore, Lee Kuan Yew became a master at appropriating racial colonialist discourses and reworking them as a basis for a new Singapore national identity. Drawing on an older British colonial rhetoric metaphorically linking Chinese culture to "hardness" and "virility" as opposed to the "soft," "feminine," as well as "lazy" character of the Malays (see Heng and Devan 1995), Lee promoted a campaign to build a "rugged society" in Singapore in the 1960s and 70s (Ong 1997: 183). What for the British were essentially Western values of individualism and meritocracy were thus refashioned by Lee into "Confucian" values of hard work and frugality. In the 1980s, the Singapore state went further, linking Confucianism with its export-oriented capitalist development policies:

> In an effort to create an authentic Chineseness among the culturally heterogeneous and Westernized population, the state employed Harvard professor Tu Wei-ming to oversee programs sponsoring instruction and research in Confucian ethics and philosophies. Ideological regulation through the educational system, and the reification of Singaporean culture as "Confucian," are disciplinary schemes to shape and control a workforce geared to state-managed economic development and "state-fathering" of the social body. State patriarchy is central to the form of state-sponsored export-oriented capitalism in Singapore.
>
> (Ong 1997: 183)

Ironically, a similar approach has been taken by the Malaysian state, where Prime Minister Mahathir advocated a "look East" policy of favoring investors from East Asia, seeking to emulate the Japanese managerial philosophy, and a broader pan-Asian Confucianism, despite both the recent history of Japanese wartime occupation and the fact that "Confucian values" were formulated in part though rhetorical opposition to the "laziness" of Malays, not to mention the fact that Malaysia is predominantly an Islamic country. Such is the need for postcolonial states to align themselves with a non-Western modernity, no matter how contradictory that alignment may be.

Such contradictions are visible in the new tourist landscapes that have accompanied the rise of Asian capitalism. In Singapore, a government-

appointed Tourism Task Force was set up in 1984, and launched a campaign
to present the city as "the epitome of oriental mystique and high-tech entertainment" (Yeoh and Teo 1996: 36). Adding to the self-orientalizing irony,
the government in 1987 began a massive restoration project for the colonial
Raffles Hotel and the infamous Bugis Street. As was noted in the *New York
Times* (10/10/91),

> The restoration of Raffles and Bugis Street is the result of a larger real-
> ization among Singaporeans that, in turning a fetid, malarial port into
> one of the most well-scrubbed nations on earth, Singapore was losing
> touch with its past.

Indeed, so important is the need to maintain a nationalistic sense of difference from the West that the government is willing to focus a nostalgic gaze
on a *colonial* past in order to generate an "imagined community" legitimized
by tourism.

   Probably the most concise tourist landscape in this regard is the Haw Par
Villa theme park (Yeoh and Teo 1996). Begun as the Tiger Balm Gardens of
the notorious entrepreneur Aw Boon Haw, Haw Par Villa was a landscape
dedicated to the visual consumption of the Singapore public for both
commercial and moral purposes. The gardens offered a vast array of
grotesque and brilliantly colored reconstructions of Chinese folk icons – the
most popular being the infamous Ten Courts of Hell and scenes from
Journey to the West – along with an idiosyncratic assortment of sculptures
representing the world beyond China, such as Sumo wrestlers, a Spanish
dancer, and a Greek discuss thrower. With its odd lack of consistency in
subject matter, Haw Par Villa was less a theme park than a reflection of the
amalgam of peoples and histories that was Singapore itself. With the park
entrance providing a stage for a virtual carnival of folk performance artists,
such as Indian snake charmers, Haw Par Villa's landscape was eccentric and
bizarre. Theme parks, on the other hand, by definition offer a landscape that
is coherent and standardized so as to soothe the visitor's gaze by erasing the
chaotic differences which render the myths of national identity and tradition
problematic (see, for example, Pemberton 1994: 245).

   When the Singapore government acquired Haw Par Villa in 1985,
however, it embarked on transforming the gardens from an eccentric folk
icon to a standardized theme park that illustrated the "Asian way" with
modern technology. Consultants from Walt Disney Productions were
engaged to draw up the master plans, and professors from Beijing University
were invited as advisors on Chinese history, culture, and mythology. The
gardens were closed in 1988 for renovation and reopened two years later as
"Dragon World," a "living testimony of rich Chinese heritage." As Yeoh and
Teo point out, in order to succeed as a theme park supporting the state's
claims to an alternative modernity in Singapore, Dragon World had to
erase the eccentric blemishes of Aw Boon Haw's original landscape while

reinforcing and embellishing the distinctly Chinese themes. What had once been a free public park acquired a high admission fee and an array of technological gadgets and diversions meant to impress the visitor that Asia, too, could have its own Disneyland. Yet, despite its pioneer status as a "hi-tech" theme park, many were not convinced that Dragon World wasn't little more than American cultural imperialism in Oriental disguise. As one *Straits Times* journalist commented, visitors encountered Chinese folklore by viewing gods do battle to the beat of American-composed music, heard famous tales of ancient China narrated by an "American robot, dressed as an old Chinese man," and found that the creators of the world, Pan Ku and Nu Wu, "have somehow acquired American accents" (Yeoh and Teo 1996: 39). Indeed, the park continued to lose money after its 1990 reopening, because, according to one analyst, it was "too westernized . . . to convey the true spirit of [a] Chinese mythological theme park" (p. 40).

Singapore's attempts to turn Haw Par Villa into a consumable landscape trumpeting the triumphant Asian appropriation of Western modernity on Asia's terms were ultimately unsuccessful. But the case offers a clear illustration of the important role invested in tourism for reinforcing the discourse of difference in Asia. There are many other cases offering similar touristic landscape encodings of Asian alternative modernities. Throughout "Greater China," dozens of theme parks have opened, many based on themes of Chinese heritage, such as Singapore's Tang Dynasty Village and Hong Kong's Song Dynasty Village. Over two hundred new theme parks are expected to be built throughout Asia by the turn of the century, "making the region the fastest growing hub for theme parks" (Yeoh and Teo 1996: 28). Many of these parks will convey one important message, regardless of their theme: Asia is becoming a major player in the global economy and in the production of global culture.

In Japan, theme parks have long been a staple of tourist activities. Disneyland opened in Tokyo in 1983, and by 1990 thirteen major theme parks had opened throughout the country. More recently, however, the construction of extravagant theme parks has become a strategy for less prosperous regions of Japan to assert their own presence on both Japan's and the world's economic and cultural stages. On the mountainous Tsugaru Peninsula on Honshu – a region of relative poverty compared to Japan's rich industrial core – the village of Morita opened its Tsugaru Earth Village in 1992 (Schattschneider 1996). Built as something of a shrine to the world's sacred stone monuments, the Earth Village offered reconstructions of such landscape icons as the pyramids of Giza, Mt. Rushmore, the Great Wall of China, and a Greco-Roman arena. As revealed in Schattschneider's account of the Earth Village's opening *Un doko* ceremony, Morita villagers invested the park with the power to represent the "global village" and Tsugaru's hoped-for place in it. The park was strategically located at the base of the Peninsula's most established folk icon, the sacred Mount Iwaki-Akakura, which provided an enveloping backdrop to the global stage laid out before it. By thus investing the site as a sacred space firmly placed within Japanese folk tradition, the park seeks to mark Morita's confident entry into the modern world on its own terms. As Schattschneider (1996: 25) argues,

> the visual excess and extravagance of the *Un doko*, repleat with strobe lights, lasers, spotlights, backlit colored dry ice clouds, and dramatic explosions of light and sound, might be read as the concrete realization of the animating forces of the culture of electronics, the foundation of the Japanese economic miracle. These modern optical displays were visibly conjoined to the spectacle and mystery of dramatized folk religious practice. At *Un doko*, these intertwined forces were performatively unleashed to manifest "traditional" Morita Village's virtual entrance into the electronic global village.

Tourism is a fundamental instrument in the orchestration of multiple modernities being played throughout East and Southeast Asia. We have, thus far, encountered two dominant versions of Asian modernity. First, there is the nation-state and its advocacy of paternalistic authoritarianism as a distinctly Asian (Confucian) value. Second, there is the transnational capitalist elite's vision of a moral, humane capitalism based on "Confucian" values of respect for authority, interpersonal relationships, concern for the welfare of workers, savings and diligence, and so on. These dominant discourses of modernity meet with considerable tension within China, where the state cultivates a legacy of socialist paternalism while attempting to take advantage of the opportunities of transnational capital. Again, tourist landscapes – primarily theme parks within China – offer a clear illustration of this tension being played out. This chapter's final section seeks to examine these tourist landscapes within China in greater detail in order to sketch the articulations between the complexities of Chinese modernity and the tourism industry.

CHINESE MODERNITY AND TOURISM

According to Aihwa Ong (1997: 172), imaginings of the possibility for and nature of modern China are currently dominated by two competing discursive systems: "the modernist imaginary of the nation-state (emphasizing essentialism, territoriality, and fixity) in tension with the modernist imaging of entrepreneurial capitalism (celebrating hybridity, deterritorialization, and fluidity)." The latter vision, promoted primarily by a transnational Chinese elite advocating "Greater China" as a new core of global capitalism, developed as a competing discourse of Chinese modernity only in the 1990s. Up to this decade, the discursive realm of Chinese modernity was primarily framed within the fixed boundaries of the nation-state, as a competition between state socialism and organized ("Fordist") capitalism. In such terms, critics of modernity could easily refer to the technologies of power marshaled by the state and by capital in their pursuit of rationality and regulation of the social body. Whether it was socialist or capitalist mattered little; modernity was, in either case, marked by a relentless pursuit of social control. Ong insists, however, that transnationalism has brought a whole new dimension to the discourses of modernity in China, in which one's identity – that is, subjectivity – may be envisioned as fixed and territorial or, alternatively, mobile and international.

While the state and capital, in their modernizing logic, are often thought to be complementary, in China the state remains wary of capital, frequently encountering moments of antagonism even as it seeks to adjust to market-oriented redistributive mechanisms. Yang (1997: 297) characterizes the situation in the following way:

> On the one hand, it is the state that initiates and sustains the new market-oriented policies and which eagerly lays out the welcome mat to overseas capital. On the other hand, the state also finds that the new forces it has unleashed often have a logic quite threatening to its own desire of fixing culture within territorial borders.

Before the reforms, there was no question of the socialist state's antagonism to capital, nor was their any doubt regarding the kind of modernity being advocated. In post-Mao China, however, the state's fitful attempts to deploy capital opens channels for new discourses of modernity to enter. These may simply be represented by new cultural products from Taiwan and Hong Kong, such as pop music and karaoke clubs. Or they may be more problematic, as the economic power of "Greater China" increasingly challenges the Chinese state's claims of sole authorship in the narrative of modern China. "On the mainland, patriotic scholars are quick to reject Greater China as a bankers' fantasy, an illusion of outsiders greedy to cash in on China's booming economy. They fear that any ideological recognition of a Chinese transnational capitalist zone will undermine China as a territorially based entity" (Ong 1997: 176). At any rate, the key conflict in China's modernization project is not the typical scenario – too often repeated uncritically by radical Western scholars – of the Third World being overrun by Western economic and cultural imperialism. Rather, it is between the Chinese state and the fluid capital of the broader East Asian region.

In the competing discursive systems represented by these two forces, however, the central problematic remains the same. This is the question of defining a modern subjectivity for China (for the nation and the enterprise, as well as the individual and community). Zhang Xudong (1997: 17–18) poses the question in these terms:

> [H]ow is it possible to define [Chinese modernity] not as a duplication of modernity as such but as something more or something else, that is to

say, as a potential alternative? The alternative in question derives not so much from the cultural, ideological difference or the uniqueness asserted by various essentialist viewpoints – these assumptions of alternativity should themselves be contemplated with cautious detachment. Rather, it must be seen as shaped by the concrete socio-economic, political, as well as cultural conditions that produced the Chinese problematic itself.

As we have seen in the previous section, the alternative modernities being articulated throughout East Asia traffic in exactly the kinds of "essentialist viewpoints" (for example, pan-Asian Confucianism) Zhang warns us to regard with caution. Zhang goes on to argue that Chinese modernism – that is, the cultural productions that struggle precisely with this problematic – is marked by what Berman (1982) has called the modernism of underdevelopment. As a non-Western society for which the nature of modernity has been primarily defined by the discursive hegemony of the West, rather than by its own indigenous experience of socioeconomic, political and cultural change, Chinese modernity "is forced to build on fantasies and dreams of modernity, to nourish itself on an intimacy and a struggle with mirages and ghosts" (Berman 1982: 232). Berman argues that such a fantastic modernity is inevitably shrill and inchoate; "it turns in on itself and tortures itself for its inability to single-handedly make history – or else throws itself into extravagant attempts to take on itself the whole burden of history."

For Zhang, Chinese modernism displays just such Olympian extravagance, revealed, for example, in the power continually invested by elites in cultural revolution as the key to China's autonomous development and modernization. Such claims can be heard throughout China's intellectual and artistic ranks, where even pop stars like Cui Jian insist that China's "problem" is not political or economic, but cultural. Zhang's analysis suggests that an authentic Chinese modernity can only start with China's own material conditions, and not the fantastic discursive imaginings of elites struggling with the "mirages and ghosts" of the West. This, then, is the fundamental struggle of Chinese modernity, "the question of how to experience the new tempospatial order (or rather disorder) as a subject" (Zhang 1997: 61). Chinese modernity, as Zhang claims, is an unfinished and open-ended project, one in which an indigenously defined "subject position" is necessary if the dislocations and displacements of a voracious global capitalism are to be transformed "into a modernity that is organic rather than traumatic."

Ever since its deliberate inclusion in China's "National Social and Economic Development Plan" of the 7th Five Year Plan (1985–1990) (see Xu 1996: 16), tourism has become an important stage in the playing out of China's modern problematic. In the tourist landscapes constructed in 1990s China can be found the symbolic markers of a chaotic and contradictory collection of actors, all insisting on a dominant voice in the representation of the modern Chinese subject. The purportedly socialist state invests theme parks, for example, with patriotic nationalism as it attempts to fix the boundaries of a unique and essential China, a nation equal and unique among a modern community of nations. Likewise, transnational capital invests in tourist landscapes that symbolize a traditional Chinese cultural core for the new Pacific Century based in flexible accumulation rather than "socialism with Chinese characteristics."

At the same time, however, an additional set of actors clamor for a voice amid these powerful competing forces in the tourist landscape. We have already encountered these additional voices in the Japanese village of Morita and their Tsugaru Earth Village. They are those with the most at stake in the modern project. For it is literally upon their bodies that the most exploitative objectifications of modernity are experienced. In this book, they are the villagers in Guizhou who struggle to refashion the tourist gaze into something they can maintain subjectivity over. Zhang's question of an authentic modernity for China – conceived primarily as an intellectual and artistic exercise – is in fact most profoundly weighed by them, in their own language and in their own locally-bound actions. As a metaphor of modernity itself, tourism objectifies them even as it paradoxically provides the materials with which they may construct their own modern subjectivity. We will get to their story in time. But before doing so, we must sketch the broader parameters of tourism in China, as an industry saturated by competing discursive systems of modernity.

Figure 1.1 Alternative modernity? Micky Mao's Café, Yangshuo

Figure 1.2 "Self-Orientalization" for tourists: *Meiyou* ("not have") Café, Yangshuo

The discursive contradictions of Chinese modernity have been observed by Anagnost (1993) in the miniaturized landscape icons of the "Splendid China" (*Jinxiu Zhonghua*) theme park in Shenzhen. Within the park's 30 hectares of detailed scale replicas of all the Chinese tourist landscape's most essential sites, one can – as the park's advertisements make clear – take in all of China within a couple hours of comfortable strolling along pathways. Not only have the park's creators made it easier to see all the necessary monumental features of China's "nationscape," but geographical inconveniences have been eradicated as well. The landmarks of Splendid China are much more efficiently arranged than their real counterparts. Thus, the miniature Potala Palace (whose inclusion itself marks the geopolitics of nationalism subsumed in the park) sits on a small hill next to the undulating Great Wall; the diverse architectural styles of Miao, Dong, and Buyi minority villages are offered in one convenient "nationality village site."

Most intriguing, however, is the juxtaposition of a miniaturized landscape of "timeless China" set within that most modern, transient, and temporal of all Chinese cities, Shenzhen. It is this juxtaposition, Anagnost suggests, that is the most compelling expression of modernity's contingencies in China. Shenzhen is the site of China's latest revolutionary rupture, the dramatic upheaval of "fast capitalism." "Shenzhen hurtling toward the telos of modernity *is* the present 'time' of the nation, but one that all the more requires the calming certainty of a timeless identity residing within"

Figure 1.3 "The next best thing to being there": miniature Potala Palace at Splendid
China theme park, Shenzhen.

(Anagnost 1993: 590). Splendid China serves as that "calming certainty," as
its position within China's earliest and most successful Special Economic
Zone signifies, perhaps, a collective ambivalence over the destabilizing open-
ness which has only intensified in the 1990s.

The opening of Splendid China on 21 September 1989, marks the real
beginning of tourism's active collaboration in the project of Chinese modernity, only the most obvious aspect of which is the intensified market
commercialism and commodification that have combined to invent a
nostalgic past upon which to build a sense of national identity and alternative modernity. In the 1990s, China experienced a veritable "theme park
fever" (*zhuti gongyuan re*). Within three years following the opening of
Splendid China, there were at least sixteen large-scale theme parks
throughout China, and hundreds of small-scale parks. The majority of these
were based – like the "Dragon World" make-over of Singapore's Haw Par
Villa – on themes of Chinese history and folk mythology. For example, by
1993 there were at least 40 parks based on Chinese folk legends, 23 of which
were devoted to the classical tale *Journey to the West*, 34 parks based on
ethnic folk culture, and 8 based on historical re-creations (Bao 1995: 7–8).

Shenzhen, however, remains China's undisputed theme park capital.
According to Bao (1995), with over 20 large-scale attractions, Shenzhen's
tourist industry had over 8 billion *yuan* in capital assets in 1995. In 1994, the
city had 29 independent travel agencies, 294 hotels (*fandian*), 550 guest-

houses (*lüdian, zhaodaisuo*), over 300 large restaurants, and 642 karaoke clubs. Ong's (1996) claim that China's modernization ought to be more appropriately labeled "karaokization" makes the most sense in Shenzhen. Her observations about the "self-orientalizing" nature of Chinese modernity also find expression in the "Oriental Mysteries" park (*Dongfang Shenqu*) and the recently opened "Dragon Garden." Indeed, in Shenzhen, even peasants and their tools are exoticized, as evidenced in the new "Agricultural Park." China's third most popular tourist destination (with over 6 million overnight arrivals in 1993) is a city that hardly existed a decade before. The almost ephemeral nature of Shenzhen itself seems perfectly matched by its most popular attractions. The theme parks that dot the new urban landscape like modern gossamers offer the tourist an excursion in hyperreality. As Pemberton (1994: 247) has observed of Indonesia's Mini (the park that no doubt inspired Splendid China), "origins are presented as recovered in a form so totally unconfusing, so endowed with an abstract miniaturized clarity, that the distance, between what represents and what is represented, in effect, collapses." Tourists themselves have come to the same conclusions about Splendid China, finding its miniatures to be more than just representations. As Bao (1995: 23–4) points out, people come because the miniatures are "artistic creations themselves." One tourist even went so far as to say that, "because Shenzhen has this Splendid China, it also has history." In 1991, a new star, discovered by the Zhijin Observatory in Nanjing, was named "Splendid China Star." The head of the observatory commented that they decided to name the star after the theme park because "Splendid China collects all the best of the Chinese people for the world to see; it represents our achievements."

But if China's glorious heritage is represented in such an "unconfusing" miniaturized way at Splendid China, the overall vision of Chinese modernity being conveyed in its burgeoning tourist landscapes is much less straightforward. The Chinese state, for its part, has offered Shenzhen its blessings through Deng Xiaoping's 1992 southern tour – heralding his support for a renewed intensity to China's open-door reforms – and through Jiang Zemin's visit to Splendid China that same year, in which he praised the theme park's patriotic message (Bao 1995: 24). But the patriotism celebrated by Jiang is not necessarily territorially-bound; it is also claimed by the transnational capitalist elite in proclaiming their allegiance to "Greater China." In these terms, Shenzhen's theme park landscape (itself developed primarily with overseas capital) conveys an attractive environment for overseas Chinese investors. Indeed, Splendid China is located within a designated region of Shenzhen, dedicated in 1985 for the explicit purpose of attracting overseas Chinese capital. This "Overseas Chinese City" (*Huaqiao Cheng*) has become a major electronics assembly zone, with the Overseas Chinese City Development Company becoming Shenzhen's fourth largest enterprise by 1993 (Bao 1995: 62–4). The location decision for Splendid China was made explicitly to help bolster investments in this special zone.

Here, overseas Chinese capitalists are encouraged to invest not simply in China, but in the modern continuation of China's rich heritage, a heritage conveniently recreated in miniature in case one needs to be reminded of the point. And so, in Splendid China, the contenders for a Chinese modernity (the nation-state, the transnational elite, market socialism, global capitalism) all meet and intertwine. The result, as Anagnost (1993: 589) notes, is a certain degree of ambivalence. The siting of Splendid China in Shenzhen exemplifies an "ambivalent temporality of the nation-state as being always caught 'between' its simultaneous desire for being both deeply historical and yet undeniably modern."

China's tourist landscape is replete with confusing signifiers of modernity, where tourists consume the past, the future, the nation, and the world, often all at the same time. Urban China has witnessed a proliferation of "old towns" (*fangujie*) throughout the 1990s. Old towns are basically shopping malls of luxury consumer items, couched within replica Ming and Qing cityscapes. These spectacles of commodity consumption are at once a rejection of the socialist architectural legacy, an invention of traditional Chinese urbanity, and an affirmation of "market Socialism" in which commodity exchange has seemingly replaced industrial production as the driver of history. Old towns thus offer another "calming certainty" of nostalgia for a China wary of entering the maelstrom of modernity. As Anagnost (1993, 595) puts it, "this juxtaposition of a nostalgia for a historical past with the commodity is not accidental; the desire for one excites the desire for the other." In the old town, the aesthetic of loss inherent in the modern experience becomes a commodity; it is a tourist landscape that apparently thrives on the experience of anxiety, ambivalence, and disorientation that modernity has brought. Yet it is also a landscape that celebrates the market and luxury consumption, and projects a China confident among the post-industrial nations of the West. It is as if socialism was only a forgotten rupture in an urban heritage that is almost timeless (see Dirlik 1997: 319).

Indeed, the socialist era of Mao is almost invisible in Chinese tourism. Rather, tourism's turn to consumable pre-modern landscapes recapitulates a *pre-socialist* struggle with formulating an alternative Chinese modernity. In the 1920s and 1930s, for example, many intellectuals celebrated the rural folk as the steadfast soul of a China weakened by centuries of feudalism and the challenges the aggressive West. Schein (1993: 110) comments that especially after the fall of the Qing there was "an intense search for alternative sources of strength and vitality to be found among the Chinese folk." This yielded "Going-to-the-people" and folk literature movements. In 1918, Gu Jiegang and Zhou Zuoren established the country's first folksong collection at Beijing University. As China seemed to collapse and break apart under imperialist domination, capitalist penetration, civil war, and finally, Japanese invasion, a national spirit was increasingly projected onto the uncorrupted lifestyle of the rural peasant. Fleeing Japanese occupation, the poet Wen Yidou led a group of 200 students through the mountains of Hunan,

Guizhou, and Yunnan, collecting over 2,000 folksongs along the way. Later publishing these folksongs, Wen wrote in the preface:

> You say these [poems] are primitive and savage. You are right, and that is just what we need today. We've been civilized too long, and now that we have nowhere left to go we shall have to pull out the last and purest card, and release the animal nature that has lain dormant in us for several thousand years, so that we can bite back.
>
> (Cited in Spence 1981: 317)

Probably the most prolific elegist of the rural folk was the West Hunan writer Shen Congwen, whose literary regionalism was driven by a primitive folk vitality in which traditional Confucian anxieties about marginal or non-Han lifestyles and behavior were recast as the very spirit which modern China needed to shake off imperial domination and reclaim a strong national identity (Oakes 1995).

What is interesting, then, about the reconstructed folk landscapes of contemporary Chinese tourism is their nearly complete effacement of the legacy of high socialism in China. This is perhaps the most confusing message being conveyed about Chinese modernity. Chinese tourists consume landscapes of folk tradition, myth, legend, and custom; they tour a self-orientalized terrain with selective amnesia. In "patriotic" Splendid China, there are no monuments to the radical socialist project of Mao Zedong. Instead, the theme park landscapes of Shenzhen offer the purportedly stable and timeless folk for tourist consumption. Two parks subsequently built next to Splendid China perfectly complement this desire for a "calming certainty" as the foundation for Chinese modernity, rather than the dislocations and ruptures of the great socialist experiment. This triad of parks conveys a false modernity that revels in the misplaced search for authenticity, rather than making sense of the destabilizing forces which have made that search necessary in the first place.

These two additional parks are "China Folk Culture Villages" (*Zhongguo Minsu Wenhuacun*) and "Window on the World" (*Shijie zhi Chuang*). The Folk Culture Villages was opened on 1 October 1991, and, much like the Indonesian Mini, it unambiguously situates ethnic minority culture within a comprehensive definition of the modern Chinese nation (note, for example, the opening date: China's national day). Featuring twenty four life-sized villages (each simply a collection of three or four "typical" dwellings), the park seeks – in true oxymoronic tourist fashion – to "authentically represent" 21 of China's 56 officially recognized *minzu* groups.[2] Anagnost's (1993: 587) reading of Splendid China is in many ways relevant to the Folk Culture Villages in that the regional, cultural, and ethnic differences which pervade China are "domesticated and rendered purely as display" for modern Chinese, whirling in the maelstrom of Shenzhen, to gaze upon in constructing a sense of modern identity. But, as if to heighten the juxtaposition between transnational modernity and the nation-state ideal of territorial uniqueness, a McDonald's restaurant has been placed right outside the gate of the Villages. Emerging from this collection of exotic and colorful ethnic spectacle, the arresting vision of the Golden Arches is perhaps all it takes to convince the visitor that modern China's identity rests squarely upon the shoulders of its "timeless" ethnic minorities.

Surrounded, as it were, by transnational capital, China Folk Culture Villages attempts to offer a coherent vision of modernity consistent with the fixed certainty of the nation-state. Like Indonesia's Mini, the Villages traffics in the selective cultural essence of a particular ethnic group, weeding out those factors which might detract from a vision of (multi)national unity. In visiting the Villages, tourists may passively collect a set of carefully crafted images and experiences which flow together with enough standardized similarity from village to village to convey a sense of the wholeness which pervades the park: modern China. A souvenir book available at the Folk Culture Villages illustrates this quite explicitly. Written in English and Chinese, it states that, "Guided by the principle of 'originating from real life but rising above it, and discarding the dross and selecting the essential' [*yuan yu shenghuo, gao yu shenghuo, huiji jingcui, you suo qushe*], the Villages attempts to reflect from various angles the folk customs and culture of China's nationalities" (Shen and Cheung 1992: 4).

Figure 1.4 Dong drum tower and covered bridge: China Folk Culture Villages theme park, Shenzhen

The book goes on to entice the visitor with descriptions of the various festival activities which are regularly performed at the Villages. The visitor's reaction to all this is quite prescribed: "Grand, romantic, rejoicing and auspicious, these festivities will enable visitors to take in the happy atmosphere of the magnificent occasions and to feel the poetic quality of the life of the Chinese nation." The touristic vision of the Chinese nation being promoted here is of a poetic and colorful mosaic, a distinctive tapestry woven by the happy and servile minorities.

Extravagantly complementing the Villages' (multi)national vision of modern China, Window on the World completes the trinity of parks with a landscape of miniaturized monuments from around the world, a collection of iconographic essences from the community of nations toward which China now seeks alignment. Thus, France is represented by a scale model of the Eiffel Tower, Denmark is a mini-Copenhagen street, while the United States, ironically, weighs in with the Statue of Liberty and the lower Manhattan collection of buildings clustered around Wall Street. The effect seems to be one of putting the supposedly "universal" aspirations of liberty, democracy, and free enterprise in their safely miniaturized place, where they can be viewed by tourists as but one version of modernity among many on display. Thus, after strolling through China's heritage of ancient monuments (Splendid China) and ancient folk cultures (the Villages) we complete the

Figure 1.5 Miao song and dance performance, the *dongfang disikou* ("Oriental Disco"): China Folk Culture Villages, Shenzhen

Figure 1.6 Ethnic costumes for rent, Li minority theme park, Hainan

journey with a triumphant return to the "Asian way" as an alternative path to modernity.

Both the nation-state and transnational capital have muscled their way into the Shenzhen tourist landscape to offer simultaneous, though not altogether mutually exclusive, visions of a Chinese modernity. Shenzhen's theme parks display both the ideal of a (multi)national modern Chinese nation, and the alternative modernity of a rising capitalist core in East Asia, where "timeless" Chinese (Confucian) heritage, rather than socialism or other state projects, forms the basis of a new subjectivity. I have focused on Shenzhen's theme parks, here, as a sort of epicenter of China's tourist landscapes, and of the conflicting discourses and contradictions those landscapes reveal. So far, those conflicts and contradictions have been defined within the framework of the Chinese nation-state and transnational Chinese capital. But throughout this chapter has been subsumed another message regarding the contingencies of modernity. For not only must we understand Shenzhen's tourist landscapes as embodying competing narratives of Chinese modernity, but we must also recognize both of these competing narratives as conveying *false* modernities. Theme park landscapes necessarily falsify place and time (Shaw and Williams 1994: 168); they erase the chaos of everyday life and replace it with essential categories, markers of the kind of modernity (and tradition) the state and capital would most benefit from. It is not simply that these parks convey messages about Chinese modernity, or even that these messages may be confusing (for example, in that they apparently ignore the decades of socialism that have most profoundly shaped modern China). Rather, the point is that they convey messages about Chinese modernity that seek to dominate the imaginings of the public (Horne 1992: 374–5). They convey that side of modernity which seeks to order and regulate through standard categories and essential abstractions. In masking modernity with a "calming certainty," they offer shrines to the misplaced search for authenticity.

Why introduce an analysis of tourism in China's impoverished mountain interior with a study of Shenzhen theme parks? In Guizhou, we can see clearly the same dominant practices at work in the tourism industry, in which village landscapes are appropriated in order to convey the same messages about Chinese modernity by offering tourists an "authentic" version of the replica they may have viewed in Shenzhen. But now the Shenzhen replica itself becomes the signified, more "real" than the original. Thus, in Guizhou, tourist villages strive to achieve a theme park-style experience on par with that provided by China Folk Culture Villages. Shenzhen has established the model that the industry seeks to emulate throughout the country, a landscape of "calming certainty" that legitimizes both the state's and capital's narratives of Chinese modernity. This, then, becomes the dominant power framework that conditions the tourist landscapes of Guizhou. It is within this framework that tourist villagers themselves must attempt to carve out their own modern subjectivity if they are to resist being completely subsumed by alienating abstractions being trafficked out of Shenzhen. Articulating their struggle for an "authentic" modernity is this book's final destination.

We must make one more stop, however, before arriving in Guizhou. Theoretical work on the geography tourism has been, for the most part, ill-equipped to deal with the possibility of "tourees" – those objects of the tourist's gaze – manipulating that gaze in order to construct a meaningful landscape or place that might offer a basis for their own subjectivity. The following chapter thus offers a critical appraisal of the relevant aspects of tourism geography in order to establish a clearer theoretical basis for the empirical chapters that follow.

2 Place and process in the tourist political economy

INTRODUCTION

Imbedded within the previous chapter lies a paradoxical conception of modernity. The attraction of theme parks may derive largely from their ability to temporarily answer a popular sense of ambivalence toward the experience of modernity. That ambivalence stems from a sense of loss as one regards the forces of rapid change. Modernity, it was suggested earlier, is an experience that enables a distanced objectivity with which to perceive a new landscape fragmented by the forces of rapid socio-economic, political, and cultural change, thus engendering an aesthetics of loss and an ironic wariness of change. Modernity drives people to grapple with the paradoxical desire to reclaim a sense of continuity with the past even as the social conditions which allow one to imagine such continuity deny the very possibility of its return. While the common response to this paradox is to invent an ideal of authentic organic continuity – a landscape or place "uncorrupted" by the dislocations of modernization – this is merely an escape from the real task of claiming subjectivity over the chaotic process of change itself. Of course, there are other ways to escape too. The nation-state provides an ideal haven from the paradox of modernity, inventing for its citizens a secure sense of identity through the mythologies of nationalism. Capital, too, provides security, by subjecting society to the behavioral norms and disciplines needed to guarantee the expropriation of surplus labor value.

Theme parks are perhaps the clearest example of how the tourist landscape reflects the modern desire for escape, for stable, essential categories of people and places that convey timelessness and security from the uncertainties of change. As such, theme park landscapes complement well the mythologizing of the nation along with the disciplining of capital. Theme parks convey a narrative of national heritage, and do so with the standardized, predictable categories needed to generate profit. For example, It wasn't until Haw Par Villa was rebuilt with significant capital investment, given a hefty admission fee, and marketed as an easily recognizable landscape of modern (alternative) Asia that it became a true theme park, a landscape dominated by the needs of the state and of capital.

If an "authentic" modern subjectivity entails not an escape from but an embracing of modern contingencies, inviting the "anxiety of form in motion" – as Goethe advocated in "Permanence of Change" (Goethe 1983: 168–9) – then what kind of landscape might actually express such authenticity? More to the point, do tourist landscapes inherently entail a misplaced search for authenticity, or can they be appropriated or manipulated to convey the real possibility of the modern subject? To address these questions, we must examine more carefully geographical conceptions of landscape and place in relation to modernity, and conceptions of tourism in relationship to modernization. This chapter is devoted to such an exploration in order to lay the theoretical groundwork for our journey into the tourist villages of Guizhou. Ultimately I will argue that the state and capital are not the sole agents in building a tourist landscape that capitalizes on public ambivalence in order to solidify their power. Rather, villagers themselves strive to mediate the construction of that landscape in order to maintain their own subjectivity, to make their experience of modernization one that is, in Zhang Xudong's terms, "organic rather than traumatic." Their struggle, ironically, represents something close to the possibilities for an authentic modern subjectivity; ironic because it is by manipulating tourism's falsifications themselves that villagers struggle to maintain their own authenticity, rather than through resistance to or escape from tourism's essentializing abstractions and objectifications. Indeed, only by facing these dislocating falsifications can an "authentic" modern subjectivity be attempted at all.

THE BETWEENNESS OF PLACE

It is often thought that place and space occupy opposite ends of a conceptual continuum representing the geographical changes associated with modernity. Giddens (1990: 18–21), as we have seen, characterizes modernity as a "disembedding of social systems," that is, the "'lifting out' of social relations from local contexts of interaction and their restructuring across infinite spans of time-space." Modernity literally dis-places social interactions, tearing "space away from place by fostering relations between 'absent' others, locationally distant from any given situation of face-to-face interaction." Thus, modernity can be thought of as a placeless terrain:

> The primacy of place in pre-modern settings has been largely destroyed by disembedding and time-space distanciation. Place has become phantasmagoric because the structures by means of which it is constituted are no longer locally organised. The local and the global, in other words, have become inextricably intertwined. Feelings of close attachment to or identification with places still persist. But these are themselves disembedded: they do not just express locally based practices

and involvements but are shot through with much more distant influences.

(Giddens 1990: 108–9)

Place was of the pre-modern world before everyone was uprooted by modernization, and remains a geographical irrelevancy, an anachronism in the modern landscape, evoked only as a spectacle or commodity: Disneyland's "Main Street, USA." In such terms, then, place itself may be the object of modernity's restless and dissatisfied search for authenticity. For precisely this reason, it seems appropriate that place be reclaimed as a geographical expression not of modernity's misplaced search for authenticity, but, paradoxically, of the radical displacements of modernity itself.

It has been a standard position of critical intellectual thought to claim place as the casualty of modernity. Place could, for example, be perceived as the all-but-lost receptacle of harmonious society unthreatened by mass media, "low brow" culture, industrial commerce, or even democratic representation. Writing in 1948, for example, T.S. Eliot was dismayed to find "mass modernity" eating away the soul of British society. "The great majority of human beings," he urged, "should go on living in the place in which they were born. Family, class, and local loyalty all support one another; and if one of these decays, the other will suffer also" (cited in Burgess and Gold 1985: 19). For Eliot, there is no progressive or regenerating force in modernity, only destruction and waste; he sees no possibility for authenticity within the experience of modernity itself. Rather, authenticity is found in a place that no longer exists, a place where people "knew their place." Edward Relph's work on the subject presents perhaps the most obvious translation of Eliot's despair into the specific language of geography. In *Place and Placelessness* (1976: 92), Relph wrote of a modernity pervaded by an "inauthentic sense of place" facilitated by tourism, kitsch, and mass media, which "are not developed and formulated by the people themselves" but are produced in "museumified" and "disneyfied" form by "manufacturers, governments, and professional designers." "The People," for Relph, are "the folk," that mythical organic community at one with the land, the true spirit and soul of the nation. Relph (1976: 117) insists that such folk are no longer recoverable in any authentic fashion:

> [I]n many cultures less technologically sophisticated than our own a profound sense of place has certainly prevailed. The depth of meaning and diversity of places associated with authentic experiences are, however, greatly weakened in most contemporary cultures. The development and diffusion of the inauthentic attitudes of place and kitsch and technique ... appear to be widespread and increasing in most of the Western world. The trend is towards an environment of few significant places – towards a placeless geography, a flatscape, a meaningless pattern of buildings.

Such a myopic and prescribed vision of modernity reflects a desire to find in place an escape from the "Permanence of Change." Relph is simply eluci- dating a much deeper trend in the scholarship of modernization, in which place becomes equated with the stable, organic communities of "tradition." Place was devalued by modernization theories of social science because it was thought to be irrelevant, an expression of the "primitive society" modernization seeks to overcome. Agnew (1989) has argued that place was relegated to a residual category because it was conflated with the idea of community. The community, of course, was thought to be the pre-modern precursor to the spatial order of state-based urban industrialism, a stage of localized social organization replaced by the "imagined community" of the nation (Anderson 1983). Indeed, envisioned in such a way, place could even be appropriated by the state (and, ultimately, by capital), as a museum-like repository of the nation's traditions, a locale of the myth of a continuous organic heritage.

Is there another way of conceiving place in the modern world? More to the point, is there a concept of place that does not ultimately submit to a discursive modernity narrated by the state and by capital? Is there a place for a "people" not relegated to quaint anachronisms or mythologized folk? Place can, I believe, be conceived as the terrain of an "authentic" modernity, where people struggle to carve an identity based not on lost tradition but on the liberating possibilities of change itself. The clues to such a place can be found by briefly returning the Wessex landscape of Thomas Hardy, a place Raymond Williams called a "border country." For Williams, Wessex was a place between, where the struggles over modernity's contradictions and contingencies found actual expression in the landscape. It was a place "between custom and education, between work and ideas," and between dwelling and displacement. The clues to what makes this a *place* – that is, invested with the meaning needed to craft a sense of identity – rather than simply a landscape, are offered in Williams's own fiction, his novels of Wales. In narrating the processes of modernization experienced by the people of Glynmawr, Williams suggests less a eulogy for the enclosed village tradition (that is, the authentic place of Relph's imagination) than a sense of place that comes to be defined as locals participate in the processes of change swirling around them. The valley dwellers play out their lives as a balancing act between integration and isolation.

For Williams, this tension yields a process of cultural production, of continuous struggles to reconstruct a place out of the ever-fragmenting terrain of modernity. Thus, Wales as a culture was produced from the multiple instances of individuals inhabiting in-between places and acting on the contradictions of their lives. *This* was the modern Welsh experience. It was defined by the many problematic and complex connections between individuals and a broader political-economy, rather than some fantasy of the organic community making its last stand against the unfeeling steam- roller of progress (see Smith 1989: 44–5). What Williams sought to articulate were the connections between different levels of abstraction (Harvey 1995), in which individuals in specific locales struggled with broader forces that operated across much vaster scales of space and time – the forces of state-sponsored nationalism, and of agricultural and industrial capitalism. Glynmawr was a "community" not because it had once been a "way of life" relatively isolated from these forces, but because it was a terrain of struggle (Eldridge and Eldridge 1994: 184–5), a place being constantly remade, a place between. Place may therefore be thought of as that spatial terrain in which levels of abstraction clash and conflict, requiring individual action (Longhurst 1991: 236). This, then, draws us closer to conceiving a geography of modernity that approaches the authentic possibilities of modernity itself, rather than misplacing that authenticity in the haze of nostalgia and tradition.

Such an approach to place diverges somewhat from critical geographies that tend to regard place simply as a terrain of resistance, a kind of oppositional spatiality that can offer some liberation from the abstract "space of flows" of capital and the state (for example, Clark 1993; Rose 1994; Cresswell 1996). These radical narratives of place-as-site-of-resistance have been inspired by a more general spatial turn in the field of cultural studies. Since the 1970s, critical theorists have been pointing out that modernity's inherent struggle – between subjectivity and objectification – is not just historical (for example, as argued by Marx) but profoundly *spatial* as well. Theoretical work on the social production of space and its cultural ramifications has led to a large body of writing on the geographies of exclusion, discipline, and visibility in modern societies (Foucault 1977; Gramsci 1971; Lefebvre 1991; Mitchell 1988; Sibley 1995; Soja 1989). Such a perspective has informed the work of Said (1979, 1993) as well, for whom modern imperialism and colonialism were most significantly projects of spatial production, representation, and control (Gregory 1995). Said's work has, in turn, helped spawn an emphasis in cultural studies on issues of diaspora, displacement, and disjuncture (Appadurai 1990) and how these experiences have led to a new regionalist politics of representation, reclaiming subjectivity over the fractured landscapes of modernity (for example, Wilson 1995). To these theoretical developments, geographers have weighed in with place as radical site of struggle.

Yet, the danger here lies in allowing the concept of place to slip into an oppositional category, thereby losing its truly radical potential. A "progressive sense of place," as Massey (1993) calls it, is not simply based on disempowered groups resisting the hegemonic power of capital and the state. As Rose (1994: 48) points out, "power relations do not neatly divide the cultural field into two opposing camps." Rather, local cultural politics are complicated by the hybrid identities resulting from complex social relations that fracture the cultural field. Place, therefore, is itself a contradictory terrain, rather than a secure refuge of resistance. Arriving at similar conclusions, Rose comments that spaces of resistance aren't simply emancipatory, but are inherently paradoxical. Indeed, places as sites of resistance "may not remain emancipatory" but instead are "insecure, precarious, and fluctuating" (Rose 1993: 159–60). Similarly, Massey (1992) has ironically observed that as long as patriarchy, imperialism, colonialism, capitalism, and nationalism have been experienced by people in places, displacement has been a fundamental part of their conceptions of place. Place is the shifting fulcrum between subjective appropriation and abstract objectification. It is the terrain upon which individuals act in attempts to secure a meaningful sense of spatial identity. Such action is grounded by an awareness of modernity's inherent paradox, in which the threats of dislocation and displacement enable a desire for organic continuity, for the "eternal and immutable," even as they render such continuity impossible.

The Guizhou tourist villages examined in this book are places of this kind. They are not simply anachronistic remnants of a "purer age" of premodern authenticity (as the state and tourism industries represent them), nor are they sites defined solely by the resistance of villagers to the dominant representations of this misplaced search for authenticity. Rather, they are paradoxical and contingent spaces in which villagers attempt to carve a sense of identity and produce a landscape that is meaningful to them, using the very tools that continuously work to alienate them and turn them into the objects rather than subjects of change. It is this latter issue that makes them truly modern places of instability, paradox, and contradiction. In their own representations of place, these villagers do not seek to "return" to a more secure past as a refuge from the disruptive forces brought to bear by the state and external capital. Instead they seek to appropriate those forces – along with the representations they come with – and craft from them an identity that is itself very modern.

Equipped with this conception of place as a dynamic and contingent *process* of change, a landscape being always remade and reinvented, we must ask whether theories of tourism are adequate for understanding tourist "impacts" in similar terms. If tourism is regarded as a fundamentally modern experience, how might tourism's locally specific effects be understood in relation to the paradox of modernity? Do critical assessments of tourism reflect a deeper understanding of modernity, or do tourism's critics too often get detoured themselves by the misplaced search for authenticity? These questions help frame the following section's evaluation of tourism studies.

PLACE AND THE TOURIST LANDSCAPE

As the previous chapter sought to demonstrate, tourism is an industry ideally suited for capitalizing on modernity's ambivalences. In partnership with the state and the needs of capital accumulation, tourism thrives by producing landscapes of security, landscapes seemingly more "real" (that is, conforming to the essential categories we construct in order to cope with the modern experience) than the confusing reality of the modern world itself. Tourist landscapes are often cloaked in an aesthetics of loss, conveying places that are not dynamic or struggled over, but frozen as leftovers of some pre-modern timelessness. Tourism is also a system of capital accumulation, commercial production, and market exchange. Tourist landscapes are not simply representations, but are commodities invested with material as well as symbolic value. The tourist experience involves two important processes. First, those whose places become the objects of the tourist gaze – for example, the Guizhou villagers of this study – must strike a balance between the colonizing forces of tourism (representations of "the folk," market penetration, commercial development, uneven capital accumulation) and maintaining a place-based sense of identity. Second, tourists themselves need to see their expectations of tradition and (misplaced) authenticity satisfied in the tourist experience. These two sides of tourism mirror the contradiction of modernity broached in the previous chapter: between the search for authenticity in other times and places – the imagined authenticity of tradition – and the struggle for authenticity within the modern experience itself.

The commodification of place

A growing field of research on tourism has dealt with the political economy of the industry itself. One common theme likens international tourism to a colonial economy (see, for example, Palmer 1994). Bandy (1996: 557), for instance, refers to ecotourism as "a kinder, gentler colonialism." This is a particularly useful approach, and it reveals much about the nature of the tourist production system. It also reveals much about the conception of modernity assumed by many of the tourism industry's critics. One of the conceptual tools most illustrative of the neo-colonial approach in the study of tourism is the "commodification of place." While this is a metaphorically rich approach for a critical geography of tourism, its use has, in fact, revealed very little about place itself. This reflects at least two general problems in tourism studies. First is the general problem, succinctly summarized by Crick (1989: 311) as a "lack of the local voice." For those addressing tourism's political and economic dimensions, the discussion of how local people fit into the tourism picture generally takes on a simplistic and emphatically critical tone, with stock phrases such as "loss of traditional culture" or "loss of a way of life" used to lament the plight of those mercilessly "impacted" by the tourist production system. Second, and resulting from the first problem, is the confusion regarding questions of culture and authenticity and their relationship to modernity. Thus, while critical studies of tourism have developed a sophisticated apparatus for understanding the political economy of the industry, their focus on this dimension often fails to account for the complex cultural negotiations being undertaken at the local level among those most directly affected by the tourism experience.

It is important to note just how well the tourist production system fits with the ideas of "late capitalism" and restructuring being debated in the social sciences. As John Urry (1990: 82) claims, the post-modern culture of post-industrial societies makes it increasingly difficult to distinguish tourism from other forms of behavior; lately, "people are much of the time tourists whether they like it or not." Culture, exoticism, and aesthetic experience have come to occupy an increasingly central position in post-industrial commercial production. In our everyday patterns of consumption, we act more and more like tourists purchasing cultural experiences, identities, and aestheticized representations of reality, along with our material commodities. With tourism, we have an industry that fits nicely with all the "flux and ephemerality" of late capitalism; it is highly fragmented and disorganized, with different services being subcontracted among a vast array of providers, and it thrives on the expansion and deepening of commodity markets currently associated with the "flexible regime" of capital accumulation, in which there has been a transfer "of the logic and rationality of commodity production to the sphere of consumption and culture" (Britton 1991: 453). Referring specifically to ecotourism, Bandy (1996: 550) finds it a "a new globalizing moment of late capitalist consumer economy." Tourism development also illustrates the ways a decentralized capitalist accumulation regime necessitates a locality-specific strategy of development. Indeed, "In this respect tourism is merely following, is perhaps in the forefront of, an important recent dynamic; the creation and marketing of experiences is becoming increasingly an overt and conscious avenue of capitalist accumulation" (Britton 1991: 465).

Tourism has thus been presented by geographers such as Stephen Britton as a process which clearly necessitates a locality-specific scale of analysis. It appears, however, that this has simply encouraged tourism to be conceptualized as a proxy for the fragmented and image-oriented nature of late capitalism. This usually yields analysis in which the local place itself, in all its social and cultural richness, becomes blurred. Place is only important in so far as it gets colonized, commodified, standardized, and uprooted by capitalism to ride the post-modern global culture industry. "We are bombarded," wrote Britton, "from all over the globe with a collage of images and snippets of insight on different places, cultures, peoples, and histories" (1991: 466). The issue, then, is whether such a critical approach to tourism doesn't unwittingly assume place to be the unfortunate casualty of modernity, articulating a kind of modernization that leaves in its wake a placeless landscape, where "authentic" place-based community identities once thrived. Britton seemed to have thought so. Sounding suspiciously like Relph, he noted that the "commodification of place" associated with tourism, "generates a 'flatness' where depth of appreciation, understanding, and especially meaning, is replaced with a new kind of superficiality in the most literal sense: a loss of depth of feeling, meaning or understanding is compensated for with transitory exhilaration, glitter, particular kinds of euphoria, and intensities of feeling" (1991: 465–6). In this appraisal, Britton was perhaps examining less the actual places where tourism develops than taking his cue from a vast literature which has bemoaned the loss of "authentic" cultural traditions to the corruption of tourism.

In this vein, the pioneering study of tourism as a process that alienates locals from the means of place production was conducted by anthropologist Davydd Greenwood. Documenting the effects of tourism development on the Basque fishing town of Fuenterrabia, Spain, Greenwood argued that tourism made a commodity out of local cultural traditions, making them meaningless to the people who once believed in them. His conclusions (1972: 87) are summarized in the following passage:

> Fuenterrabia's cultural heritage has become a commodity, a neo-Basque facade packaged and promoted for tourists. As for the Basques them-selves, some have identified with the new consumer way of life, whereas the rest appear to be receding into ever more private cultural worlds, leaving only the outward forms of their life for touristic consumption. In the future Fuenterrabia promises to become nearly indistinguishable from all the other tourist towns on the coast of Spain.

Later, Greenwood (1977) documented the effects of tourism on the annual Alarde festival in Fuenterrabia, claiming the festival was essentially killed by the local municipal government's decision to promote it as a public perfor-mance for tourists. His conclusions helped establish in anthropology a normative framework for evaluating tourism in negative terms, in which cultural authenticity is replaced with "staged authenticity" (MacCannell 1989: 91–107). This framework has been one that does not question the idea of "authenticity" as a modern discursive construction, but as a simple fact of pre-modern (or, at least, pre-tourist) life. Anthropologists focusing on "ethnic tourism" have been particularly good at reinforcing this misplaced search for authenticity. "The tourist quest for authenticity is . . . doomed by the very presence of tourists," wrote van den Berghe and Keyes (1984: 346). "But for the ethnic tourist, tourism destroys the very thing he has come to see: the unspoiled native." Similarly, in a later study, van den Berghe (1992: 247) wrote, "The ultimate irony of ethnic tourism is that, as it invades the last isolated refuges beyond the pale of the global village, it threatens to destroy the very commodity it seeks: the unspoiled, authentic other." Van den Berghe and Keyes do not necessarily take to heart this common tourist myth of "pre-contact purity," but neither do they allow for the possibility of authenticity being defined in any other way. Tourists and "the industry," in other words, get exclusively rights to define modern subjectivity on *their* terms, with "tourees" relegated to the status of objectified victims.

Focusing on the political economy of tourism as an inherently colonialist industry, geographers have come to the same pessimistic conclusion as Greenwood by substituting an "authentic sense of place" for his "authentic cultural heritage." My point here is not to deny the neo-colonial nature of tourism, especially concerning international tourism in the developing world. Indeed, we will examine tourism in Guizhou specifically in these terms in Chapter 4. However, there has been little done in the way of combining the political-economic dimensions of tourism with a more detailed focus on place and the meaning of authenticity. There appear to be two reasons for this. One is that the "commodification of place" approach tends to become analytically confused with the assumption that places themselves – in a reified sense – are being bought and sold in an increasingly standardized fashion. Another is that place-based identity is often assumed to be something authentic and organic, developed out of some natural pre-modern link between people and the landscape and thus subject to displacement by the "disembedding" forces of modernization.

Influenced by Jameson's (1984) approach to postmodernity, and Harvey's (1989) theory of "flexible accumulation" in late capitalism, Britton (1991) characterized the "commodification of place" as a situation in which places are marketed by the tourist industry as desirable products. Tourism, he argued, must "sell" the features of a particular place by persuading the consumer that by buying the tourist product (such as hotel accommodation, guided tour, or transport fare), he or she will receive more than the product is itself capable of delivering. The consumer receives meaning and experience which can't be gained in other ways. Significant, though, is the qualification that places are not necessarily sold as ends in themselves, "but because visits to them, and the seeking of anticipated signs and symbols, are a vehicle for experiences which are to be collected, consumed, and compared" (1991: 465). Put in plain terms, what is really being sold is simply a collection of services; these are marketed with the promise of an experience, supported by a phalanx of images and representations of place. As a means of understanding the nature of the tourist production system, the "commodification of place" reveals much about how representations of place relate to the marketing of a service. But it is a major leap from this to the claim that *places themselves* are being casually bought and sold. People in tourist places are, of course, subject to the commercial standardization and rationalism of capitalist expansion. Those forces work to displace locals, attempting to eclipse their own place representations with those generated by the tourism industry. Yet, as the previous section's discussion sought to argue, such displacement is merely a fact of place in the landscape of modernity. It does not render that landscape placeless or "fake." Instead, tourism's colonizations are but one aspect of the broader forces of abstraction that are struggled over in the on-going reconstruction of places. Place is not a given unit of geographical terrain, like a piece of property; it is a social construction, a field of meaning built out of the betweenness of modern life.

In his analysis of tourism in Bali, Connell (1993: 652) notes that in all the tourist developments on the island, "Bali" itself is "conspicuously missing." Connell's analysis is a good example of the "commodification of place" approach taken in tourism studies. To his credit, Connell approaches authenticity as nothing more than a game played between tourists and industry suppliers, and much of his analysis is devoted to discounting the idea that "authentic" Balinese culture has been displaced by tourism. After all, what we expect as "authentic" Balinese culture is but a representation initiated by the Dutch colonists at the beginning of the twentieth century (Picard 1993). Nevertheless, Connell offers a decidedly negative assessment of Bali's prospects of remaining a distinctive place. He does not, in other words, envision the possibility of another form of authenticity emerging within Bali's tourist landscape itself. For Connell, place commodification is simply tourism's version of the inevitable rationalism and standardization of modernity. He thus writes that, "Not only have international forms of tourism and spectacles – from surfing to river rafting – replaced rather than supplemented local forms, but local cultural forms have been displaced to the tourist periphery" (p. 653). Connell (1993: 658) goes on to argue that,

> The commodification of place and culture – the mystic, spiritual, and scenic qualities that are the essence of place – has given way to the resort as commodity triumphant. As Bali has become a 'cultural icon,' with the image, and reference points of a very wide society, its actual distinctiveness – rather less elusive – is denied.

Quoting Urry (1990: 61), Connell (1993: 658) adds that tourism has led to "'the casual eradication of distinctive places and the generation of a standardized landscape.' At the same time the organization of tourism has shifted further away from Bali through the internationalization of the tourist industry, and some of the distinctiveness of Bali has gone as package tourists travel in environmental bubbles of free-spending uninterest."

Modernity, of course, is well known for its oppressive demand for rationality and standardization. But this is only part of the story. The threat and experience of rationality, the sense of loss that it generates, yields in people a tremendous amount of creativity and insistence on freedom. Not only does Connell's analysis equate the increasingly standardized representations of Bali with the loss of "Bali itself," but it is convinced enough of the power of capital that we don't even need to hear what the locals might be saying about all of this. The experience of tourism development isn't nearly the clear picture of dislocation and placelessness which Connell or Britton make it out to be. For one thing, tourism, like modernity, is itself fraught with contradictions. Crick (1989: 337) offers one perspective on these contradictions:

> For almost any effect of tourism discovered in one case, one can find a counterexample. For instance, tourism ought to have a symbiotic rela-

tionship with the environment: An area often becomes a tourist destination precisely because of its scenic beauty, wildlife, and so on. That attractiveness must survive to lure tourists. Some studies show that tourism indeed preserves wildlife, but many others report that tourism has ruined the very environment that created it. Likewise tourism is said to weaken tradition; but it may also, by raising historical consciousness, lead to restoration of ancient monuments and the like. Ethnic art tells a similar two-faced story, for tourism brings both the degradation of traditional technique for the mass production of airport art, and the reinvigoration of artistic skill.

Given this process of contradictory effects, it has become clear to many that tourism "is not a universal juggernaut, flattening everything in its path in the intentional or unintentional service of global homogenization and uniformity. Study after study has documented how individuals and groups have responded actively to both the constraints and opportunities brought by tourism development" (Wood 1997: 5). It is interesting to note, in this light, that Greenwood's pessimistic conclusions regarding the "death" of the Alarde festival in Fuenterrabia have been challenged by Wilson (1993). In 1988, he points out, the festival was alive and well, a thriving symbol of Basque separatism. Indeed, he argues, Basque nationalism has appropriated tourism as a means of promoting the cause of regional separatism.

Cultural politics of place in tourism

Much research has begun to conceptualize tourism as not a strictly "outside" force impacting a local culture, but as a dynamic component of that culture itself. This perspective not only reveals the shortcomings inherent in interpretations of the "commodification of place," but also helps us integrate a more dynamic conception of place into tourism studies. As summarized by Wood (1993: 57), there has been an overdue shift away from the "normative problematic" in tourism studies toward three new directions in assessing the relationship between tourism and culture: First, "an increased awareness of the social construction and invention of both tradition and authenticity has undercut the distinction between positive and negative impacts central to the normative problematic"; second, "an increased awareness of how tourism both engenders and becomes implicated in a broad range of cultural politics has brought attention to domestic stratification and conflict much more to the fore of tourism studies, exposing concepts of society-wide interests as naive and obfuscating"; and third, "various 'post-modern' observations about culture highlight the positional nature of cultural judgments and suggest interesting and productive ways to reframe the questions we ask about the relationship between tourism, culture, and development."

Wood's summary suggests a set of research imperatives that mesh nicely with those laid out earlier dealing with the study of place. To begin with, "cultural tradition" is, like place itself, an on-going process. Similarly, concerning evaluations of tourism's "impacts" on traditional culture, Wood (1993: 58) points out that:

> what is traditional in culture, the specification of links between an invented present and an imagined past, is constantly being symbolically recreated and contested. There is no objective, bounded thing that we can identify as "traditional culture" against which to measure and judge change. What is defined as traditional culture, both for the past and for the present, is constantly being reformulated.

In the relentless "commodification of place" described in critical geographies of tourism, there has been little attention to the local appropriation of touristic place representations. The local cultural politics of place tend to be ignored in focusing on the symbolic packaging of place for tourist consumption. Thus, Wood (1993: 66) lays out the research agenda in the following manner:

> Not tradition but its on-going symbolic reconstruction; not authenticity but its attribution; not inherited identities but relational, improvised and contested ones; not internalized values as much as available templates and strategies of action; not culture but cultural invention and local discourses – the central questions to be asked are about process, and about the complex ways tourism enters and becomes part of an already on-going process of symbolic meaning and appropriation.

The "contradictions" of tourism are not that it both "destroys" and "preserves" culture, as suggested above by Crick (1989: 337). Rather, tourism is itself part of the inherently contradictory process of cultural change associated with modernity. "Even the natives read *National Geographic*," Wood quips (1993: 68), and thus modernization replaces one cultural diversity with another. Modernity is not simply a story about the decimation of the old ways, but is also a story about the profound sense of loss that inspires a recreated tradition, place, and identity based on the new possibilities of interrelation and integration. The experience of tourism is but one of the more profound examples of how this story plays out.

This brings us back to the idea of place-based identity as the product of an on-going struggle between extra-local forces of change and the local need to maintain subjectivity over those forces. Tourism is a process of commercial development and integration in which the idea of place may be "commodified" through the marketing of increasingly standardized images. But it also injects a whole new set of possibilities that may be appropriated by locals as they reconstruct a sense of place. The key to relating tourism to the study of place, then, is to maintain a focus on place-based identity as a process in which the representations developed and marketed by the broader tourism industry are subject to appropriation by locals who are, ironically, aware that their local cultural traditions have indeed changed and thus are in need of reinvention.

A final point to be covered in relating the study of tourism to the concept of place involves the differentiated quality of local society. Locals share an uneven degree of access to the extra-local forces that condition their sense of place. In this case, we are talking primarily about access to the means of representing and marketing a place to tourists. Locals who enjoy such access will have considerably more power in constructing a particular place-based identity. Others, however, may construct alternative identities to contest those constructed by their more powerful neighbors. Complicating the picture is the fact that these local representations may, in many ways, resist and/or accommodate those dominating the broader tourist industry itself. Even more complicating is the fact that this process may be going on, simultaneously, at many different scales; locals may be constructing and contesting place identities for their village, region, province, or nation, all at the same time, but with very different issues concerning resistance and accommodation. I do not propose to present a typology that deals with all the possibilities inherent in this situation. I simply wish to alert the reader to be aware that, in the Guizhou cases discussed later, the analysis will not be confined to one particular scale of place-identity. Indeed, any study of place must foreground such local social complexities, for these complexities are what make modern places such landscapes of betweenness; the more abstract fragmentations of modernity are played out locally through social cleavages that erupt as people engage broader forces differentially.

The approach taken in this study focuses on the linkages across space and *across scale* that characterize the complex constructions of place-based identity associated with tourism development. Rather than assuming "local society" as an undifferentiated entity, I have focused on key local actors who display differential access to the broader tourist industry. The result is an analysis in which a whole range of place representations are revealed, promoted by different individuals or groups who maintain different linkages to the broader political economy of tourism. The point is that it is these integrative linkages which condition the different constructions of place-identity, rather than, say, the collective sentiments of the "local society." Perhaps even more important than this, though, is revealing the dynamic situation these actors find themselves in. As will be discussed in the chapters that follow, the experience of modernization in Guizhou (illustrated most succinctly by, but not limited to, the development of commercial tourism) provides a crucial context to understanding the ways these place representations are constructed and made meaningful.

It is thus an intriguing double irony in which we find ourselves. Tourism, on the one hand, comes about as an expression of the modern tourist's own sense of loss, a search for the "eternal and immutable" in some other place.

Travel to some authentic place is required to reinvigorate modern life with meaning, tradition, security, identity, and so on. Yet, as has been pointed out in the previous chapter, modern subjectivity cannot be limited to the tourist. The process of tourism development, as an experience of modernity, engenders a similar sense of loss for those on the supply side of the tourism equation, and thus generates a situation in which new representations of place and constructions of place-identity are asserted. While the tourist gaze seeks to construct a landscape of stasis, isolated from the world of change – something akin to the hyperreal landscapes of Shenzhen's theme parks – the fact remains that the place upon which the gaze rests is characterized by dynamic process. Ironically, in tourist landscapes that are actually lived in, the on-going process of constructing a place-based identity out of the insta-bilities of modernity leads to the appropriation of those very representations of stasis and (misplaced) authenticity that the tourist gaze thrives on. Paradoxically, authentic subjectivity is made possible, in this case, by embracing inauthenticity itself. Ultimately, both tourist and host find them-selves in similar aesthetic worlds: the touristic culture of modernity. Searching for other places, and constructing those places, are two facets of the same general experience. The rational and standardizing "colonial economy" inherent in that search for other places is also a fertile breeding ground for the creative assertion of new place-based identities.

Beyond theme parks: landscapes of heritage

Before moving on to Guizhou, it might be helpful to examine a few cases that reveal more explicitly these conceptions of place, modernity, and authenticity. The remainder of this chapter is therefore devoted to a brief look at the heritage industry as a field of tourism in which the above issues can be clearly illustrated. Whereas theme parks provide excellent illustration of the dominant visions of modernity promoted by the state and by capital, we need to examine some tourist landscapes that are actually lived in, in order to understand better the ways locals struggle to define their place and their authenticity in modern terms. Efforts at historical preservation for the purposes of tourism development offer perhaps the ideal situation for exploring these struggles. For the questions of historical preservation go far beyond the needs of a tourism economy to incorporate much broader issues of place-identity in relationship to tradition and modernity. Furthermore, some analysis of the heritage industry here will help with later interpreta-tions of Guizhou village sites, since much of the tourism being promoted there is based on the deliberate preservation of cultural and ethnic heritage, and the cultural politics of Guizhou's ethnic tourism development tend to revolve primarily around questions of heritage.

As we have already seen in the previous chapter, reconstructions of the past – the home of the "authentic folk" – have long been a staple of nation-state and capitalist interests. With every post-colonial independence movement, for example, we are again reminded of nationalism's power to shape public historical imagination. States deliberately foster a sense of national identity through the reformulation and interpretation of the surviving relics of history (Ashworth and Larkham 1994: 7). As Ashworth (1994: 13) states, "History ... is widely used to fulfill a number of major modern functions, one of which is shaping socio-cultural place identities in support of particular state structures." This can be achieved simply with propaganda campaigns through official media channels, but in capitalist states it has been primarily the work of the heritage industry to inculcate a place-based identity in association with the nation-state (along with state structures at other scales). If history is the remembered past, then heritage is "a contemporary commodity purposefully created to satisfy contemporary consumption" (p. 16). The heritage industry requires a specific kind of historical interpretation in order to thrive. Lowenthal (1985: xvii) reminds us that, for those whirling in the experience of modernity, the past is a "precious and endangered resource" that is "venerated as a fount of communal identity." As a resource, the past itself may be regarded as a modern product. "We may fancy an exotic past that contrasts with a humdrum or unhappy present, but we forge it with modern tools. The past is a foreign country whose features are shaped by today's predilections, its strangeness domesticated by our own preservation of its vestiges. It is no longer the presence of the past that speaks to us, but its pastness." "Pastness" is a product whose entry into the marketplace of public culture and commercial tourism supports the accumulation of symbolic and material capital for both the state and capitalist investors.

Yet, as Ashworth and Larkham's study makes clear, neither the nation-state nor powerful capitalist interests "own" the past, no matter how hard they may try. "Pastness" is subject to different productions supporting different scales of identity (for example, local or regional as opposed to national) or different inventions of historical continuity (for example, conflicting interpretations of national history from the perspective of ethnic minorities). Ultimately, "each individual necessarily determines the constitution of each unique heritage product at the moment of consumption." It is ultimately the consumer of heritage who authenticates the product, not the producer (Ashworth 1994: 17–18). The past is thus subject to continuous reinvention to suit the needs of modern subjectivity (see Urry 1995: 163–70). Based on the contradictions of modernity itself, these needs often clash violently and pose troubling dilemmas for heritage producers (see Tunbridge 1994). In what ways, then, does the past speak to the needs of the present? In what ways do particular productions of "pastness" support the needs of certain political or economic interests? How are attempts to "own" the past diverted, resisted, or appropriated by marginalized interests? Two cases below offer answers to these questions that help to disclose how struggles over heritage reveal the deeper struggle over modernity, and how these struggles reveal place to be a terrain of betweenness.

The first case is offered by Herzfeld (1991) whose fine study of the Cretan town of Rethemnos focuses on the disputed ownership of history among the complex and conflicting interests of the Greek state, local and regional capitalists, and old town residents. Herzfeld (1991: xi) prefaces his story thus:

> It is about the efforts of the present-day inhabitants of an old but well-preserved town, Rethemnos, to come to terms with the significance that others have foisted on the physical fabric of their homes. Possibly the best preserved example of Renaissance Venetian domestic architecture to be found outside Italy, the Old Town of Rethemnos survived the economic boom of the early 1970s and the frantic development mania that came with it. Not that its inhabitants did not want to join the boom. They were prevented from doing so, in part by circumstances – the lack of a good harbor, fierce competition from the two larger towns on the island – that condemned Rethemnos to poverty for a little longer. When, from about 1970 on, the Rethemniots found the prospect of money coming their way, so that they did not have to chase after it in distant places, they also encountered a severe setback. The government had not only forbidden virtually all new building within the Renaissance limits of the town but had strictly enforced a ban on even minor alterations to the fabric of their homes.

Herzfeld's story is about the efforts of Rethemniots to reclaim their subjectivity in an environment that has conspired to make them objects of "pastness." Modernity has presented them with a paradoxical situation. The unevenness of capital accumulation has resulted – by means of default – in the preservation of a landscape long regarded as a sign of poverty by its contemporary inhabitants. But the old buildings that came to symbolize the Rethemniots' imprisonment within the harsh logic of market capitalism soon took on another kind of symbolic value in the eyes of a Greek state increasingly eager to assert its presence as an equal among the progressive community of European nations. Being Venetian, Rethemnos represented a history of Greek integration with Europe, a time when important merchants from Venice established themselves within the space of what has become the Greek nation. This "pastness" of Greece as a nation firmly entrenched within a broader European heritage was produced for the purposes of attracting the increasingly mobile capital (both political and material) of the new European Union. The inhabitants of the Old Town were thus caught between their continuing impoverishment at the hands of capital and their monumentalization at the hands of the state. Either way, they were faced with objectifications of modernity, and the need to somehow craft their own subjectivity within the narrow confines of the highly charged symbolic space of the Old Town.

The task of crafting subjectivity in such circumstances is fraught with contradictions. Its inhabitants could simply invest Rethemnos Old Town with the oppositional symbolism of resistance – following the idea of place-as-site-of-resistance – perhaps by destroying their homes or otherwise subverting the state's project of monumentalizing their lived space. Such acts of resistance, of course, do occur regularly in Herzfeld's account. But resistance is not the point here. As the discussion in this chapter's first section attempted to argue, oppositional resistance does not provide much with which to build an authentic subjectivity. For in doing this, they would also be denying a significant component of their identity as Greeks. As Herzfeld points out, "The people within the walled space of old Rethemnos resent the town's compression of their lives and at the same time defend it against all critics." They might find their lives increasingly objectified by the state, but it is nevertheless a state that most Rethemniots would "defend to the death" (p. 4). Nor would they want to resist inclusion in the vision of a "timeless" European (as opposed to parochial local) history, a pastness capable of conveying urbane cosmopolitanism rather than backwardness and abject poverty. Yet at the same time, to simply "play their part" as the picturesque folk happily preserving tradition on a stage built for powerful interests far removed from their own daily lives – that is, to simply go along with modernity's "disembedding" logic – is equally humiliating. The task is not simply to resist, but involves a much more difficult struggle to strike a balance and create a place of betweenness.

Herzfeld characterizes the struggle over the Old Town as one articulating two different conceptions of time (and, we should add, space): monumental and social. Social time is the "grist of everyday experience," while monumental time is "the time frame of the nation state" (p. 10). Between these lies a "discursive chasm" that separates official from popular historical imaginations. It is that chasm itself that Rethemniots must inhabit if they are to claim any subjectivity over their modern lives. The social spaces that Rethemniots inhabit and experience through social time are always shifting and unstable, as people are born, die, grow rich, grow poor, get married, have children, and otherwise carry out their lives. The state, however, in its purveyance of instrumental rationalism, strives to recast such social spaces as monuments, frozen in time, to national mythology. As Herzfeld (p. 6) puts it, "they succumb to the bureaucratic nation-state's insatiable taxonomic appetite":

> By recasting past and future in terms of a monolithic present, the state creates "traditional neighborhoods" and "archaeological monuments," out of what, for residents, are the streets where their friends and enemies live and die. As the state encroaches even further, residents increasingly adopt its rhetorical tactics in self-defense.

It is with this move of "self-defense," this act of subjectivity, that inhabitants of the Old Town begin to bridge and occupy for themselves that "discursive chasm" between the space of the nation and the space of the everyday.

The realization of a new, modern authenticity for Rethemniots thus lies not in the complete rejection of the nation-state's hegemony of "monumental" time and space, nor can it be found simply in the social spaces of everyday life, for such spaces have been irrevocably marked by the monumental project itself. Instead, "social time appears to slip away" as the people of old Rethemnos get caught up in the discursive narratives of modern Greece and Europe. In telling his story, Herzfeld notes that, "it is not enough to simply record acts of resistance against conservation alone. On the contrary, we must see . . . that the monumental version of time is in fact extremely vulnerable to creative reuse by the same social forces that it seeks to control" (p. 15). It is in such "creative reuse" that an authentic modern subjectivity is possible for Rethemniots. Accordingly, such a subjectivity is highly unstable and contradictory; how could a modern identity be anything but paradoxical?

It is important to remember that Rethemniots face not only the state and its monumental nationalism in this struggle, but the standardizing logic of capital accumulation as well. The symbolic capital of Old Town Rethemnos is accumulated by the state only by marshaling the commercial power of the tourism industry, by turning the Old Town into the commodity of heritage. Along with the state's direct representative in Rethemnos – the historical conservation agency – tourists themselves come to represent the most invasive aspects of the state and its collaborating capitalists, and it is towards tourists and the increasing social fragmentations they bring that townspeople express many of their greatest frustrations. Tourism in Rethemnos brought a massive revaluation of land, turning formerly useless beach front and cramped Old Town property into immensely valuable assets, with their owners becoming a lucky class of local nouveaux riches, most of whom subsequently abandoned the Old Town for more comfortable modern quarters in the New Town. They either sold their property to outsiders capable of paying the high prices, or remained absentee landlords. Either way, wealth was steadily siphoned out of the Old Town itself. Tourism also brought about a new level of aggressiveness in economic competition within the Old Town. As local trade increasingly catered to the needs and desires of tourists, previous trades – such as tailors and barbers – that catered to local clientele grew depleted. Survival often depended upon one's willingness to succumb to the seductions of the tourist economy, as did numerous shoemakers who abandoned their craft to make tourist handbags. Tourism also invited an increasing amount of competition from outside entrepreneurs with greater access to capital and greater ability to pay the increasing rents in the Old Town.

Faced with the oppressive rationality of the state conservation project and the alienating logic of tourism development, many inhabitants sought to claim for themselves the rhetoric of conservation and heritage in order to assert their defiance of the abstract forces bearing down upon them. One way of doing this, according to Herzfeld, was to recast the whole idea of national heritage as that of a dowry. A common practice in the Old Town was for men to dower their daughters by building an additional floor on their house. With the conservation law making this illegal, residents appealed by invoking the state's own rhetoric of heritage. Heritage, many disgruntled fathers claimed, should be the state's dowry to its citizens, something to exploit for future benefits, not a restriction guaranteeing their future poverty. Poor residents of the Old Town used other rhetorical strategies as well, often turning the bureaucratic rhetoric of the conservation agency against itself as they sought to subvert the ban on alteration by capitalizing on the law's vagueness. In addition, many claimed that the state was simply acting as an agent for the rich, who themselves destroyed much of old Rethemnos with their building and "beautification" of the New Town. Now, enlisting the state, the rich sought to "preserve" what was left, the poorest quarter, knowing the poor would be unable to resist. Here, the poor again appealed to the idea of heritage, claiming the rich, in their greed, had already destroyed most of the town's "real" heritage; to call the decaying Old Town domestic quarters of the poor "archaeology" worth preserving (a term that conjures monumental images such as the Acropolis in Athens) is a travesty of "true" Greek heritage.

This is not, then, a simple struggle between the imposition of an official time and space and its populist resistance. It is rather a struggle to claim subjectivity over a new political and economic order. The state's efforts at historical conservation and its definitions of "tradition" are not simply rejected by Rethemniots, but reinterpreted in a familiar sense. The heritage industry is not something to be shunned by Old Town residents as much as it is something they strive to control and exploit for themselves. "The official past may be in the process of gaining control of the living present; but the living population has domesticated substantial areas of the official – and once alien – historical past. These are 'our' buildings now" (p. 259). Instead of defying monumentalization, residents seek to monumentalize themselves. There is no return, in other words, only a struggle over how to move ahead.

The second case brings us closer to China and examines the permutations of Taiwan's heritage industry revealed in a sustained critique by Johnson (1994). Johnson's analysis focuses on the tortuous complexities of the Taiwanese state's imaginings of "pastness" due to the Nationalist government's removal from the ultimate source of its very legitimacy, mainland China. In its claims of legitimacy as a nation-state, the Republic of China (ROC) constructed a pastness of absent China, rather than present Taiwan. In so doing, it effaced any conceptions of a distinctly Taiwanese past; instead, Taiwan was represented as "a place without history" (p. 186). Its pastness was inseparable and inescapable from that of China. Even geological history was enlisted to establish this point; according to official accounts, fossils discovered in Taiwanese archaeological digs reveal that the island was connected to the mainland in prehistoric times. As Johnson quips, "Nowhere else do fossils testify to the legitimacy of the state. In

another Taiwan Miracle, nature is mobilized to enforce Taiwan's incorpora-
tion into the Chinese nation-state, even before there were Chinese" (p. 188).
ROC geologists thus see Taiwan as "cut off" from the mainland relatively
recently by glaciation and tectonic shift.

In constructing a landscape of heritage on Taiwan, the ROC has thus
been at pains to represent the island's historical relics simply as extensions of
China. In the implementation of its Law on the Preservation of Cultural
Assets, Johnson argues that the ROC's dictatorial regime monumentalized a
state-military history marking both state control and Chinese conquest of
Taiwan. This is most obviously found in heritage sites marking the recap-
turing of Taiwan, first by Koxinga, who in the seventeenth century drove the
Dutch off the island and subsequently refused to yield to the newly installed
(and "foreign") Manchu Dynasty on the mainland, and second by Chiang
Kai Shek, who arrived on the heels of a new foreign intrusion on Chinese
soil (the Japanese) and likewise refused to submit to the newly installed
Communist Dynasty on the mainland. Another example can be found in the
state's invoking the importance of "native place" in its selection of sites
worthy of preservation or restoration. Recognized sites such as temples, resi-
dences, and guild and ancestral halls, emphasize their importance as
uprooted vestiges of "home" on the mainland.

Since the decline of the Nationalist dictatorship on Taiwan, however, the
historical preservation project has taken a new, populist turn. New spaces
have opened up in the discursive realm of pastness in which competing
conceptions of heritage are advocated. Important changes have taken place
on Taiwan, all of which conspire to recast the field of historical preservation, and redirect pastness to even newer modern uses. Deregulation of the
market economy has brought about an explosion of commercial development; Taiwan's economy increasingly looks like one dominated by the
"flexible accumulation" of late capitalism. Taiwanese capital has been
seeking new investment frontiers on the mainland, which is regarded less
and less as home to a displaced Taiwan, but as home to cheap labor
resources. Commodification has also dislodged the heritage industry from
its previous control by the state to a shifting, competitive arena of capital
accumulation, into which new entrepreneurs increasingly enter, bringing a
new diversity of sites and pasts. Demographic change has also meant that
the majority of Taiwan's population was born on the island, rather than the
mainland; the meaning invested in "native place" is being challenged by a
new generation with a different conception of home.

These changes have resulted in a number of different futures for the past.
As Johnson points out, one of these is simply a commodified, less violent
version of the dictatorship's earlier project. China as the "source" becomes a
heritage commodity marshaled more for capital than the state (see Shih
1995). Another is the production of a heritage for Taiwan as a nation itself,
apart from China. Still another possibility is a pastness that speaks to
"Greater China," that is, a distinctly "nonnational" heritage. Within this

shifting new terrain of historical preservation, we find the local assertion of heritage on the part of those who seek to tap into any and all of these possible futures and claim subjectivity over them. The important heart of this struggle lies in claiming authority to interpret the authenticity of relics and heritage sites. The field of historical preservation in Taiwan has been dominated by what Johnson refers to as a "techno-orthodox" paradigm, and populist challenges to that paradigm seek to invert it, claiming that people at the local level are the agents of remembering, of marking what is "real" about the past.

This struggle has been waged on a vast array of fronts in Taiwan's heritage industry. One example would be the efforts of aboriginals to inject themselves back into the historical imagination of Taiwan, an island once marked by the absence of history apart from China. Thus there was a struggle over the inclusion of the Shih-san-hang archaeological site, a relic that suggested Taiwan "had contact with peoples to the west, had developed significant technologies, and had supported a sizable population – all independent of China" (Johnson 1994: 226). Significantly, the inclusion of such aboriginal sites in the state's official catalogue of heritage has been mirrored by the rapid commodification of those sites as well. Giving a past to "the people without a past" has become a distinct avenue of capital accumulation – most of which is controlled not by aboriginals, but by Chinese entrepreneurs. And so the struggle goes on. The situation is one ripe for the kind of paradoxical assertions of subjectivity encountered among the Rethemniots.

Another example would be the Chiu-fen campaign. Here, a declining mining town on Taiwan's east coast faced a real-estate boom brought on by wealthy Taipei and Keelung professionals seeking a nostalgic weekend getaway. Rapid land speculation threatened to decimate the local economy and drive out long term residents. In an effort to arrest this very real process of modern dislocation, residents "launched a counterattack through the authoritative language of historic preservation and comprehensive planning" (p. 233). But in doing so, they sought to reformulate that language into something not obsessed with "objects" or "nostalgia simulation" but as a "social practice" aimed at constructing "local subjectivities." Their strategy was not to deny the monumental rhetoric of state-sponsored heritage, but to appropriate and mediate that rhetoric to their own ends.

> The key element of the resulting plan is social. A local preservation organization is to supervise development and institutionalize autonomy. The original layout of cultural space is to be preserved, while specific areas are marked to service (and bring in money from) the cultural tourism industry. The longer term aim of the plan is to enable local people to "rediscover the use value of the settlement space. This value will later supersede the value of commodity exchange."
>
> (Johnson 1994: 233–4)

As Johnson comments, this is especially significant because it marks a struggle that does not revolve around nation-based discourses, but instead seeks to reformulate these in terms of local autonomy. This, of course, is a paradoxical move, for the rhetoric of historic preservation is itself wrapped up first in the discursive monumentalism of the state and second in the rationalizations of capital. But the residents of Chiu-fen have attempted to carve a space of subjectivity amid these hegemonic narratives, rather than in complete opposition to them.

As the above cases suggest, in the landscapes of the heritage industry can be found the terrain of modernity itself. They offer testimony to the significance of tourism as a powerful medium through which modernity's contradictions are experienced and struggled over. In each case, we see the rationalism inherent in the modern project, expressed both by the state and by capital in their efforts to colonize certain spaces for the production of pastness. For the state, heritage serves to legitimize the rationality of the nation as a basis of identity for its citizens; heritage helps convey the "naturalness" of the nation as an "age-old" product of tradition, of historical continuity. Indeed, heritage is marshaled by the state as an ideology – a misplaced search for authenticity – attempting to deny the very contingencies that make up the modern experience itself. Likewise, for capital, heritage serves to discipline the social body into participating in its own fossilization for the benefits of capital accumulation – that is, tourism. In each instance, we see dominant agents attempting to divert social process toward something that can be controlled, predicted, and standardized; something, in other words, that responds to *reason*. Such acts of domination, however, only result in the objectification and imprisonment of the social body. This "imprisonment" would be more easily recognized if it wasn't accompanied by the enticements of newfound liberties. Modernity promises new opportunities for economic prosperity and, more important, new ways of defining one's subjectivity. In Old Town Rethemnos and in Chiu-fen, those promises were found in the pocketbooks of tourists and in the celebrated valorization of those places themselves. The ensuing struggle was therefore not some banal attempt by locals to reify tradition and use it as a club to beat the modern present. Rather, it was over the right to *define* for themselves the newfound modern liberties brought by the greater forces of change. It is not a struggle that rejects those liberties themselves, only their exclusive purveyance by the powerful. But because the struggle is waged not simply materially but rhetorically as well, its strategies are paradoxical and contradictory. At issue is not just who gets to benefit from the profits, but who gets to articulate the representations of place that have become so important in the "flexible accumulation" strategies of late capitalism.

This is the issue, and the struggle, we will see in Guizhou's tourist villages. In China in general, and Guizhou specifically, there is a profound awareness of modernity's incompleteness, its unfulfilled promises, and its open-ended nature. For villagers in Guizhou, the enticements of modernity are acutely felt, if only because they have for so long been beyond reach. Because of this, the stakes are incredibly high for villagers participating in tourism development; few are willing to let this long-awaited opportunity for genuine modernity to pass without a fight. And it clearly is a fight, for along with the first vestiges of modernization comes its oppressive, standardizing logic, threatening to imprison villagers in a trap of instrumental rationality. They understand, better than many of us it seems, that claiming subjectivity over the modern experience means embarking on a confusing and paradoxical path of tension, of reconstructing a place constantly in flux, in balance between the objectification of modernity's misplaced search for authenticity and the liberation of a newfound subjectivity.

3 Colonizing a "barren and profitless" place

INTRODUCTION

The competing narratives of Chinese modernity introduced in Chapter 1 –
the nationalist project of the state and the neo-Confucianist project of
Chinese transnational capitalists – all share the problem, and potential, of
modernity as an unfinished project, an open-ended process. In that chapter,
it was suggested that the task of defining an authentic modern Chinese
subjectivity must be conceived specifically in terms of China's own historical
and geographical experience, rather than via "self-orientalizing" or otherwise essentialist narratives that merely confirm the West's dominance in
defining modernity's discursive playing field. It was also suggested that the
alternative modernities conveyed by the Chinese state and by transnational
Chinese capital are "false" modernities because they derive their claims of
difference from a misplaced search for authenticity – the mythic (and now
monumentalized) landscapes of the folk and their celebrated heritage.
Tourism collaborates in this construction of false modernities, but it is also
subject to appropriation by those seeking to transform their objectification
at the hands of the state and capital into a completely new modern subjectivity.

If we are to understand what an authentic modern subjectivity might
look like in China – in the terms of tourism and place explored in the
previous chapter – we must first understand China's particular historical
and geographical experience itself. But more important, we must begin by
recognizing that there is no single Chinese modernity, but many. We need
not, in other words, reinforce the state's construction of one modern nation
out of a vast space of extremely diverse peoples and places. This is not to
deny the incredible integrating power of the Chinese state. Indeed, this and
the following chapter will offer much evidence of that power. But to understand the real struggles over modernity, we must focus on a local scale, and
examine not the landscape of the nation, but of place. The remainder of the
book therefore focuses on Guizhou as a site of struggle over Chinese modernity (Figure 3.1). Admittedly, focusing on a province with over 30 million
people and a great diversity of environments and economies hardly achieves

a place-oriented scale of analysis. Guizhou province is merely a convenient set of upper geographical limits. It provides a general frame of reference for more detailed examination of the southeastern region of the province (Qiandongnan), and the four case-study sites within this region. It is only at the level of the case-study villages explored in Chapter 5 that we finally reach the scale needed to understand the struggles for authenticity.

To better understand those struggles, however, we need to sketch the history and geography of broader forces conditioning the places in which they take place. But this is not simply an exercise of painting scenes to back-drop the dramas that ultimately unfold in Chapter 5. Chapters 4 and 5 also provide an argument about power relations. The struggles over modernity take place on a terrain in which power is distributed extremely unevenly. The context of these struggles is thus not simply a historical geography of modernization in Guizhou, but of Guizhou's *colonization*, first by the Chinese state, and more recently by Chinese capital. The process of internal

Figure 3.1 Location of Guizhou

colonization has left a distinctive mark on the kind of modernization experienced in Guizhou, and on the imaginings of modernity among its people. This chapter, then, examines the history and geography of Guizhou's colonization and explores the consequences of this for the kind of modernity pursued in Guizhou in the 1990s.

On one level, the chapter concludes that Guizhou's contemporary political economy is dominated by two key problems: First, the region's economy is threatened by an impending agricultural crisis brought about by chronic rural poverty, lack of investments, limited land resources, and rapidly increasing population. Second, a simmering fiscal crisis resulting from fiscal decentralization and decline throughout China has pushed Guizhou toward increased dependence on an inadequate local revenue base. In attempting to deal with these problems, post-Mao provincial leaders have advocated a modernization plan emphasizing the commercial integration of Guizhou's economy with external markets. Liberalized economic policies initiated in 1992 set off a brief boom in Guizhou's urban economy, and intensified concern over the need for commercial development of the lagging countryside. Such concerns have paved the way for the uneasy pursuit of external capital and, consequently, a competing narrative of modernity not just in the cities but in the countryside as well.

On another level, however, the chapter ultimately argues that the experience of internal colonialism has left a legacy in which the contemporary contradictions of modernity are articulated most profoundly in the changing relations between dominant Han society and ethnic non-Han minority groups. The colonizing state in Guizhou has, throughout the past few centuries, sought to integrate the region's non-Han periphery into the political and economic space of the Chinese empire-nation. In the latter part of the twentieth century, this has been translated into a sustained pursuit of a rational, standardized (socialist) modernity. The critical barriers to achieving this have long been conceived not so much in terms of the typical political and economic disadvantages of a colonial region, but as the inherent *cultural* problems of a people locked in the tight grip of tradition. Modernization, then, has been largely conceived by the state in terms of "cultural development," and ethnic relations within Guizhou have been mediated primarily by a culturalist discourse, under which fear, discrimination, and difference are all subsumed. With the advent of market reforms, however, a somewhat different narrative of modernity has arrived on the scene. Cultural traditions long regarded by the state as impediments to rationalization have become exploitable commodities at the hands of capital. Thus, the additional modern discourse of commercialism marks a gap between the competing narratives of modernity offered by the state and by capital. In Chapter 5, we will see how villagers occupy and exploit this gap as a space in which to claim their own modern subjectivity.

Guizhou, then, offers something of a microcosm of the broader modern problematic experienced by China as a whole. In Guizhou, we see the same tension between the state and capital over the kind of modernity imagined for the future. We see the open-ended character of Chinese modernity. In the changing discourse of cultural development we see the shifting terrain of modernity, from one dominated by the state and its exclusive rhetoric of empire, nation, and socialist rationality, to one complicated by the challenge of capital and its reworking of "traditional culture" into a marketable (and, paradoxically, modern) commodity. And amidst these dominant contenders for the right to represent the modern subject, we see the actions of the less powerful, claiming the competing rhetorics of cultural development for themselves and an autonomously defined modern subjectivity. This chapter lays the foundation for understanding these competing rhetorics. Chapter 4 then takes a closer look at the narratives of modernity purveyed by the tourism industry in Guizhou, while Chapter 5 explores the appropriations of these narratives by the less powerful inhabitants of Guizhou's ethnic tourist villages.

HISTORICAL GEOGRAPHY: COLONIZING GUIZHOU

In the Spring of 1882, the British trade representative for Chongqing, Alexander Hosie, was underway on one of his numerous sedan-chair expeditions of southwest China. His route took him from Chongqing south through the poppy-rich hills of southern Sichuan and into Guizhou. Upon reaching the border, Hosie (1890: 25) made the following observation:

> It was like a transformation scene. From smiling fields of poppy, wheat and beans, we were suddenly brought face to face with hill-side patches of the same crops sadly stunted. The poppy, which to the north was being bled, had not even burst into flower, and the scanty soil looked barren and profitless.

That night, Hosie endured the most pathetic lodgings of all his travels in China, and the remainder of his journey to Guiyang impressed him to conclude that, "Northern Kuei-chow is a huge graveyard" (p. 32). Hosie's imagery of a ghostly and impecunious place has been echoed by countless officials, scholars, and travelers in their descriptions of Guizhou throughout history. Few can write about the province, for example, without referring to the infamous proverb: *tian wu san ri qing, di wu san chi ping, ren wu san fen yin* ("No three days are clear, no three feet of land are flat, no person has three cents").

Hosie's poor impressions of Guizhou were in part due to several decades of disastrous rebellions which preceded his travels (Jenks 1994). But such social disorder had, by that time, become common in a region whose relative inaccessibility and poverty made banditry and rebellion an attractive alternative for many locals. Chronically unstable, Guizhou's integration and assimilation to more "civilized" Chinese ways had long been an objective of imperial governments. For the Chinese state, Guizhou needed not only economic assistance but *cultural development* as well. Curing Guizhou's ills of poverty and social disorder was legitimized as a cultural project aimed at the large proportion of non-Han peoples who inhabited the province. Accounting for Guizhou's poverty, and explaining its need for development, became a project in which non-Han ethnicity figured prominently. This was particularly true with respect to the region's largest ethnic group, the Miao. For the Chinese, the Miao seemed to exemplify Guizhou's poverty and need for benevolent outside help. Accounts commonly referred to Miao so poor they worked naked in their fields. In *The Long March* (1985: 106), Harrison Salisbury recounted his informants' impressions of Guizhou when the Red Army passed through in 1934 in the following way:

> They had come to the land of the Miao, a minority race that antedated the Hans and had been driven into these remote stony hills, there to live lives so poor that women could not emerge from their huts – they had no clothes. They sat huddled in nakedness beside straw cooking fires, with the smoke issuing from a hole in the roof. Girls of seventeen and eighteen worked naked in the fields. Many families had only one pair of trousers to share among three or four adult males.

But the Miao were compelling not simply for their poverty, but for their association with wilderness and "savagery" as well (Diamond 1995). Nakedness has been a common trope for identifying not just poverty, but naturalness, primeval ancientness, and anything else distinctly non-Confucian (for instance, sexual promiscuity). It was a common claim during the eighteenth- and nineteenth-century rebellions in Guizhou, that "many of the Miao tribesmen went so far as to kill their own wives and children before embarking upon the revolt, so as to feel completely reckless of the consequences" (Weins 1967: 190). Such passionate savagery would certainly point to the need for a culturally civilizing influence of the Chinese state in this frontier region.

Culturalist representations of Guizhou's endemic poverty have been the staple of the region's historiography. The presence of ethnic non-Han peoples has long been the primary factor legitimizing Guizhou's colonization. It remains the state's primary explanation of why Guizhou requires further integration and development. Furthermore, the image of isolated and primitive minority cultures remains a fundamental component of Guizhou's contemporary landscape, and continues to be tied quite explicitly to the region's poverty. But the story of Guizhou's colonization is not simply about the subjugation of tribal peoples and exploitation of their land. More important, the colonial project of "civilizing the natives" helped define the boundaries of indigenous identity with representations of remote, exotic, primitive, and hostile peoples.[1] These representations – later translated by the PRC's ethnic identification (*minzu shibie*) project into cultural categories scientifically marking social distance from the Han Chinese – continue to fuel the imaginations of tourists visiting the province today. The images of a "barren and profitless place" where girls worked naked in the fields and warriors killed their own families before going into battle sustained the state's colonialist narrative justifying integration and rationalization. But they also shaped the contours of ethnic identity in Guizhou and, ultimately, have become marketable images under the new regime of capital accumulation in post-Mao China. The relationship between the construction of exotic peripheral or marginal cultures – worthy of both discrimination and commodification – and colonial projects of exploitation, integration and development is certainly not unique to the experience of Guizhou. Representing an extreme standpoint in this vein, Dirks (1992) has argued that the whole idea of culture itself is wrapped up in the history of European colonialism. Something similar is evident in the Chinese situation, where the idea of cultural difference has developed as a product of China's historically expanding frontiers. The imagining of a Chinese cultural center, in other words, was wrapped up in the demarcation of its peripheries.

Guizhou as a physiographic periphery

According to Skinner (1985: 288), Chinese history has been "an internested hierarchy of local and regional histories whose scope in each case is grounded in the spatial patterning of human interaction." Skinner grouped these local and regional histories into nine physiographic macro-regions, each characterized by a core area of agricultural accumulation and urban networks. Macro-regional boundaries tended to be defined by major drainage divides, since rivers provided the dominant medium of transport in China before the twentieth century. Looking at the administrative region defined as Guizhou on the map quickly reveals something of its peripheral nature in physiographic terms. It is entirely a hinterland region, straddling the borders of no less than four of Skinner's macro-regions (see Figure 3.2). Thus, each part of Guizhou was historically oriented economically toward core areas beyond the province. Throughout Guizhou, river transport was found to be virtually absent, severely inhibiting commercial integration.

Several other aspects of the macro-regional approach apply in explaining the physical situation in Guizhou. The majority of the province occupies the eastern portion of the Yun-Gui macro-region, something of a residual in Skinner's framework. Yun-Gui, he noted, was characterized by a "deficit of centrality" in its urban system and marketing hierarchy; it had the lowest urbanization rate in China, estimated at 4.1 per cent in 1843 (Skinner 1977: 230). Its boundaries were defined not according to drainage divides, but as the region *beyond which* one could navigate up-river from the Changjiang (Yangtze) or Zhujiang (Pearl) systems. In Skinnerian terms, much of Yun-Gui's deficit was also the result of the region's poor agricultural

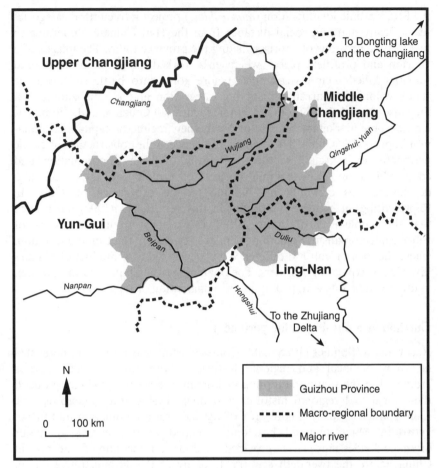

Figure 3.2 Guizhou's situation in relation to macro-regions of SW China

productivity, its shortage of flat fertile valleys and plains, and its limestone mountains which criss-cross the plateau, effectively cutting off from each other the few fertile valleys that do exist. The commercial development of urban centers was constrained by high transport costs; cities remained relatively isolated from each other in terms of trade, and rural markets were very limited. While it took less than a week on a Changjiang river junk to reach Shanghai from Hankou (Wuhan), it took over 40 days on foot to get from Guiyang to Kunming. This does not mean that commercial activity did not exist, but peripheral conditions effectively stunted commercialism, making the local economy extremely volatile and vulnerable to disruption.

Skinner's model implies another important aspect of Guizhou's peripheral nature. Throughout history, by virtue of its serving as hinterland to four different core areas, the region was a stage for the competing interests of those cores. Thus, at different periods, Guizhou territory was under the influence of independent power centers to the west (Dian, Nanzhao, Dali), south (Nanyue), east (Chu, Hunan), and north (Shu). The rise and fall of these power centers greatly affected Guizhou in terms of military activities, migration, and disruptions in trade. Such geopolitical ruptures were a mere prelude, however, to sustained late-imperial colonization and integration by the Chinese government, which established Guizhou as a province in 1413 and has been developing it as a periphery ever since. The selected details of this history offered below are organized topically rather than chronologically. They include migration, political colonization, and economic integration. The focus is on how these processes, all of which linked Guizhou's history to more distant sources of power, helped condition the cultural boundaries of local identities in Guizhou.

Migration

At the beginning of the Yuan Dynasty in the thirteenth century, it is estimated that the majority of people living in southwest China were found in Yunnan, concentrated on the fertile plains and valleys around Erhai and Dian lakes. Inspired to hyperbole as he was, Marco Polo himself marveled at the large urban population of Dali on the fertile shores of Erhai. In contrast, according to James Lee, Mongol generals had found Guizhou to be deserted or, at best, sparsely inhabited (Lee 1982: 713). They reported a population of 300,000 in Guizhou (a figure Lee suspects is overestimated), compared to almost 1.3 million in Yunnan. It would be difficult to say what the trend before 1250 was, but after the thirteenth century the population on the Yun-Gui Plateau began to increase steadily. This was due to a sustained government effort to settle and colonize the region. The policy was known as *wei suo tun tian* or "defending the empire through military-agricultural colonization." These colonies tended to concentrate on fertile valley lands and plains where Chinese-style "peasant-gardening" (Whitney 1980) agriculture could be practiced. The government was to provide seeds, draft animals, and tools, though Lee (1982: 720) claims that a chronic shortage of these implements continually plagued the plateau region. According to Lee, *tun tian* development only increased population pressures on lands that were already under indigenous cultivation. As valley dwellers were displaced, increasing amounts of hillside land came under shifting cultivation, requiring extensive land use. Settlers competed with natives for the most productive lands in a region lacking in this resource, and the social repercussions were often severe.

By the sixteenth century, according to Lee (1982: 716), the population of Guizhou had increased to about 1.5 million. He contends, however, that over the next couple of centuries people remained highly concentrated on fertile plains and valleys, and that population growth was not sustained but discontinuous. Migration was still predominantly government regulated and agricultural production increased only in terms of expanded acreage. However, during the eighteenth and nineteenth centuries the region witnessed incredible population growth. In 150 years (from 1700 to 1850) the population in southwest China increased roughly five-fold; a rate of growth surpassed in China only by the Sichuan basin (Ho 1959). The rate of growth in Guizhou itself was not quite this staggering, but was still impressive. Lee estimates 3 million people in 1733 (double the sixteenth-century figure) and about 7 million by 1850.[2] Overall, it has been estimated that in the 427 years from Guizhou's founding in 1413 to 1840, land under cultivation expanded five-fold, productivity doubled, and population increased ten-fold (Chen 1989: 14).

Migration was the dominant factor in this growth. New World crops played a role in bringing marginal land into cultivation, and double-cropping and other techniques were imported and implemented on a larger scale, especially during the eighteenth and nineteenth centuries (see Ho 1959: 136–68).[3] But Lee (1982: 740) argues that these techniques were in fact long available in the southwest, and received widespread use only when population increase demanded them. He goes on to argue that the pressures brought to bear by migration meant that fertile lands were increasingly devoted to rice and commercial crop production. This intensified the socio-economic gap between valley and mountain dwellers. Thus, New World crops, concentrated in mountain areas, took on the derogatory status of "mountain food" fit only for non-Han and independent mountain settlers even as trade in these crops enabled the further development of valley economies. In this process we find some clues to the dynamic construction of mountain and valley identities based not simply on primordial cultural affinities but on the interplay of settlement, production, and social power relations.

During the Qing Dynasty, independent migration became an increasingly significant factor in how these processes were played out in Guizhou. Guizhou was particularly vulnerable to this type of migration, due to its proximity to the middle and upper Changjiang regions, both of which were becoming densely populated. Ho (1959) identifies the settling of the "Yangtze highlands" as one of the most significant interregional migration patterns in late-imperial China. He further points out that independent migration was the dominant type in these movements. The increasing availability of New World crops such as maize and potatoes, and their suitability for cultivation in more marginal mountain lands, fueled an increasing presence in the highlands of what officials called *pengmin*, or "shack people." In official sources cited by Ho, most contemporary accounts depicted the *pengmin* as desperate, land-hungry peasants trying to get maximum short-term results on soil they had no intention of cultivating permanently. New World crops did bring relatively good returns over the short run, but at a high cost to a delicate mountain environment that valley dwellers failed to understand. Unlike indigenous shifting cultivators, migrant farmers monocropped in straight deep rows, yielding bumper harvests for several seasons until rains washed the topsoil off the steep mountain slopes. Various memorials cited by Ho complained of massive erosion, flooding, water pollution, and the leaching of soil nutrients, all as a result of the *pengmin*. So severe was the damage, in fact, that the Changjiang highlanders probably grew more food in the early nineteenth century than they did in the 1950s (Ho 1959: 148).

Intensified migration also brought about much conflict between settlers and indigenous groups, whose extensive land-use patterns were disrupted by settled farmers operating under a vastly different conception of land tenure. Ho (1959: 146) has this to say regarding ethnic conflict in the Changjiang highlands:

> As the economic advantages of maize and sweet potatoes became more evident, even native poor peasants trekked toward the mountains. So much of the hilly land of inland Yangtze had been taken up during the early eighteenth century that, from about the middle of the century, natives and immigrants encroached upon the area of hilly western Hunan, the home of the Miao. Local officials in general paid little heed to Miao complaints, with the result that Miao rebellions broke out in the latter half of the eighteenth century.

Officially, the central government regarded Han encroachment on Miao land as a serious problem. The ensuing conflicts undermined its ability to maintain adequate control and prevented further integration via the government's own soldier-settler colonies. But, unable to prevent independent migration or effectively control local officials, there was little the government could do beyond resorting to repression. This it did, many times. Rebellions in the late eighteenth century in western Hunan, for example, were brutally suppressed; garrisons and *tun tian* were enlarged, and a long wall with watchtowers was built to maintain order (Jenks 1994: 67). Western Hunan, however, was much more easily managed than Guizhou. Rebellions there erupted most fiercely in the mid-nineteenth century, and were far more severe than they had been in western Hunan. These uprisings, collectively called the "Miao rebellion," were in fact motivated, according to Robert Jenks, by a complex set of interrelated factors, and the rebels were by no means limited to the Miao. As he notes (1994: 4), however, "The Qing authorities were well aware that the Han played a major role in the rebellion. By labeling it a 'Miao' rebellion in official historiography, the authorities made sure that the stigma of having rebelled and caused vast destruction and misery was attached squarely to the Miao and not to the Han." The Miao, in these terms, were represented as those who rebelled, the barbarians rejecting civilization (see also Diamond 1995).

This is in fact a consistent theme in Chinese accounts of the Miao. Miao identity could be acquired by repudiating Confucian civility and "going native." For example, in *Qiannan Chifang Zhilue*, an encyclopedic account of Guizhou compiled by governor-general Le Raotian (1773–1854) and translated by Lin Yaohua, we find a number of interesting comments. Le's account of the origin of the Miao – some three thousand years ago – is indicative (Lin 1941: 271):

> During the decline [of the region] of Kao-hsin, a certain San-Miao chieftain, seizing the region between [the lakes] Tung-t'ing and P'eng-li, established a state. He, in turn, followed the governing policy of Ch'ih-yu, liked imprecation and believed in ghosts. His influence and power extended to the present provinces of Yunnan, Kweichow, Szechwan, and Kwangtung, and all the people [of those places] followed his customs. Thereupon this state of [good] reputation and [high] civilization became barbarous in customs; from this fact the name 'Miao' arose.

Similarly, there are several other instances in which soldier-settlers were sent to certain places, where they took on a specific identity to distinguish themselves from the earlier inhabitants (for example, by adopting the surname of their military commander). Over time, however, they would simply come to be called a certain type of Miao, such as Zhong Miao, by still newer inhabitants. On-going migration thus contributed to the development of Miao sub-groups, and the on-going process of distinguishing the civilized from the savage.

Land alienation was a fundamental issue which further informed the representations of Miao identity in curious ways. Jenks (1994: 48) claims that, "Officials acknowledged that ethnic minority groups had lost a considerable amount of land. They placed most of the blame on unprincipled merchants and userers who were alleged to be taking advantage of the simple-minded Miao." The Miao were depicted as helpless and unable to understand the scheming trickery of merchants who put them into debt and then claimed their land. It is no doubt true that many were clearly at a loss when faced with the new system of Chinese land tenure and private ownership. But official descriptions of Miao victims were standardized and played a role in distinguishing (savage, but innocent) Miao from (civilized, but sneaky) Chinese. Actually, it seems that the Miao were quite aware of their rights and indeed were famous for pressing their claims in courts (Clarke 1911: 25). The courts tended, however, to favor Chinese settlers in land disputes, giving the government, as much as tricky merchants, a major role in land alienation.

Another factor related to migration in Guizhou was intermarriage between migrant farmers (the majority of which were men) and indigenous women. Norma Diamond (1988: 21) has argued that this was a source of anxiety for the Chinese, and played a role in defining Miao identity. The necessities of survival in a mountain environment meant, among other things, that women were much more socially visible than Chinese settlers might be used to. Migrants who married natives "would have literally been laughed out of court had they brought charges that a woman was not a virgin at marriage, or that she refused to stay within the confines of house and courtyard all day" as Confucian morality dictated. Most mountain people practiced some form of delayed-transfer marriage. Thus, Chinese men often regarded the first born in a Miao marriage to be illegitimate, because these marriages seemed to lack the contractual characteristics of Chinese marriages. This view is made explicit in a late Qing account translated by Lin (1941: 332–3):

> Shortly after [the marriage], [the bride] returns to her mother's home and does not see her husband. She summons another man – called the "wild husband" – to live with her in her parent's house. When she experiences pregnancy, she secretly tells her husband to build the Ma-lan. Thereupon, she forsakes the "wild husband" and goes back to her husband's home; and they dwell together to their old age. Therefore, the "wild husband" is also called the "sad husband."

Political colonization

In her historical geography of the Zhujiang Delta region of Guangdong, Helen Siu (1989) wrote of a "delicate balance between autonomy and control" maintained in relations between local society and the central government. Such a balance was preserved by the presence of autonomous local social institutions which mediated central state power and diffused it to "multiple centers" at the local level. These local institutions did not exist in a peripheral region such as Guizhou, where agricultural accumulation was limited, rural markets weak, and urban networks minimal. The only viably autonomous institution which did exist – the *tusi* system of native chieftainship – was itself a primary target of imperial colonization efforts. The gradual disintegration of this system left a vacuum which ultimately left Guizhou increasingly vulnerable to political and economic subordination.

Prior to the thirteenth century, political integration in this region was less the government's concern than general frontier security. With limited resources, the simplest way to ensure security was to empower local frontier elites to rule their domains autonomously while paying tribute and perhaps a nominal tax to the center. This approach was taken as early as the Han Dynasty, when various independent kingdoms of the southwest were for the first time conquered by the Chinese, and turned into prefectures (*jun*). Prior to the Han, the region of Guizhou had first been dominated by a kingdom identified by the Chinese as Yanke, which rose up in the river valleys of the Guizhou-Yunnan-Guangxi border area. During the Warring States period another kingdom, Yelang, rose to prominence in much of central Guizhou and northern Guangxi, while in eastern Guizhou, Qianzhong was the dominant state. Even for these early kingdoms, the imperial presence to the north was a potent one. Yanke, for example, paid tribute to the Zhou court as early as the seventh century BC (Lin 1941: 272). In the struggles between these southwestern states and their neighbors to the north, the region of Guizhou remained somewhat of a transition zone, for the kingdoms were generally based in the fertile lowlands of Guangxi with the mountainous plateau of Guizhou serving as an effective buffer to their increasingly powerful northern neighbors.

As the Han government established control over the region it both empowered local chieftains to rule their native lands as well as brought in "great families" from the north to establish a civilizing influence (Lin 1941: 273). Thus even in a system of indirect rule, the mechanisms were being put into place for distinguishing between native and newcomer. By the late Song, indirect rule had been institutionalized as the system of native chieftainship (*tusi zhidu*). The system consisted of three categories: *tuguan* (native administrators, such as magistrates), *tusi* proper (chieftains invested with military titles, hereditary offices, private armies, and tax collecting autonomy), and *tuli* (minor native officials such as jail wardens or registrars). For Guizhou, Jenks (1994: 40) notes that, "Most *tusi* paid the government a nominal amount of land tax annually, although large areas of southeastern Kweichow were exempted from this obligation. In addition, they sent in tribute, which consisted, in the case of Kweichow, of small quotas of local products like horses and beeswax." In terms of local taxes within *tusi* domains, each class or rank of the populace entailed certain tribute obligations to the *tusi*. Apparently, the local populace was subject to much abuse by *tusi* in collecting tribute, conscription, corvee, and so on (Jenks 1994: 41).

The *tusi* system was widely implemented by the Mongols (Yuan), and during the early part of the Ming. But problems began with the intensified development of military-agricultural colonization. The *tun tian* system met much resistance from local *tusi*. Outside armies were often brought in to quell resistance as more and more valley land was placed under the authority of soldier-settler colonies. By the sixteenth century about one-half to two-thirds of Guizhou was still under *tusi* administration (Lee 1982: 716), and resistance to increased Han encroachment on native lands remained strong. By the beginning of the Qing, the government was committed to the ultimate removal of all *tusi* and the implementation of direct administration of their lands. This policy came to be known as *gai tu gui liu*.

The establishment of Guizhou as a province in 1413 and the ensuing implementation of *gai tu gui liu* became the fundamental basis for its colonization during the Ming and Qing Dynasties. But *gai tu gui liu* was slow and incomplete in Guizhou, and a large portion of the province, centered in the rumpled and incised folds of its mountainous southeast region, distinguished itself as a stubborn knot of resistance to direct administration. This region, the boundaries of which were considerably vague and shifting, came to be known as the *Miaojiang*, the "Miao borderlands." In both symbolic and practical terms, it represented the antithesis of everything the Chinese empire stood for: its inhabitants were shifting cultivators, non-commercialized subsistence producers, and uncivilized warriors who would rather cling to their primitive ways than embrace the light of heaven emanating from the emperor. According to Jenks (1994: 66–7), the *Miaojiang* was a region "populated solely by unassimilated Miao who were completely beyond the reach of Chinese officialdom. Few Han had ever set foot in the area." Bringing such a region to heel became, by the eighteenth century, an exceptionally important priority of the provincial and imperial governments (Yu 1997). But the process of colonizing the *Miaojiang* was, at the same time, one which helped solidify the boundaries of Miao identity even as it sought to break them down.

According to Lin Jianzeng (1992), the opening of the *Miaojiang* was characterized by a policy of *xianfu houjiao* ("first appease and pacify, then suppress"). It was initially hoped that appeasement and non-interference would convince the region's leaders to accept direct rule. The region was declared to be in perpetual remission of land tax, and quotas regarding the ratio of Miao to Han were established in an effort to control Han encroachment (*Qiandongnan Gaikuang* 1986). Native leaders were given titles as "Miao officials" (*Miao guan*), customary law was allowed to continue, and no imperial roads were opened through the region. Only the Qingshui River, which cuts through the heart of the region, was opened to trade, in hopes of spurring the development of economic crops and timber. The government was, however, increasingly dissatisfied with this approach, and in 1726 a campaign to directly subdue the region was launched by Ortai, governor-general of the Yun-Gui region. Miao in pacified areas were no longer allowed to keep arms and were forced to assimilate to various Han ways; a ring of walled garrisons was established (with considerable resistance), encircling the region. The legacy of these forts continues to this day, in that they have become the seats for most of the counties in southeast Guizhou.

Along with the pacification campaign came the practice of distinguishing the region's inhabitants as either *sheng* (raw) or *shu* (cooked). *Sheng* Miao were unassimilated, rebellious, and primitive. *Shu* Miao were assimilated, and were regarded by officials as important propagandists in spreading the virtues of Chinese civilization throughout the area. These categories initiated a long standing practice of ethnic classification – which continues in the form of the PRC's *minzu shibie* ("ethnic identification") project – in order to facilitate socio-cultural integration. Such categorization was necessary, for example, for appropriate collection of taxes, grain procurement, and corvée draft. *Sheng* Miao were meant to be spared many of these imperial appropriations in order to keep them pacified. Local fiscal pressures, however, only resulted in increasing vulnerability to such actions for most of the region's inhabitants. Repeated rebellion, rather than voluntary acceptance of direct administration, was their answer.

By the mid-eighteenth century, the Qing financial system was increasingly unable to meet the fiscal needs of the empire adequately. Guizhou offers an extreme case of the central government's fiscal problems. It was the lowest revenue province in the empire, and offered the lowest yields in land tax per county of any province. In 1753, according to Wang Yejian (1973), Guizhou yielded 6,000 taels per county compared to 130,000 taels per county in Jiangsu, the highest yielding province. The imperial average was 36,100 taels. Much of Guizhou's land was either exempt from the land tax or went unregistered. This was well known, and it was often quipped by officials such as Hong Liangji in 1795 that the farmers of Guizhou "till tax-free land" (Ho 1959: 118). This was not, however, a happy consequence for the peasant. The Qing's inability to meet Guizhou's revenue needs meant that local officials had to devise all sorts of surcharges which proved quite onerous and typically were most burdensome for the lowest strata of society.

In the *Miaojiang* disguised taxation, along with the trend in commuting taxes from kind to cash, worked increasing hardship on the populace. For example, a "chicken-grain"(*jiliang*) tax in this region evolved out of the *tusi* custom of peasants providing a chicken to leaders as a token of sincerity. With the implementation of direct rule, this became institutionalized as a requirement. Eventually it was paid in rice, then silver, then copper cash. Those without land had to pay a "household tax." Farmers were also subject to government procurement of grain to supply the army at artificially low prices. The heaviest burden fell on the *sheng* Miao, who apparently were seldom even paid for such grain (Jenks 1994: 51–2). Ethnic prejudice was clearly a factor in the abusive collection of taxes by local yamen runners entering Miao regions, and the government actually tried to limit local tax collecting autonomy in these cases. But resistance to these administrative abuses was officially regarded as a characteristic of being Miao. Ironically, Miao identity maintained one's distance from civilization even as it further wrapped one in that civilization's abuses. Rebellions, often instigated not by those most destitute but by local elites with distinct political interests, were invariably interpreted in ethnic terms, and consequences for the destitute were most severe. This pattern was eloquently captured by Shen Congwen in his *Congwen Zizhuan* (1934). A failed 1911 attempt to capture the west Hunan garrison of Fenghuang by anti-imperialist townsmen was proclaimed a "Miao rebellion." As a result, the government proceeded to summarily execute a hundred Miao peasants per day for over a month until the town gentry finally appealed for constraint.

Rebellions in the *Miaojiang* were even more severe. The first half of the nineteenth century witnessed severe deflation which created an excessive tax burden on the Guizhou peasantry in the form of increased surcharges (Wang 1973). Burdens were increased further by the Taiping rebellion, which served to reduce further the limited central funds allocated to Guizhou. Many simply gave up to join the numerous groups of bandits that infested the area, preying on what little wealth there was. The struggle for survival was becoming so acute that in 1853 local magistrate Hu Linyi wrote with melancholy, "They die as bandits or they die from starvation, but they die and that is all. If they break the law, they can postpone death; if they simply endure starvation, they will die forthwith" (cited in Jenks 1994: 71). Rebellion intensified, and from 1855 to the late 1860s nearly all of southeast Guizhou, including the ring of walled garrisons, was in rebel hands.[4] While the causes of rebellion were clearly tied to the failures of a broader political economy, official accounts primarily concentrated on the inherent resistance of the Miao to Chinese civilization as the leading factor. To the Chinese, the Miao were the worthy foes of the civilized world; ancient folks who left the lap of heaven's kindness early and had been on the run ever since. What better evidence of this could there be than some two decades of utter destruction in the *Miaojiang*?

The incomplete implementation of *gai tu gui liu* had resulted in a situation in which much land, such as in the *Miaojiang*, remained under the control of semi-autonomous local chiefs. Military suppression of rebellions in these regions resulted in state confiscation of these lands. According to Lin (1992), most of the confiscated land went to wealthy landlords who moved in from Sichuan, Hunan, and Guangxi; some was also offered to Guizhou landlords who sided with the government in the rebellions. The Miao, who, in the eyes of the state, bore responsibility for the revolts, were dispossessed of much land during this time. The legacy of the rebellions was thus one in which those identified as Miao were increasingly impoverished and alienated by the early twentieth century, when geographer Joe Spencer visited Guizhou and called it an "internal Chinese colony" (Spencer 1940).

Economic integration

Peripheral status does not mean economic isolation. Rather, core-periphery economic linkages mean increased economic subordination and dependence for the peripheral region as its integration with core regions ensues. Jenks (1994: 21) identifies two impediments to the independent development of commerce in Guizhou: poor transport conditions, and a lack of economic surplus. This should not mean, however, that trade did not affect local social patterns or that subsistence production precluded commercialism. Huang (1990), for example, has argued that subsistence farming and commercialism went hand-in-hand in China. More at issue here, though, is that the *degree* of commerce and trade is not as important in the periphery as its *nature*. In Guizhou, as with most peripheral regions, these economic linkages would best be characterized by resource extraction.

Guizhou's economic integration with broader markets did not become significant on a macro-regional scale until the eighteenth century, but *tun tian* colonies, the establishment of a provincial government in 1413, *gai tu gui liu*, and the Yuan-Ming construction of post-roads crossing the province north to south and east to west, all contributed to the establishment of economic linkages with distant markets. By the early eighteenth century, standard markets regularly carried imported salt, cotton yarn and cloth, and silk. Guizhou's export items at this time included: mercury, cinnabar, lead, raw silk, horse hides, tong oil, wax, timber, *wubeizi* and mugwort powder (medicinal herbs), tea, and raw lacquer (Chen 1989: 13).

As early as the fourteenth century in the *Miaojiang*, despite its official representation as an isolated region of purely subsistence producers, logs were being floated down either the Qingshui River into Hunan, or the Duliu River into Guangxi (*Qiandongnan Gaikuang* 1986). Timber production thus linked the "impenetrable" borderlands quite significantly with two different macro-regional cores in Lingnan and Middle Changjiang. By the sixteenth century commercial centers had developed at key points on the two different river systems draining southeast Guizhou. Zhenyuan became a dominant trade center, located at the upper-most navigable point on the Wuyang River (a more placid tributary to the Qingshui, which was too swift for large junks). It became the major trans-shipment point in the region. Numerous markets developed at key put-in points along the Qingshui (such as Chonganjiang, Panghai, Shidongkou, and Yuankou), in which timber was the dominant item traded. The timber trade was extremely lucrative for merchants and brokers, who took advantage of the government's pacification of the Qingshui corridor. The division of labor in this trade was often organized along ethnic lines, with upland activities like woodcutting and hauling identified as Miao work, and river-valley activities carried out by merchants, brokers, and others identified as Han (*Qidandongnan Gaikuang* 1986: 26; see also Clarke 1907: 264; Lin 1941: 289).

Timber was a crucial aspect of upland people's ability to support themselves, and as the timber trade increased, local incomes became increasingly dependent on it. These were shifting cultivators who relied on commercial trade not for profit, but for survival. Therein lay the vulnerability of their status, for if trade were to be cut, their survival would be at stake. This is exactly what happened during the Taiping Rebellion. Chaos in Hunan and along the Changjiang corridor had by 1855 severely disrupted the timber trade. After the rise of the Taiping, according to a memorial by the local prefect in Taigong, "the waterways became blocked and the timber piled up like mountains and began to rot. The local Miao became so destitute that they were reduced to digging up their family graves to obtain silver funerary ornaments that could be used to buy sustenance and to pay taxes until the waterways were opened and timber could be sold again" (Jenks 1994: 89).

Eighteenth- and nineteenth-century rebellions had so devastated Guizhou's countryside that whatever vestiges of rural capital accumulation there might have been were all but obliterated. Thus Guizhou became increasingly vulnerable to the unevenness of its trade relations with the rest of China. In addition to the example of timber just discussed, this vulnerability can be illustrated by looking at the development of commercial crops in Guizhou during the nineteenth and twentieth centuries, and the increased concentration of landholdings that resulted.

The penetration of imported cotton yarn and cloth, much of it from India, created a new division of labor in the rural household economy by the late nineteenth century. Because of the higher quality of the imported cotton, most households stopped growing and spinning their own. Instead, a local weaving industry developed rapidly. A survey in Xingyi, which was one of Guizhou's principal cotton markets due to its proximity to both Yunnan and Guangxi, indicated that households with looms jumped from 10 per cent in 1861 to 80 per cent in 1896 (Chen *et al.* 1993: 41). Another survey indicated that by 1890, 80 per cent of all yarn sold in Guizhou was imported, while this was true for only 10–20 per cent of the woven cloth sold (Chen 1989: 16). Industrial development along the coast was also creating a demand for many raw materials which Guizhou could provide. By 1900, one hundred log rafts per day were floating down the Qingshui River into Hunan. The missionary Samuel Clarke (1907: 264) wrote that the upper Qingshui hills were being deforested at an alarming rate. Tong oil production increased dramatically, as did exports of tea, tobacco, and medicinal herbs. Guizhou, in fact, became one of the country's major sources of the medicinal herb *wubeizi*, 97 per cent of which was sold to external markets (Chen *et al.* 1993: 42). But by far the most significant development in Guizhou's commercial crop production was the spread of opium.

Throughout China, after 1856, domestic opium production was deliberately encouraged by the Qing government as a way to counter the drain on state silver reserves due to illegal opium imports. For Guizhou, as well as many other mountainous peripheral regions, opium quickly became *the* major cash crop, and the population became notoriously "opium sodden." As Hosie quipped in 1882, "A lazier set of people it would be difficult to find anywhere" (Hosie 1890: 29). Opium originally arrived in Guizhou via Yunnan, and was first planted commercially around 1820. Hosie (1914: 286) claimed that between 1863 and 1900 annual output in Guizhou rose from an estimated 2,400 kg to nearly 300,000 kg. Guizhou historians, however, claim that 2 million kilograms were produced in 1896, and 2.4 million in 1906 (Chen 1989: 18). Whatever the exact figure, the increase was exceptional. The key to this phenomenal development lay in opium's high value, low bulk, and durability during transport. Here was the perfect commodity for Guizhou's treacherous and transport inhibiting topography. Most of the households that stopped growing cotton during this time found it very convenient to simply switch their fields to poppy cultivation. Furthermore, opium production didn't necessarily preclude food production; it could be double cropped with New World staples. This meant, as Huang (1990) has documented with cash crop production in North China and the Lower Changjiang regions, fuller employment of household labor. Hosie's observations (1890: 15) confirm that women and children tended to be in charge of poppy cultivation in most peasant households. The consequences of addiction notwithstanding, poppy growing must have been a boon for mountain peoples relegated to marginal lands. One report estimates that poppy growing increased the average rural household's income by three to five times (Zhou *et al.* 1987: 25).

By the turn of the century, Guizhou was the third largest opium producing province in China. As poppy cultivation intensified, however, it appears that grain production began to decrease significantly. As Zhou *et al.* (1987) point out, this resulted in increasing grain prices, causing greater hardship for those whose households were not self-sufficient in grain. Poppy growers were also vulnerable to the suppression campaigns which began in 1906 and were carried out off and on until 1949 when opium production was systematically banned by the communists. Guizhou, in fact, was particularly hard hit by inconsistencies in the official attitude toward the poppy. Spencer (1940: 168) commented that, "In Kueichou even more than in other provinces of the southwest, unscrupulous military interests in the first two decades of the Chinese republic alternately enforced poppy growing and suppressed it, each time taking a money levy out of the population." Though the official crusade against domestic opium production began in 1906, enforcement in Guizhou was initially left up to local officials who were loathe to give up their chief revenue source. Hence, output did not begin to decrease until 1910 when outside troops were brought in to scour the province. This not only worked much hardship on poppy cultivators themselves, but depressed the region generally. In 1914, Hosie (1914: 152) observed that Guizhou roads were significantly devoid of traffic compared to his previous visits two decades earlier.

> This [my men] attributed to the suppression of opium. Opium, they said, brought buyers, brought money, and brought other trade where there was money to purchase. Now there is no opium to dispose of, no money, and no trade. This was perfectly true, and there is little hope for the Keuichou farmer being able to make up for the loss of opium by extending the cultivation of cereals and pulse, which cannot be profitably moved and disposed of in such a mountainous province.

The loss of opium revenues was a hardship even for the provincial government. In 1906, opium had accounted for 40 per cent of the province's revenues (Chen 1989: 18). Guiyang had a considerable amount of opium stockpiled and repeatedly petitioned the central government to sell it (as the going price was about five times what it had been before prohibition); these requests were consistently refused (Hosie 1914: 286).

But with the fall of the Qing and the disintegration of the fledgling republic, Guizhou warlords reversed the campaign against opium in order to increase their own revenues. So much opium wealth was being amassed around Zunyi, in the hands of warlord Bai Huizhang, that the region came to be known in the 1930s as Guizhou's "Northwest Kingdom" (Salisbury

1985: 115). In 1935, it is estimated that as much as two-thirds of Guizhou's cultivated land was producing poppy (Chen *et al.* 1993: 44). Such expansion was possible, by this time, given the increasing concentration of landholdings among a wealthy elite; they simply forced their tenants to grow the poppy. Annual production reached as high as 5 million kilograms, and accounted for 65 per cent of provincial revenues (7.8 million silver dollars in 1935) (Chen 1989: 19). Then, with the rising power of the Kuomintang (KMT), and especially with its wartime move to Chongqing, opium was again suppressed. This alternating rise and fall of opium worked to keep tenant farmers vulnerable, discouraged long-term investments, and further structured the unequal exchange between Guizhou and China's wealthier regions.

Combined with land alienation associated with the suppression of rebellions and *tun tian* colonization, opium production and suppression was the final measure needed to fully subordinate Guizhou's rural economy and contribute to an already stratified and impoverished society. By 1940, Spencer would write of the Miao as having born the brunt of Guizhou's hardships. Upland cultivators survived the rebellions only to lose their land as an increasingly commercialized economy placed resource control in the hands of a dominant minority. Data from Perkins (1969: 101) reveal a rapid increase in tenancy in Guizhou, from "small" in 1888 to 80 per cent by the 1930s. By 1949, the lower 51.5 per cent of the population owned 13.5 per cent of the land, whereas the upper 10 per cent owned 43 per cent (Chen 1989: 22). Rent in Guizhou (unlike the rest of the south but like the more unstable North China region) was collected as a share of the harvest, thereby discouraging increased productivity (Perkins 1969: 101). "It is quite certain," Spencer (1940: 167–8) wrote, "that practically all the rice lands are in the hands of the Chinese, for the most part Chinese of the landlord class who live in cities, towns and villages. This means that all the really good land in the province is in the hands of a relatively small group." He also observed much land that wasn't under cultivation, having previously been devoted to poppy. "Such land," he added, "is for the most part held by wealthy Chinese of the landlord class who have no particular incentive to use it, under conditions which have existed in the recent past."

The extraction-based economic order of the periphery lent itself well to the ordering of local society along ethnic lines. It was especially the volatility of that economy, as evidenced by local dependence on both timber and opium production, which helped lay the foundations upon which local society was organized. The legacy of Guizhou's colonization has, in sum, been profoundly cultural as well as economic and political. The militarized and impoverished frontier landscape that increasingly characterized Guizhou during the late Qing and Republican periods was legitimized by emphasizing cultural differences between the Chinese and indigenous groups, even as the colonial project professed to erase those differences. Although cultural distance between indigenous groups and the Chinese was accepted in *a priori* terms by the colonizers, it was in fact a distance constructed by colonialism itself. The boundaries of ethnic identity were drawn according to social distinctions engendered through aspects of the colonial experience such as land alienation, onerous taxation, new divisions of labor based on cash crop production, and especially the harsh implementation of direct rule. Place-identity in Guizhou has likewise inherited a profound legacy of remoteness. The sense of living in a geographically peripheral space remains a potent feature of local culture in Guizhou today.

THE PROJECT OF ETHNIC IDENTIFICATION (*MINZU SHIBIE*)

The paradoxical legacy of defining the boundaries of ethnic identity in the pursuit socio-cultural integration and assimilation came to be institutionalized once the Communist Party (CPC) took power in 1949. By this time, however, the "civilizing project" (Harrell 1995) of imperial China, in which non-Han peoples were expected to embrace the virtues of *acting* Chinese, came to be articulated as a nationalist project, in which ethnic minorities were to become citizens of a single nation-state. This idea was initially articulated by Sun Yat-sen, who exclaimed that,

> The name "Republic of Five Nationalities" exists only because a certain racial distinction which distorts the meaning of a single republic. We must facilitate the dying out of all names of individual peoples inhabiting China, i.e. Manchus, Tibetans, etc. . . . We must satisfy the demands of all races and unite them in a single cultural and political whole.
>
> (Cited in Dreyer 1976: 16)

Sun later amended these views after learning of the model of multinationalism being developed in the Soviet Union. The Nationalists, however, maintained this approach, changing the Republican flag from the five-banners to a single white sun, and declaring that all nationalities in China were of the same racial stock.

The CPC, on the other hand, more astutely adopted the Soviet model of multinational unity as the foundation to building an integrated nation-state. As the Chinese communists began to implement their own version of this model in the liberated areas during the 1940s, their approach toward non-Han peoples reflected the decidedly practical goal of achieving geopolitical security and national integration, regardless of the contradictions with Marxist theory their methods entailed. A "united front" with minority elites was forged, and the upper classes of minority society (in particular the Hui and Mongols) were given preferential treatment during the land reform process. "Han chauvinism" was officially condemned, and "local nationalism" was tolerated to prevent discord from erupting along China's sensitive borders.

These pragmatic tactics did not, however, deter the CPC from pursuing a vision of a culturally, socially, economically, and politically integrated nation-state. The projects of *minzu shibie* and regional autonomy were promoted in order to facilitate the realization of this vision, not to guarantee the self-determination of minority groups. In 1956, party theorist Zhang Zhiyi wrote that only by employing a policy that recognized minority "special characteristics" (*tedian*) could "the ways of life of each of the nationalities be brought closer together and improved; in this way, they can more easily be induced to cast off their backwardness" (Zhang 1966: 97). The final stage of integration would be achieved once the nationalities overcame their mutual alienation, and the various groups "recognize their kinship, join clans, and select a name for the whole people" (1966: 39). What would bring about this crystallization of the "collective body of the Chinese people" (Fei 1981: 30), the *zhonghua minzu*, was socialist modernization and cultural development (*wenhua fazhan*), and in these the Han were the clear leaders.

Initially, economic development and socialist modernization was to be governed by the particular needs of minority groups themselves. Based on the model developed under Stalin in the Soviet Union, National Minority Autonomous Regions were created as spaces in which the "special characteristics" of non-Han peoples could be recognized and condition the "pace" of socialist transformation. Unlike the Soviet prototype, however, Chinese autonomy policy explicitly declared minority areas to be an inseparable part of the People's Republic (Conner 1984; Dreyer 1976). Rather than delimiting self-determination, these were spaces in which "backward" cultures and economies were symbolically juxtaposed with the ideals of socialist modernization in order to reveal the distance which separated them from nationalist integration (Hsieh 1995). The General Program for Regional Autonomy of 1952, for example, stated that governments in these regions should, "utilize different appropriate forms to introduce to people of various regions the experiences and conditions of political, economic, and cultural construction in the advanced regions" (cited in Solinger 1977: 183).

Establishment of autonomous regions required the scientific identification of minority nationalities, bringing about the need for the *minzu shibie* project in which an astonishing number of groups claiming separate ethnic identity (over 400) were classified into 55 *minzu* categories (Fei 1981). *Minzu shibie* was carried out primarily for political reasons, and the philosophy underlying its implementation reflected the state's commitments to cultural development and socialist modernization. Again working from the Soviet model, Chinese ethnologists used classification criteria laid out by Stalin himself. Although these criteria were derived from a basically materialist approach to identity, they were in fact largely ignored by the Chinese in their efforts to scientifically measure the socio-cultural distance between minorities and Han Chinese.[5] This was because the goal of *minzu shibie* was simply to identify those people who had some "catching up" to do in achieving the ultimate goal of socialist transformation. In order to recognize them and grant them territory where their "special characteristics" would temper the speed of their transformation, they needed to be scientifically identified. In this the Chinese relied heavily on the "stages of development" model attributed to Lewis Henry Morgan (1877), a model which in fact inspired Marx and Engels (see Engels 1884). As China's pre-eminent ethnologist Fei Xiaotong (1981: 65) commented, "The state of the nationalities in China in the early post-liberation years provided researchers with a living textbook on the history of social development."

Morgan's evolutionary framework became important not only in terms of identifying where a particular group stood along the path of social development, but in providing a standard set of cultural markers which the state could expect to find in such a group given its stage of development. These cultural markers became the primary determinants of *minzu* status since few groups exhibited Stalin's other characteristics in any consistent fashion. *Minzu* categories came to be defined primarily according to cultural criteria (Harrell 1990). This established a very important aspect of state-sanctioned ethnicity in China, especially in the southwest. Because Chinese people had historically "seeped" into the various tribal domains of southwest China over an extended period of time, the cultural traditions of that region have in many ways long been influenced by Han Chinese culture. Although Barth reminds us that the "sharing of a common culture should not be constructed as the essential definitional criterion of ethnic groups" (cited in Okamura 1981: 457), the Chinese state proceeded from the assumption that *minzu* groups could be identified according to essential non-Han cultural markers. Fei (1981) notes that the major problem confronted by *minzu shibie* involved separating from everybody else those who, despite claiming otherwise, were really Han. These were generally groups who could not claim sufficient cultural distinctiveness from dominant Chinese markers. Thus, more than anything, *minzu* groups were defined according to cultural distance from the Han.

Norma Diamond (1995: 108–9) illustrates this in her analysis of how the Miao were classified during *minzu shibie*:

> That the Miao were initially identified as an example of primitive communal society is somewhat surprising, since the bulk of the survey work on the Miao was carried out in Guizhou. It was the absence of clear-cut class stratification within many Miao communities, the absence of "big landlords," full time artisans, and merchants; and the existence of communal lands that were the basis for viewing Miao populations as representative of an early stage of society. The investigators underplayed Miao involvement in local marketing systems and their use of currency, stressing instead the self-sufficiency of the household economy.

Given the contentious history of Chinese–Miao relations, it is not surprising that investigators would be looking for certain cultural markers which indicated the Miao were a primitive people. "Miao" was simply a category used by Chinese, consolidating many geographically, culturally, linguistically, and economically different groups under a collective derogatory label meaning "sprouts" or "weeds." Glossing over actual differences, ethnologists described all Miao as pre-literate, primitive, and communal representatives of an earlier stage of society, one locked in a "natural economy" (*ziran jingji*) which impeded socialist modernization.

In Guizhou, *minzu shibie* work teams confronted at least 87 different groups who either themselves claimed separate status, or had long been identified by neighbors and officials as distinct. Fieldwork was conducted between 1953 and 1956, and concentrated on weeding out those groups who – despite claiming otherwise – were really Han, on consolidating dozens of geographically and linguistically distinct groups under the classification of Miao, and on finding other names for those – such as the Bouyei, Gelao, and Dong – who had long been popularly thought of as Miao subgroups (Jiang 1985). Work was halted after 1958 as Maoist radicalism began gearing up for the Great Leap Forward and condemning "local nationalism" as counter-revolutionary. *Minzu shibie* resumed in 1965, but was once again halted, this time by the Cultural Revolution. In 1980, when work again resumed, 22 different groups still awaited classification. *Minzu shibie* in the reform era became somewhat less ideologically bound, and adopted a mildly critical stance towards work which had been conducted in the 1950s, but remained committed to cultural development and national integration as the overriding objectives of the project.

A report by Jiang Yongxing (1985), for example, was critical of early PRC ethnologists for trying to blindly apply "Marxist–Leninist nationality theory" to the Chinese situation, and for focusing too much on genealogy and not enough on the aspirations of the minority groups themselves. Jiang argued that Stalin's four principles of nationality identity applied only to the modern European context, and he criticized *minzu shibie* work for not recognizing the aspirations of ethnic groups themselves. This certainly was the case, as Cheung (1994) has argued, concerning the Ge of southeast Guizhou, a group that, since the 1950s, has been contesting its classification as a branch of the Miao. Yet while Jiang calls for "scientifically" recognizing *minzu* aspirations, he cautions against making this the sole basis for classification, and reminds his audience that the most important point is to create a solution which best meets the needs of economic development, progress in science and technology, and social equality. This leaves unstated the underlying assumption that continues to inform the *minzu shibie* project, which is to create a systematic basis for a culturally integrated and ethnically unified nation-state. The result, ironically, has been a state-sanctioned construction of firm ethnic boundaries which serve to continually remind minority groups of their backwardness, but which have, in fact, achieved little in the way of meaningful economic development. Integration has only achieved the perpetuation of their poverty. As Diamond (1995: 114) concludes,

> being Miao means living in areas where schooling is often unavailable, being excluded from jobs in the modern sector (even when these do not require even basic literacy), and being controlled by state policies into which they have had little or no input. Most particularly, it now means restricted access to pasturage, woodlands, and farmland at the same time that they are experiencing population growth, and very firm restrictions on moving into unsettled mountain areas to open up new lands as they have done in the past.

In Guizhou, two autonomous prefectures – Qiandongnan and Qiannan – were established in 1956. A third, Qianxinan, was established in 1981. Ironically, though not surprisingly, Qiandongnan and Qiannan were established at the outset of China's "high-tide" of collectivization. Any earlier concessions made to minority regions in terms of the "pace" of land reform and social transformation soon became meaningless as the entire Guizhou countryside was caught up in the formation of agricultural producer cooperatives and, ultimately, communes. By the end of 1958, all of rural Guizhou had been carved up into 534 communes, each averaging close to 30,000 people (Chen 1989: 50). For all practical purposes, between 1956 and 1978 minority autonomy was a complete fiction. Rapid collectivization caused a tremendous amount of resentment among minority groups, especially since it was coupled with an intense campaign against "local nationalism." According to Goodman (1986: 131), popular resistance and resentment, combined with economic chaos in the agricultural sector, fundamentally undermined political leadership in the province, which was condemned by Mao in 1964 as thoroughly "rotten." In 1965, Guizhou's leadership was reorganized by the Southwest Regional Bureau, based in Sichuan. Needless to say, the plight of the poorest strata of rural society went unrecognized as Guizhou's colonization continued.

REGIONAL DEVELOPMENT DURING THE MAOIST ERA

The fiction of minority autonomy in Guizhou shouldn't have been surprising given the central state's designs on Guizhou as a resource-rich province of considerable potential, especially in terms of energy, mineral, and timber production. The province was also to serve as a prime site for Mao's *san xian* ("Third Line") defense industrial relocation policy. The three decades of Maoist rule saw in Guizhou – as in the majority of rural China – a general stagnation and decline in agricultural production and a failure to adequately address the high rates of rural poverty throughout the province. Along with the chaos that accompanied the implementation of collectivization, the province's inability to provide the needed inputs in the rural economy can be related to a broader political economy of unequal exchange which developed under state socialism in China. Under Maoist regional development strategies, Guizhou's links to the center came to be dominated by industrial developments which did not fully articulate with the local agricultural economy, and the province survived on subsidies rather than developing a structurally diverse economy. While these structural features conspired to perpetuate rural poverty, official state development discourse generally blamed "traditional thinking" and a "low cultural level" on the part of minority and Han peasants, thereby shifting the causal focus on endemic rather than broader problems (see Wang and Bai 1991; Ran 1991: 221; Li 1991: 2). As we will see, this remains the dominant explanation for rural Guizhou's continuing "resistance" to modernization.

Economic development strategies adopted by China after 1949 were drawn from the Soviet Union and its emphasis on heavy industrialization, high rates of accumulation and investment, and rapid industrial growth at the expense of agriculture (Chan 1994: 59–63). As indicated by Table 3.1, China's investment patterns have been characterized by accumulation rates averaging between 25 per cent and 35 per cent. The overwhelming bulk of this accumulation has been reinvested into heavy industry. Under Mao, the emphasis on rapid industrialization was combined with perceived national security needs to produce a deliberate strategy of interior industrial development. While the party's focus on interior regions at the expense of the more developed coast has been interpreted by some as a geographical expression of Maoist egalitarianism, it appears that pragmatism, more than any theories of regional social equality, was the governing principle in the PRC's regional development program. As Kirkby and Cannon (1989: 5) conclude, "never in the Mao period is the theme of regional equity *per se* elevated to a matter of principle and policy." Instead, regional development policy was dictated by what was perceived as the efficient realization of rapid industrialization and national defense requirements (see also Leung and Chan 1986).

Initially, during the First FYP (1953–7), regional development was highly planned and directed by a central government which controlled – as indicated in Table 3.2 – as much as 78 per cent of state expenditures (Lardy 1978: 38). It focused on the so-called "156 key projects" which utilized Soviet aid and expertise. Seventy percent of these projects were located in interior provinces away from the coast, and 58 per cent of First FYP industrial investments went to interior provinces (Kirkby and Cannon 1989: 5). Many of these were iron and steel projects, including enormous steel works in Taiyuan, Baotou, and Wuhan. Iron and steel production was thought to be an important indicator of socialist modernization, and by the mid-1960s every provincial capital except Lhasa had its own iron and steel works. As Kirkby and Cannon comment, "no modern socialist city could hold its head up without its own steel-making facilities."

Table 3.1 China: investment patterns, 1952–90

Shares of NMP (guomin shouru) based on current price	1953– 57	1958– 60	1961– 62	1963– 65	1966– 70	1971– 75	1976– 80	1981– 85	1986– 90
Consumption	75.8	60.7	85.0	77.3	73.7	67.0	66.8	68.7	65.7
Accumulation	24.2	39.3	15.0	22.7	26.3	33.0	33.2	31.3	34.3
Sectoral shares of state capital investment									
Heavy industry	36.2[a]	54.0[b]		45.9	51.1	49.6	45.9	38.5	44.3
Light industry	6.4	6.4		3.9	4.4	5.8	6.7	6.9	7.5
Agriculture	7.1	11.3		17.6	10.7	9.8	10.5	5.0	3.3
Transport and communications	15.3	13.5		12.7	15.4	18.0	12.9	13.3	13.0
Commerce and services	3.6	2.0		2.5	2.1	2.9	3.7	5.9	3.2
Housing	9.1	4.1		6.9	4.0	5.7	11.8	21.3	12.7

Source: Chan (1994: 61; computed from *China Statistical Yearbook 1991*).

Notes:
[a] This column based on averages for 1953–60.
[b] This column based on averages for 1960–2.

Table 3.2 China: central and local shares of state expenditure, 1955–94 (%)

	1955	1959	1965	1971	1984	1990	1993	1994
Central	78.1	47.6	62.2	59.5	46.6	39.8	37.0	30.1
Local	21.9	52.4	37.8	40.5	53.4	60.2	63.0	69.9

Source: *Zhongguo Tongji Nianjian* (China Statistical Yearbook), 1995, p. 21.

But it wasn't just symbolism that spurred such rapid industrial expansion throughout the interior. The horizontal expansion of facilities was encouraged by two important features of China's economic development plan: a macroeconomic condition of shortage, and the political legacy of the party's revolutionary experience and continuing priorities of national defense. Regarding the first, Kornai (1986) has characterized the socialist economy in terms of the continuous reproduction of shortage. According to this interpretation, state-owned enterprises operate on "soft budgetary constraints," and are thus not sensitive to costs, face little investment risk, and display an insatiable investment hunger. Shortage is reproduced not because of absolute scarcity in raw materials, but because of the systemic nature of the relationship between producers and consumers, and between central planners and local governments. With firms in constant demand for increasing amounts of inputs (a demand encouraged by increasing output quotas), regardless of their actual economic situation, supplies for other buyers – specifically household consumers who operate on "hard budgetary constraints" – are in constant shortage. One of the important features of this system is that economic growth does not depend on internal accumulation, but on investment in new productive capacity. This provides a partial explanation for the rapid horizontal expansion of industrial development into China's interior; it was a systemic consequence of a Soviet-style centrally planned economy. Planners favored investment in new facilities because these could be immediately translated into statistics on economic growth; new facilities could easily be planned, and they allowed the government to expand its ownership of enterprises at a time when it did not have complete control over the economy (Tang 1991: 33).

The other important feature of regional industrial expansion was the political legacy of the revolution and the continuing perception of a hostile world beyond China. Local self-reliance was a constant theme running through Maoist politics, and was encouraged by the perception of constant danger from the outside. It was also reinforced by the vertical nature of the administrative and industrial system. After 1957, when Maoist radicalism began to dominate the Chinese political economy, the exercise of vertical authority became increasingly entrenched, particularly at the provincial level, producing a legacy of "local encystment" (Wong 1991: 712). The expansion of the iron and steel industry to over 2,000 state and collective enterprises by the mid-1980s reflects the fact that it was deemed important that local regions be equipped with all the necessary instruments of self-sufficient socialist modernity (Kirkby and Cannon 1989: 11).

While the perception of a hostile geopolitical environment helped justify the idea of local self-reliance, it also encouraged the massive relocation of China's defense industry away from the coast to the "Third Line" (*san xian*) provinces of the interior: namely, Guizhou, Yunnan, Sichuan, Shaanxi, Gansu, and parts of Henan, Hubei, and Hunan. Beginning in 1959, and gaining momentum with the Sino-Soviet split in the early 1960s, the *san xian* policy thrived as Mao began to reassert his authority by criticizing the economic liberalism which followed the Great Leap Forward fiasco (Kirkby and Cannon 1989: 8). The linchpin and symbolic heart of the Third Line was the iron and steel works at Panzhihua, Sichuan, which was initiated in 1964 and is now China's fifth largest. Some 29,000 state enterprises were built during this period, mobilizing a workforce of 16 million. Naughton (1988: 366) estimates that at its peak in the late 1960s and early 1970s, two-thirds of the state's industrial budget was going to *san xian* investments.

Projects were especially costly due to their remote mountainous locations and almost non-existent infrastructure. The cost of laying railroad track (between, for example, Kunming and Chengdu) was between four and five times higher than normal for other parts of China.

It is unlikely, however, that Third Line industrialization contributed much to regional self-sufficiency. As Naughton points out, the project was highly centralized; local governments had little say in the use of *san xian* funds. The command structure of the project had the authority to "cut across functional and regional administrative boundaries, an extraordinary dispensation that was made acceptable by the urgency accorded the construction itself" (1988: 367). Third Line projects also bypassed normal material allocation procedures, sometimes skipping provincial governments entirely (as in the case of Panzhihua). Nor did the construction of these industries necessarily contribute to local economic development; few projects articulated significantly with the local economies which surrounded them, and most of the labor force was shipped in from other parts of the country. Indeed, Third Line industrialization, with its "*san bian*" principle of simultaneous design, construction, and operation, reinforced the dependence of interior provinces on state subsidies, saddling them with poorly built, inefficiently managed, and unprofitable industries. Even the railroads became a burden. From 1978 to 1988, RMB 40 million was spent repairing defects on the Chengdu–Kunming line, and over a hundred serious problem spots were still awaiting attention. The Chongqing–Xiangfan line was opened in 1973, but had to be closed a year later due to multiple cave-ins, and was not reopened until 1978 (Naughton 1988: 376).

Thus, even though cellularized self-sufficiency was reinforced in various ways by Maoist economic planning, the *san xian* experience indicates that centralization remained a significant factor in the development of interior regions. Yet, dependence on the center did little for the long-term economic development of Guizhou during the Maoist era. Although the central government sought to redistribute wealth in China, richer provinces seeking industrial maximization were able to significantly determine spatial patterns of accumulation (Leung and Chan 1986). The central government's attention to development in Guizhou tended to be dominated by turning the province, with its large coal and iron ore reserves, into a center of extraction for fueling rapid industrial development and integration throughout southwest China (Goodman 1983: 119). During the Great Leap Forward (1958–60), nearly all state investments were diverted to mining and mineral processing, the result being a decrease in agricultural production and an increased dependence on central financial assistance (Chen *et al.* 1993: 60–3). Ironically, Guizhou's leaders perceived the GLF as a turning point in provincial integration, and welcomed it as an opportunity for Guizhou to cast off its colonial status. Guizhou was even promoted as a model of the virtues of having been "poor and blank" (Goodman 1986: 111). Ultimately, however, rapid collectivization of agriculture and the excessive investment focus on extractive industry only led to economic and political chaos in Guizhou. It was at this time, in 1965, that Guizhou's entire leadership was dismissed and replaced with functionaries from Sichuan. It would be 15 years before a Guizhou native would once again serve among the province's leaders (Goodman 1986: 131).

This made the industrialization of the *san xian* policy, which followed on the heels of the GLF, even more likely to disregard the basic rural develop-ment needs of the province itself. Indeed, defense industrialization only perpetuated Guizhou's economic chaos (Chen *et al.* 1993: 64–7). Between 1964 and 1966 100 major capital construction projects were carried out, and in 1966 an additional 117 projects were initiated. Yet the poor planning, design, and construction of these projects, along with their enormous cost and diversion of investments, resulted in a 12 per cent decline in industrial and agricultural output from 1966 to 1969. Heavy industrial output alone declined 26 per cent, translating into a 47 per cent decline in revenues. This represented a return to 1955 levels of revenue and resulted in a RMB 214 million budgetary deficit for Guizhou. To compensate, *san xian* investments in Guizhou were stepped up, and peaked in 1971 at RMB 1.46 billion. This did little, however, to alter the dependency structure of the economy which defense industrialization and resource extraction created. Guizhou simply survived on subsidies – which primarily went to urban residents for the purchase of manufactured goods from wealthier provinces and food at deflated prices (Wang and Bai 1991: 73; Tang 1991).

"GOING TO THE WORLD": GUIZHOU IN THE DENG ERA

The utopian modernity pursued by the Maoist state in China had, by the late 1970s, exhausted itself as a viable image for China's future. Its efforts to implement, through "high socialism," a completely rational, objective, and (literally) reasonable modernity failed, theoretically, because of its failure to recognize in modernity the tension between rationalism and the need for subjectivity. Mao's utopian collectivism, what Croll (1994) calls an "imaged heaven," lost its credibility as a narrative for modern China when, after 30 years of effort, the gap between the dream of future prosperity and present austerity remained as wide as ever for most Chinese. For the people of Guizhou, Maoist modernity was a failure because, in wrapping Guizhou's future prospects within those of the nation as a whole, a historical pattern of internal colonialism was never significantly altered. If, as Croll states, "deferred gratification" became a permanent condition for China on the whole under Mao, such deferment was particularly poignant in Guizhou, where resources of the earth had always been shipped out for the gratifica-tion of wealthier regions.

Deferred gratification, in fact, continued as Guizhou fitfully entered the post-Mao era. Croll contrasts the "aspiring to heaven" of the Maoist era to the more practical "resourcing the earth" of the Deng era. But dreams of future prosperity had always been far off for the farmers of Guizhou, while resourcing the earth had long been only for the benefit of powerful interests far removed. This was summarized by one Guizhou cadre who in the 1980s complained to reporters, "Guizhou transports its coal to Sichuan in exchange for Sichuan's mud!" (Wang and Bai 1991: 24). The internal colonial structure of Guizhou's relationship to China's core remained essentially unchanged in the Deng era. Central control of natural resources and lack of attention to rural needs remained the order of the day throughout the 1980s and well into the 1990s. Aware of the increasing desperation of subsidy-dependent provinces such as Guizhou, the center allowed a significant degree of economic liberalization, which finally got underway in 1992 following Deng's well-known southern tour. But while this prompted significant growth in urban areas, rural Guizhou has simply been left to its own devices, instructed to seize the opportunities that have been now made available to it. Its slowness in doing so has consistently been blamed on the cultural "backwardness" of the population, a charge directly explicitly toward the large proportion of non-Han minorities in the province. Thus, the state's narrative of modernity as a rational project of teleological socio-cultural transformation remains a potent force in the Guizhou countryside. It has simply been repackaged in post-Mao rhetoric. Rather than calling for a utopian socialism, modernity is now a smoothly functioning marketplace. The rationality of high collectivism has been replaced by the rationality of the commodity economy.

The legacy of the Third Line

Post-Mao Guizhou still displays many of the characteristics of a province dominated by the legacy of defense industrialization and resource extraction. It still ranks third, behind Sichuan and Shaanxi, in the size of its defense science and technology industry (Liang 1993: 13). In 1990, 84.9 per cent of Guizhou's industrial output value came from the state sector. China's average, at this time, was considerably lower at 54.6 per cent (GS 1993: 142; ZTN 1995: 375). By 1994, the state share had dropped to about 70 per cent, yet the national average had declined even more, to 34 per cent (ZTN 1995: 375, 378–9). Outside of Guiyang, the state's share of industrial output was still as high as 82 per cent in 1995 (GN 1996: 640–710). Besides the dominance the state-owned enterprises, another feature of Third Line regions is the continuing low productivity of their industries. A recent World Bank (1992: 55–6) study found a close relationship between Total Factor Productivity (TFP) and the proportion of non-state industry; the study claimed that "provinces with very low shares of non-state industry . . . had the lowest productivity." Guizhou's TFP index was found to be around 84, compared with Guangdong, Jiangsu, and Zhejiang, all with indices of over

125. Guizhou's low performance was shared by other Third Line provinces, including Shaanxi, Shanxi, Gansu, and Sichuan.

Table 3.3 gives an indication of the historical pattern of state investments in Guizhou, in which heavy industry has been overwhelmingly emphasized. In 1992, the state sector claimed 74.6 per cent of total fixed capital investments in Guizhou; only 2.5 per cent went to agriculture, while 65.8 per cent went to industry.[6] Throughout the 1980s and into the 1990s, the vast majority of industrial investment has gone toward mining, mineral processing, energy, and military industrial development. In 1992, 50.2 per cent of total industrial investments went to extractive industries.[7] With their large investment appetite met by central allocations, these industries have been seeing considerable growth in output (for example, 12.3 per cent in 1995) (GN 1996: 59).

As part of the Eighth FYP's "Key Regions of the Comprehensive National Development Plan" (*Quanguo guotu zongti guihua zonghe kaifa zhongdianchu*) put forth by the National Planning Commission, three key regions were selected in Guizhou for the large-scale development of energy and mineral resources. Finalized in August 1990, this plan, which covered nearly two-thirds of Guizhou's territory and 70 per cent of its population, brought the intensification of resource extraction to a new level. The plan was to centrally administer 19 key regions throughout China. In Guizhou, it called for the development of 14 major hydroelectric power stations, 12 major coal-fire power stations, and intensification of coal, aluminum, iron ore, manganese, phosphorus, sulfur, and gold mining (*Guizhou Sheng Guotu Zongti Guihua* 1992). The plan also called for the creation of "processing chains," vertically integrated sets of industries taking advantage of their geographic proximity in key mining cities such as Liupanshui (Deng 1993). This represented a recognition that, "because of low prices for the primary products," Guizhou's mining centers "cannot build up a sufficient urban infrastructure" (Ye 1993: 129).

At the same time, the comprehensive development plan further emphasizes the center's prescription for Guizhou as a net energy and raw materials provider in light of the increasing obsolescence of its industrial

Table 3.3 Guizhou: total state sector investments, 1950–90 (RMB¥ × 1,000,000)

	1950–7	*1958–78*	*1979–90*
Agriculture	25	580	647
Light industry	15	345	2,457
Heavy industry	66	8,226	11,323

Source: *Guizhou Shenqing* (Guizhou Provincial Gazeteer), p. 36.

manufacturing sector left over from the Third Line era. These enterprises have seen almost no growth in output in the 1990s, and are recognized as one of the weak links in Guizhou's modernization efforts (GN 1996: 61). In an effort to make these industries profitable, many have been converted to consumer goods production and moved to new development zones near Guiyang, Anshun, and Zunyi. Yet this transformation of Guizhou's ordnance industry has also entailed a weaning from central investments (Liang 1993: 14). Thus, the comprehensive development plan means an increased concentration of central investment in the energy and mining sectors, while the province is given the responsibility of reviving a derelict manufacturing industry. Despite the rhetoric of market reform, then, post-Mao central planning represents significant continuity with historical patterns of Guizhou's internal colonial exploitation.

The impact of fiscal decentralization and decline

During the reform era the redistributive effectiveness of the central government has declined considerably with the retreat of the Maoist welfare state. Since 1980, a trend toward local self-financing has generated growing regional economic disparities (Wong *et al.* 1995). As previously indicated in Table 3.2, the central government's share of the budget has dropped from roughly 47 per cent in 1984 to 30 per cent in 1994. At the same time, government revenues have declined to 12.7 per cent of GNP in 1994. Mirroring a pattern that has become familiar throughout provincial China, Guizhou is faced with increasing fiscal responsibilities and increasingly inadequate revenues; it has thus taken to reaching "beyond the budget" to generate revenues through extra-budgetary and self-raised funds.[8] At the same time, the center's ability to address regional economic disparities through budgetary manipulation has declined. Of the center's budgetary transfers to provinces, only quota subsidies are based on need, and by 1990 these accounted for only 15 per cent of total transfers. Over 50 per cent of transfers were earmarked grants, the overwhelming majority of which were absorbed as price subsidies in grain, oil, and cotton for relatively prosperous urban populations (Wong *et al.* 1995: 96).

Between 1988 and 1994, Guizhou received annual fixed quota subsidies of RMB 740 million, representing a significant proportional decline in central transfers as the provincial budget expanded (Wong *et al.* 1995: 92). As indicated in a recent Asian Development Bank (ADB) report, in the early 1980s subsidies financed nearly 60 per cent of Guizhou's total budget. By 1993, this figure was down to less than 20 per cent. In 1995, 70 per cent of total fixed capital investments were financed by the province, a significant increase over the 1992 figure of 48 per cent. (GN 1996: 60; GTN 1993: 102). By the 1990s, the provincial government was no longer able to transfer its diminishing subsidies to counties and instead was extracting a surplus from them to finance provincial outlays. This has resulted not only in inadequate attention to agricultural investment and rural poverty, but to a proliferation of damaging fees and surcharges on rural households and industries as counties scramble to meet their remittance quotas. The ADB's report charges that, "in Guizhou, since 1988, the entire rural sector has acquired net remitter status, so that the rural sector may be supporting the urban sector" (Wong 1995: 11). Poor counties have thus seen very little growth in expenditures, while even relatively wealthy counties are strapped with heavy revenue-sharing burdens which dampen whatever comparative advantages they've been able to muster.

In an effort to arrest fiscal decline and increase central revenue shares, a new tax-sharing arrangement was introduced by the Ministry of Finance in 1994. This shifted the bulk of turnover taxes (value added tax, business tax, and product tax) to the center, and created a new consumption tax on luxury goods, including alcohol and tobacco, also to be remitted directly to the center. This recentralization of revenues has in fact been an on-going trend throughout China in the reform era; whereas in 1980 the center collected only 19 per cent of state revenues, by 1994 it was collecting nearly 58 per cent (ZTN 1995: 21). According to the ADB, in the short run at least, these developments exacerbate Guizhou's financial difficulties. The majority of revenue expansion for counties has come from turnover taxes, and the loss of these indirect revenues in the rural sector will put significant stress on counties to find new sources of income. At the same time, many Guizhou counties have been able to capitalize on a comparative advantage in tobacco and liquor production. They now face the loss of the majority of these revenues to the center.

During the 1980s, the central government tried to compensate for economic difficulties in the interior by introducing a number of development funds for minority regions, revolutionary base areas, and impoverished counties. In terms of direct aid, however, these funds did not amount to much. In 1986, they equaled only 0.1 per cent of China's national income, and were being distributed to 60 per cent of all of China's counties (Ferdinand 1989: 46). The meager amount of these funds were yet another indication "that the center is severely strained in its fiscal resources, and its transfers are generally insufficient or ineffective in raising the growth of capital investment in these poor regions to match the national level" (Leung and Chan 1986: 44). In the 1990s, these development funds continue to be the primary source of central investment in most counties, but their effectiveness remains minimal. They're now typically used to cover the everyday expenditures of county budgets, such as salaries for teachers and government cadres, rather than stimulating the development projects for which they're intended.

The persistence of rural poverty

Fiscal decentralization and decline, along with the internal colonial legacies of defense industrialization and resource extraction, contributed to the continuing stagnation of the rural economy throughout the early phase of the post-Mao reforms. For Guizhou's farmers, the 1980s was a decade of unfulfilled promise. With environmental conditions, population growth, and lack of investments resulting in an increasingly dismal reality in the country-side, the official response has consistently been to emphasize the "backwardness" of the rural population and the need for cultural develop-ment to instill a rational sense of entrepreneurship among peasant farmers. Modernity, then, continues to be articulated as a cultural project, one in which – as in the Maoist years – non-Han ethnicity becomes the major problem. Before exploring how cultural development has been marshaled as a modernization project in Guizhou, however, let us examine the conditions that the province's farmers found themselves in after a decade and a half of post-Mao reforms.

Only about 3 per cent of Guizhou's mountainous, rocky topography – classified by local geographers as "plains" or *bazi* – is suitable for generating an agricultural surplus. In addition, 73 per cent of the landscape consists of highly porous carbonate rocks, which not only creates problems for water supply but, given the relatively wet climate (1,000–1,500 mm annually), leads to a deeply dissected landscape of sheer cliffs, gorges, enormous caverns, and sinkholes. We have already encountered the historical difficulties such a landscape has imposed on Guizhou's trade and commerce. Cultivators them-selves are faced with thin, acidic soils that are often isolated amid rocky karst cones. Thirty-five percent of cultivated land is classified in the lowest of China's three productivity categories. In 1994, about 10.5 per cent of Guizhou was cultivated (1.84 Mh). Based on the 1994 population estimate of 34.58 million, this works out to 0.053 ha per capita, or 67 per cent of China's average.[9] In 1985, the figure was 0.063 ha per capita, indicating a 16 per cent reduction in less than a decade (GTN 1993: 5 and 7). The majority of this reduction is explained by population increase, but land loss due to erosion remains a critical problem as well. By 1994, at least 40 per cent of the land area was experiencing moderate to severe erosion – up from 11.3 per cent in 1975 (Edmonds 1994: 67) – and as land use intensifies, particu-larly on steep slopes, erosion rates are accelerating. With increasing population pressures local leaders find it difficult, however, to limit peasants to farming land which is less susceptible to erosion. As one report concluded, "The harder people work, the more wasteland they reclaim and the more land is reclaimed, the harder they toil. The consequence is drought when it doesn't rain and flood when it does" (Wang and Bai 1991: 26). In the 1980s, bare areas degraded by erosion were expanding at a rate of over 300 ha annually in Qingzhen county, and over 500 ha in Puding county (p. 25). Incidents of massive erosion disasters have increased as well, the worst recorded being a downpour in Leishan county that washed away over 1,300 ha of newly terraced slope in a matter of hours (p. 26).

Since the early 1980s, diversification in commercial crops, livestock, and timber has been stressed as the primary means for local counties to raise capital for investments as they are weaned from central subsidies. "Leading sectors" and "growth poles" have been development buzzwords used to encourage this idea (Chen and Wang 1990; Huang 1991). With one-quarter of the land classified as "grassland," a considerable portion of Guizhou's agricultural output value already comes from animal husbandry (see Table 3.4). Livestock raising became the major "leading sector" during the first decade of reforms, accounting for 27.5 per cent of agricultural output value in 1992, up from 19 per cent in 1980 (GTN 1993: 191). Yet there have been signs of severe overgrazing in certain counties. Beyond livestock, however, the major problem with developing a commercial agricultural sector has been the inability to take prime land out of subsistence production.

While rural poverty is often blamed on a lack of incentive among peasant farmers to "jump into the sea of commerce" (*xiahai*), this remains difficult for the majority of households who have trouble growing enough to eat. Nearly all cultivated land remains devoted to staple foods for local consumption: primarily rice, wheat, canola, corn, and tubers. What little surplus some households do grow is sold to the state at procurement prices that remain artificially low. The lack of income results in an inability to buy fertilizer. Many farmers are left with the choice of going into debt or going hungry, and in some cases the latter alternative is the only option. With the Agricultural Bank acting more and more "businesslike" in the spirit of market reforms, poor farmers are increasingly denied credit on the grounds that repayment is deemed unlikely nor do they possess sufficient collateral (Unger 1994: 48–9).[10] Grain production has thus remained well below China's average (see Table 3.5), and grain subsidies have accounted for a substantial portion of total food consumption in the province, averaging between 500,000 and 1 million tonnes annually.[11] Imported grain was costing the province an average of RMB 700–800 million annually in the late 1980s, a figure roughly equal to Guizhou's annual quota subsidies from the central government.

While government officials have focused their concern on the Malthusian trend of population growth outpacing food production on a declining resource base, the larger issue appears to be access to the resources necessary to increase productivity. Certainly, Guizhou's population growth rate has remained well above China's average (see the demographic data for Guizhou given in Tables 3.6a–d). Between 1970 and 1982 China's Total Fertility Rate declined by 54 per cent whereas Guizhou's declined by only 36 per cent (Hill 1993: 6). Population growth has been highest in minority regions, where one study estimated a rate of natural increase at 23 per thousand between 1949 and 1989 (Ran 1991: 221). Local geographers estimate annual growth rates of up to 3.5 per cent in some minority regions. Thus, between 1985 and 1988, for example, population in minority areas grew by 4 per cent whereas grain output grew by only 2.7 per cent; per capita output dropped from 372 to 366 *jin* (Ran 1991: 230). This, however, was during a period when growth rates in grain

Table 3.4 Guizhou: shares of industrial and agricultural output, rural GMP, and
farmland, 1980–92 (%)

	1980	1985	1990	1992
Shares of GVIAO				
Agriculture	44.6	41.7	40.0	37.0
Industry	55.4	58.3	60.0	63.0
Light industry	19.5	23.2	25.4	24.9
Heavy industry	35.9	35.1	34.6	38.2
Shares of rural GMP[a]				
Agriculture	83.8	74.5	75.0	70.2
Industry	5.5	11.3	14.6	18.0
Construction	6.7	7.8	3.4	3.8
Transport	0.9	2.6	3.3	3.9
Commerce/Trade	3.1	3.8	3.7	4.1
Shares of GVAO				
Cultivation	66.5	55.4	53.5	52.1
Livestock	19.0	22.5	24.3	27.5
Sidelines	10.5	14.0	16.4	12.6
Forestry	4.0	7.8	5.5	7.4
Share of farmland				
Irrigated paddy				41.8
Dry field				58.2

Source: *Guizhou Tongji Nianjian* (Guizhou Statistical Yearbook), 1993, pp. 28, 188, 191, 198.

Note:
[a] GMP, or Gross Material Product (*Shehui Zongchanzhi*), is the total output value of the five
   major material production sectors: agriculture, industry, construction, transport, and
   commerce. It differs from Gross National Product (GNP) in that it excludes net income from
   non-material services but includes the consumption of material inputs, such as raw materials
   and energy resources, in its calculation.

production declined throughout China due to changes in state procurement
procedures in 1985. At issue is not population growth *per se* but inadequate access to additional sources of income, with increasing labor power
being the only viable response for many peasant families.

The prospects for joining the "commodity economy" also remain slim

Table 3.5 Guizhou: grain output and productivity, 1990–4

	Productivity (kg/ha)		Output (kg/cap)	
	1990	*1994*	*1990*	*1994*
Guizhou	2,835	3,849	235	271
China	3,930	4,500	390	371

Source: *Zhongguo Tongji Nianjian* (China Statistical Yearbook), 1991, pp. 345–8; 1995, pp. 347, 350.

Table 3.6a Guizhou: ethnic composition

	(× 1,000)			% of total	
	1990 census	*1982 census*	*% change[a]*	*1990*	*1982*
Total	32,391.1	28,552.9	13.4	100.0	100.0
Han	21,148.8	21,129.5	0.1	65.3	74.0
Miao	3,668.8	2,582.6	42.8	11.3	9.0
Bouyei	2,478.1	2,098.9	18.1	7.7	7.4
Dong	1,400.0	851.1	64.5	4.3	3.0
Tujia	1,045.5	1.6	63173.2	3.2	0.0
Yi	704.7	564.6	25.3	2.2	2.0
Gelao	430.6	51.5	735.6	1.3	0.2
Shui	323.1	275.7	17.0	1.0	1.0
Hui	127.1	98.5	28.5	0.4	0.3
Bai	123.3	4.9	2414.7	0.4	0.0

Sources: *Guizhou Shengqing* (Guizhou Provincial Gazetteer), p. 430.

Note:
[a] The outstanding population growth of many minority groups in Guizhou (particularly the Tujia, Bai, and Gelao) is due to the return of the *minzu shibie* project in the 1980s and the subsequent determination of many "pending" cases of *minzu* classification.

given both the lack of resources invested in poor regions of Guizhou and the lack of articulation between rural and urban areas (Wang and Bai 1991: 104). This has particularly been the case in minority regions. The autonomous prefectures of Qiandongnan, Qiannan, and Qianxinan make up the southern half of Guizhou. In addition there are ten minority

Table 3.6b Guizhou: total fertility rate

	Guizhou	China
1970	7.0	5.8
1982	4.5	2.6

Source: Hill (1993: 6).

Table 3.6c Guizhou: rural infant mortality rate (per thousand)

	Guizhou	China
UNICEF survey of 300 poor counties, 1989	108.0	68.0
Ministry of Public Health rural survey, 1994	73.2	21.5

Source: Wong (1995).

Table 3.6d Guizhou: population growth (per thousand)

	Guizhou		China	
	Birth rate	*Natural increase*	*Birth rate*	*Natural increase*
1981	28.0	19.4	21.0	14.5
1992	22.4	13.9	18.2	11.6
1994	22.9	14.8	17.7	11.2

Source: Hill (1993: 6); *Zhongguo Tongji Nianjian* (China Statistical Yearbook), 1995, p. 60.

autonomous counties outside of these prefectures. Combined, these regions make up 55.5 per cent of Guizhou's territory and just over 40 per cent of the total population. As indicated by investment and income statistics, conditions here reflect a growing gap between minority and Han regions during the reform era.[12] Net Material Product (*Guomin shouru* or NMP) per capita in Guizhou's minority regions in 1985 was 43.6 per cent of China's average, and 79 per cent of the provincial average.[13] By 1990, the proportions had dropped to 30.4 per cent and 65 per cent respectively (Li 1991: 3). Relative to population distribution, state investments in minority regions have clearly been lacking. Only 10.5 per cent of Guizhou's total investment during the Sixth FYP went to minority regions. During the Seventh FYP, the proportion declined to 8.4 per cent. Minority region shares of fixed capital invest-ments also dropped from 12 per cent during the Sixth FYP to 9.5 per cent during the Seventh (Li 1991: 5). Of the 49 counties comprising these regions, 39 depend on subsidies from either the province or the central government. In 1989, revenues in minority regions amounted to a mere 54 per cent of outlays, and on a per capita basis were only 16 per cent of China's average and 31 per cent of the provincial average.

The majority of what is officially defined as "absolute poverty" in Guizhou is concentrated in minority regions.[14] In 1990, Guizhou's population accounted for about 2.8 per cent of China's total, yet it had 9.2 per cent of China's population living below the poverty line. Of the 31 counties in Guizhou (out of a total of 86) that are designated as "impoverished counties" (*pinkun xian*), 21 are in minority regions, accounting for half of the total minority population in Guizhou. Impoverished counties are entitled to special assis-tance from the province and the central government. This typically means special engineering projects (referred to as *wen bao gongcheng*, or "food and shelter projects") to help increase agricultural productivity. As part of the overall trend in fiscal decentralization, however, central aid to impoverished regions has been declining. In 1990 state assistance amounted to just over RMB 212 million, down from over 300 million in 1987 (Ran 1991: 222).[15] Declining assistance notwithstanding, poverty alleviation loans (accompanied by subsidized low interest rates) seldom go to the neediest households, and many projects focusing on fruit trees and animal husbandry have failed due to poor technical assistance and insufficient start-up capital (Croll 1994: 148).

Indeed, according to Croll (p. 152), poverty alleviation efforts throughout China have focused too much on jump-starting commercial projects, rather than treating more basic problems such as lack of primary health care. One plan, for example, has called for 70 per cent of all state poverty alleviation investments in Guizhou to finance new cash cropping schemes (Ran 1991: 229). But raising some pigs, planting an orchard, or clearing a slope for a new crop of soybeans, merely earns the farmer a place in a weak market that by no means guarantees success. The value of agricultural and livestock products can seldom overcome high transport costs of Guizhou's moun-tainous terrain, nor is there a significant market for these products beyond the local region anyway (Wang and Bai 1991: 153–61). This is especially true considering the popularity of such income-generating schemes throughout China's rural areas. As these larger structural problems conspire to swallow up whatever money the government throws at the problem of rural poverty, peasants are left with the blame for failed projects due to their "traditional attitudes" and "lack of entrepreneurship" (Wang and Bai 1991: 38).

Pursuing market socialism in Guizhou

Poverty in rural Guizhou, then, remains envisioned by the state as the problem of an incomplete modernity. Rural development is saturated with the rhetoric of rationalism and progress toward an ultimately ordered future made reasonable for the subjugating purposes of the state and capital. Villagers are left with little choice but to embrace this narrative if they are to achieve any success in turning its objectifying logic to their advantage. Their identity – as "backward peasants," "traditional minorities," and so on – has, once again, been conceived as Other to the modern state and its progressive society. As the 1990s brought about a significant economic liberalization in Guizhou, the rhetoric of "backwardness" only increased as rural Guizhou found itself lagging further and further behind urban areas and their incipient prosperity.

Economic liberalization came about as a series of tentative steps aimed at addressing Guizhou's dependent relationship to the center. Throughout China, local governments have been faced with the contradictory combination of fiscal decentralization (giving them more responsibility for managing their budgets) and fiscal decline (making it necessary for them to cover more of their expenditures). The fiscal burdens of this situation have resulted in a tremendous amount of local activity in independently promoting regional economic development, especially by expanding the light industrial sector. This has often led to irrational duplication and regional protectionism (Wong 1991). It has also led to a flurry of real estate and trade speculation aimed at attracting increasingly mobile capital from domestic and foreign sources. In Guizhou, efforts to attract external capital and "align" the local economy with broader markets was perhaps most clearly manifest in rapid expansion of special economic development zones and glitzy trade fairs in 1992–3. The year 1992 marked the real beginning of economic reform in Guizhou's urban-industrial sector. With encouragement from the State Council, and the appointment of a new governor (Liu Shineng), the province attempted to ride the coat-tails of Deng's 1992 southern tour by cashing in on the southern China development boom.

While the bulk of Guizhou's external economic activities continued to be dominated by investments in energy and mineral resource extraction, the provincial capital quickly became the site of intense land speculation. Provincial leadership managed in July 1992 to negotiate with the State Council for Guiyang's preferential status as an "interior open city" (*neilu kaifang chengshi*). This set off a small real estate boom, and by May 1993, 25 real estate development companies had been established, half of them with external funds. Indeed, with land one-third to two-thirds less expensive in Guiyang than Guangdong, 45 per cent of all private external investments in Guizhou in 1993 were in real estate (*Xingdao Ribao* 16 May 1993). The sudden flurry of construction was quite noticeable to the citizens of Guiyang, who by 1993 were comparing their city to a frontier town where wealth easily comes and goes. An even more indicative example of Guizhou's pursuit of fast capital is found in the 1992 purchase of 330 hectares of land at the booming Guangxi port of Beihai, ostensibly for an export development and processing zone but more likely as a simple attempt at land speculation (Hendrischke 1997). This turned out to be a poor invest-ment that nevertheless created quite a stir. Entrepreneurs in Guiyang talked glowingly of Guizhou's new link to world trade, despite the fact that in the late 1990s the land remained undeveloped.

Much of the real estate boom took place in newly established economic development zones outside of Guiyang. These zones were initiated by the relocation of many Third Line enterprises, referred to as the *xiashan chugou* policy ("coming down from the mountains and out of the valleys"). Along with their relocation, these enterprises began switching to consumer goods production. In 1979, 10 per cent of Guizhou's military industrial production was in consumer goods; by 1992 the proportion was up to 72 per cent (Liang 1993: 15). Faced with the state's expectations of accountability, these firms hoped their new location in "hi-tech development zones" would act as a springboard for attracting external investment. By 1993, for example, they had established linkages with over 150 "window enterprises" in the open cities along the coast in order to facilitate export-oriented production and attract investment deals. The first and largest of these zones was at Xintianzhai – the *Guiyang Gaoxin Jishu Chanye Kaifaqu* ("Guiyang Hi-Tech Industries Development Zone") – which was established, with State Council approval, by the 1992 relocation of the Zhenhua Electronics Group (*Guizhou Huabao* 1993: 18–23). An additional three zones were established the same year by the provincial government; they were located in Guiyang (at Xiaohe), Zunyi, and Anshun. Determined not to miss out, Guiyang's municipal government also established its own zone at Baiyun, and other municipalities and counties quickly followed suit. The entire Bijie Prefecture was granted state-level status as a "Poverty Alleviation Experimental Zone." Then, in 1994, Qiandongnan Miao and Dong Autonomous Prefecture was designated a state-level "Experimental Development Zone" for minority regions by the Nationalities Affairs Commission (*Guojia Minwei*) (*Qiandongnan Bao* 15 April 1994; Zhang 1995).

Bolstered by the establishment of this experimental zone in Qiandongnan, the prefectural capital of Kaili in turn established its own "Economic and Technological Development Zone." The zone's policies, outlined in draft version provided by a city official in 1994, give an indica-tion of how localities tried to attract mobile capital. Tax policies in Kaili include five-year income tax holidays followed by another five years of reduced taxes (tax holidays are even longer for "hi-tech firms"), value-added tax reductions and waivers, subsidies for firms that face tax hardships, and tax holidays of various lengths for land, property, transportation, and employment. In addition, the majority of taxes for the first six years (following the tax holiday) will be returned to the place from which the new firm's investments came. Land rents and utility fees are reduced, especially for "hi-tech" and tourist enterprises. Kaili, which in 1965 became a center for Third Line electronics enterprises, is especially hoping to capitalize on this legacy by attracting investment in modern electronics production.

All of this development had a noticeable impact in Guizhou's urban sector. Provincial exports increased 64 per cent between 1990 and 1993, while imports jumped 94 per cent. Urban consumer spending was up 34 per cent during the same period, matching similar growth in urban per capita incomes (GTN 1993: 159, 161, 338–9). Yet, overall per capita consumption for the province in 1994 remained the lowest in China at 735 *yuan* (42 per cent of the national average) indicating the influence of rural Guizhou's stagnant growth; rural per capital expenditures in Guizhou were the third lowest in China in 1995.[16] Urban–rural disparities only increased during the 1990s. Development zones primarily benefited urban residents, whose lives were already subsidized by the state in many ways.[17] From 1990 to 1993, nominal incomes per capita in rural households increased 16 per cent, less than half the figure for urban residents (GTN 1993: 168). Similarly, investments in Guizhou's energy production only benefited urban heavy industries (consuming roughly 78 per cent of all commercial electricity in the province). The other major beneficiary – urban households – consumed ten times as much electricity as rural households in 1995, despite the fact that they accounted for merely 14 per cent of the total population (GN 1996: 357, 598). Furthermore, the focus on speculative development in trade and real estate resulted in the virtual ignoring of agriculture's continuing plight.

By the mid-1990s, the government was responding with increasingly symbolic gestures aimed more at shoring up its legitimacy than actually alleviating rural poverty. On a 1996 visit to Bijie, General Secretary Jiang Zemin – in the midst of passing out token blankets and coats to the half-dressed inhabitants of each miserable hovel he visited – made a point of reassuring his local hosts that, "China is still a socialist country." But upon investigating impoverished villages near Guiyang, a group of Beijing reporters covering Jiang's visit rhetorically asked if Guizhou even *had* a communist party. For how could such wretchedness be tolerated if it did? Despite all the efforts of the early 1990s, the overall picture of Guizhou's economy had changed little in structural terms. While industry and agriculture contributed nearly equal parts to the provincial output value in 1994, they did so with vastly different employment figures: industry accounted for roughly 8 per cent of the workforce whereas agriculture accounted for nearly 75 per cent (ZTN 1995: 86, 332, 381). State-level investments continued to be dominated by mining and energy development (GN 1996: 231). Rural commercialism remained stubbornly undeveloped and calls for "cultural development" (*wenhua fazhan*) as the remedy only intensified.

The discourse of cultural development, in fact, represents an interesting field in which to see the shifting narratives of modernity in Guizhou. As the Deng era project of modernizing rural society retreated almost exclusively to the realm of symbolism and rhetoric (having largely failed in its poverty alleviation efforts), capital came to play an increasingly significant, and in many ways contradictory, role in the imaginings of a future, prosperous modernity. While minority groups continue to occupy the symbolic heart of campaigns that call for changing the "traditional thinking" of the rural sector, they ironically have emerged as bearers of a new kind of modernity, one cautiously distant from the paternal state and reservedly attracted to the mobile capital of a "Greater China." Tourism has been the catalyst for this shift in the discourse of modernity in Guizhou.

The touristic spectacle of modernity in Guizhou

The establishment of suburban development zones in Guizhou between 1992 and 1994 was accompanied by a marketing and promotional blitz unlike anything the province had ever witnessed before. For provincial leaders, Guizhou's modernization was to become a spectacular event, attracting tourist/investors from the wealthier regions of China and the world. Tourism, in fact, was slated to become one of the province's "pillar industries," with plans calling for tourism revenues to contribute as much as 20 per cent to Guizhou's income by 2010 (in 1993, tourism contributed about 5 per cent) (Sun 1994). If successful, such a plan would lift tourism to the same level of importance as the province's other recognized "pillars": coal mining, hydroelectricity, mineral processing, defense industry, and agriculture. In the 1990s, the role of tourism in Guizhou shifted from a convenient way to foreign exchange (most of which left the province anyway), to a comprehensive modernization strategy in its own right. This also marked a shift in which tourism came to be seen as a strategy serving local development needs more than national needs. Tourism was to be a vanguard industry, opening the way for other processes to gain a foothold in Guizhou, particularly external investment and commercial integration of the rural economy with external markets. This idea was championed by the phrase *lüyou tatai, jingmao changxi* ("economic trade performing on a stage built by tourism"), which was soon found in nearly all local media coverage of commercial development projects. Tourism was to be the principle vehicle by which potential investors and consumers were brought to Guizhou. It would also serve as a primary means by which the countryside could cast off its "traditional thinking" and adopt a "commercial conscience" in order to solve its impending subsistence crisis. Through its "demonstration effects," it could raise expectations for improved living standards, and introduce a medium of exchange that could overcome the trasnport inhibiting terrain (Wang and Bai 1991: 169). Symbolically illustrating the important role of tourism, Guizhou's only high-grade highway was completed in 1991, between Guiyang and Huangguoshu Falls, the province's most popular tourist attraction. When this highway was built, 20 per cent of Guizhou's administrative village seats were still roadless (Li 1991). With primitive transport conditions throughout the province, the construction of a high-grade highway to a site of "non-productive" economic activity represented a significant commitment to initiating the basic infrastructure investments necessary for "selling Guizhou."

Ethnic minority culture – long regarded as an impediment to modernity – became a fundamental feature of Guizhou's promotional activities, both in terms of using exotic cultural representations as enticements for potential investments, and as a feature of market socialism's potential for rural development in minority regions. Indeed, tourism itself was thought to be ideally suited for these regions by taking advantage of the conditions which made them so poor: harsh but scenic mountainous environments and socio-cultural distance from modern Chinese economies and lifestyles. The representations of minority culture that became ubiquitous features of promoting the province would not only make Guizhou more interesting to outsiders, but were meant to establish a model for the cultural development of minority groups themselves, conditioning them to articulate symbolic cultural practices with commercial projects. Tourism was thus seen not simply as a propaganda and marketing tool for Guizhou, but also as a process of development and integration encouraging minority regions to become more modern.

The associate director of China International Travel Service (CITS) in Guiyang, for example, saw tourism helping peasants achieve a "commercial conscience." It did this by opening up particular villages to tourism, allowing them to earn a cash income and learn the value of money, and giving them a sense of ethnic pride. Once village thinking had been "turned around" another village would be selected and the process would start over. She pointed out that it was good business for her too, since once a village became "modernized," tourists would be less interested in seeing it anyway, and it would be time to find a new one that was still "primitive." There were certain villages which the Guizhou Tourism Bureau (GTB) promoted as "models" of how this process worked. One was the Miao village of Heitu, which had been relocated in 1958 when Hongfenghu reservoir was built. Heitu was given only two-thirds of its original landholdings after relocation, and had been very poor until being opened to tourism in 1991. With funds provided by the National Tourism Administration (NTA), RMB 300,000 was used to build a road to the village, and the county minority affairs commission (*minwei*) chipped in another 4,000 to beautify the village. Soon tour groups were arriving to be treated to an elaborate village welcoming ceremony and song and dance performance. According to the county *minwei*, in two years Heitu's per capita net peasant income (*nongmin chunshouru*) jumped from RMB 167 to 670.

But the most visible signs of Guizhou's touristic modernity were found not in rural villages but in urban and suburban regions. Tourism was an explicit component of the economic development zones that popped up around Guizhou in the early 1990s. Each of these zones featured plans for a holiday and vacation resort, catering to the zone's prospective free-spending investors. Throughout China, holiday villages and special vacation zones became the fastest growing sector of the tourism industry in the 1990s. These relatively luxurious resort sites, officially sanctioned by the NTA as

"Tourism and Vacation Zones," represent the rapid growth of domestic tourism beyond the traditional "meeting tourism" (*gongfei lüyou*) of bureaucrats that has traditionally dominated the domestic tourist market. Increased wealth, especially along the coast, has created a great demand for vacation resorts. Twelve of these were approved by the NTA as state level zones (Zhang 1995: 55–6), but every province and city was busy creating its own versions, and Guizhou was no exception. Numerous vacation zones for Guiyang, Zunyi, and Anshun were planned. In Guiyang's Xiaohe economic development zone, "Guiyang Recreation City" and "Yelang Ancient Tourist Scenery Zone" were established. Both of these holiday camps were glossed in various ways with ethnic cultural features, and were meant to present amenities which further enticed investors contemplating doing business at Xiaohe. Similarly, Kaili's plans called for preferential policies for all tourism-oriented projects. In particular, projects that exploited local ethnic culture were looked upon favorably.

In Yunnan, this resort-building trend developed much more rapidly than in Guizhou, and provided something of a model for hopeful resort builders in its poorer neighbor. At the state-level resort of Yangzonghai, southeast of Kunming, plans included a golf course, a convalescence hot spring, a horse racing track, and a diving center. Over US$ 900 million was poured into the site by "Greater China" investors from Singapore, Taiwan, and Hong Kong. Another resort, "geared to overseas tourists," was also planned closer to Kunming. It included holiday villas, a recreation center, a beach, fishing center, zoo, and a "reproduction of a typical village depicting the architecture and lifestyles of 25 minority groups in Yunnan" (*China Daily* 7 March 1994). This in addition to Yunnan's "Folk Culture Village" ethnic theme park already built in the same area. Guizhou's leaders expect similar developments in the future, and are planning a similar emphasis on theme-park style ethnic cultural attractions.

Despite these rapidly growing resorts, China's domestic tourism market continues to be driven primarily by "meeting tourism" (*gongfei lüyou*) and a large responsibility of the GTB has been in attracting this market, much as a city's convention bureau would in the US. The primary issue here, as one GTB official claimed, is the fact that Guizhou retains all of its domestic tourist receipts, whereas a large portion of international receipts still flow to the central government, or to agencies beyond Guizhou. The province tries to attract this increasingly lucrative tourist market by offering cheaper prices, and by emphasizing its cooler summer climate, its magnificent scenery, and charming ethnic customs as an enticement for government or business units looking for meeting sites. Indeed, at the state-level scenic area of Hongfenghu, just 30 minutes west of Guiyang, a series of replica ethnic villages have been built; they are primarily used for entertaining conference-goers with a conveniently staged version of Guizhou's ethnic hospitality. They feature a number of hotels built in traditional Miao, Dong, Yi, and Bouyei architectural styles, restaurants, souvenir shops, performance arenas, and karaoke lounges.

Tourism, however, is more than a collection of vacation resorts and conference sites. More importantly, it is through the medium of tourism that many in Guizhou imagine what modernity must be like. Tourism is both a language and canvas for finishing China's incomplete modernity. In Guizhou, its role as such was celebrated in a rash of flashy trade fairs in 1992 and 1993. While these can be interpreted, in part, as manifestations of the local initiative spurred by Deng's southern tour, they were also orchestrated as part of several centrally promoted tourism campaigns sponsored by the NTA. In 1992, the province held a "batik festival" (*laran jie*) in Anshun, and a "liquor culture festival" (*jiu wenhua jie*) in Zunyi. The following year, there was an "azalea blossom festival," while the former "liquor culture festival" was combined with a "Huangguoshu sightseeing festival." This latter event was partly funded by the NTA and was one of five official events throughout the country marking "China Scenery Tourism Year" (*Zhongguo shanshui fengguang lüyounian*). Guizhou's selection for NTA funding in 1993 was treated as a crucial opportunity for economic development; "Huangguoshu Sightseeing and International Famous Liquor Festival" became the largest commercial event in Guizhou's history, promoted with the phrase *rang shijie liaojie Guizhou, rang Guizhou zouxiang shijie* ("let the world understand Guizhou, let Guizhou go to the world").

These festivals were very large-scale undertakings which combined ethnic cultural performances, traditional crafts demonstrations, and numerous exhibitions of local products, especially liquor. The azalea festival, for example, sought to combine tourism and trade under the principle of *yi jie yin shang, zhao shang yin zi, fazhan maoyi, kuoda duiwai jingji hezuo* ("lure business through festivals, lure investment by favoring business, develop trade, expand external economic cooperation"). The festival focused on Guizhou's "100 *li* azalea belt," a scenic attraction along the border between Dafang and Qianxi counties. Dafang is one of Guizhou's 31 impoverished counties. During the festival, *Guizhou Ribao* (14 to 18 April 1993) ran an article titled "Economy Performing on a Stage of Flowers" which described Dafang's various natural resources awaiting investment and exploitation. Other articles followed, over the course of the week, on investment opportunities throughout the Dafang region. The paper also ran full color pages of advertisements for Guizhou enterprises, most of which were participating in the commodities exhibition. *Guizhou Ribao* also emphasized ethnic activities in its coverage, pointing out that the region's rich minority culture made it an ideal place to invest in ethnic tourism development.

The Huangguoshu festival was an even bigger event. With the extra boost of NTA funds, millions of *yuan* were spent beautifying Guiyang and the nearby scenic sites for the week-long festival. The festival featured an "International Children's Crafts Festival" (with children's performance troupes from China, USA, Vietnam, Laos, Burma, Japan, and France), a parade featuring elaborate floats sponsored by various local distilleries, ethnic song and dance performances at Huangguoshu Falls, and no less than seven different commodities and crafts exhibitions. The largest of these was held in the provincial exhibition center, which was renamed the "International Economic and Technological Trade Center" to better capture the heady spirit of the fair. The festival was attended by the head of the NTA, along with numerous central party officials, and a random assortment of foreign ambassadors. It was covered by *Guizhou Ribao* (8 to 12 August 1993) with four consecutive days of color photographs and advertisements. As with the azalea festival, it also provided an opportunity to print numerous stories on development and modernization throughout the province. The unprecedented extravagance of the festival, however, compelled the newspaper to run an editorial cautioning enterprise managers against the flagrant waste of valuable funds on lavish banquets and, ironically, the use of "too many advertisements."

In trying to insure their success as public relations events, the provincial government arranged to have RMB 1.85 billion worth of economic cooperation projects, which had actually been negotiated throughout the preceding year, to be finalized during the festivals. *Guizhou Ribao* (17 August 1993) reported that the total business volume for the 1993 festivals exceeded RMB 3.65 billion, that nearly 10,000 tourists and business representatives attended, and that over US$ 70 million in foreign direct investment was negotiated. A total of 33 joint venture/cooperation projects were negotiated, a number which, if finalized, would account for 15.5 per cent of all such contracts in Guizhou between 1980 and 1992. By 1996, however, officials in the provincial government privately acknowledged that many of these business deals were never finalized. Looking back on the festivals, one official commented bluntly that the trade fairs had been "a huge waste of money" for the province.[18] Indeed, since 1993 there have been no more large-scale trade fairs held in Guizhou. Yet, while the festivals were perhaps a failure in economic terms, reinforcing Guizhou's disadvantaged position in pursuing the newly mobile capital of post-1992 China, they were nevertheless profoundly cultural events, not simply for the tourists visiting the province, but especially for people in Guizhou itself. The festivals provided a brief tangible model of cultural development and commercial integration combined with celebrations of tradition and symbolic cultural diversity.

"Going to the world" did not simply herald the (perhaps premature) birth of the commodity economy in Guizhou. More important, it attempted to resolve the profound sense of isolation and dependence that centuries of internal colonialism helped produce. It is no wonder that the festivals of 1993, which might be scoffed at by Westerners as crass commercialism, were so enthusiastically celebrated by the citizens of Guiyang. Students at Guizhou Normal University, for example, referred to the Huangguoshu Sightseeing and Famous Wine Festival as "one of the most exciting days" of their lives. Tourism, for them, was the hoped-for purveyor of modernity, an agent of change long overdue in a backward province. Yet, while Guizhou's urban residents may have briefly reveled in the spectacular allure of capital as a long-awaited alternative to decades of subsidized dependence under state socialism, a karaoke-filled future offered an even more significant alternative modernity for non-Han minorities in the countryside and their elite urban representatives. Touristic modernity has opened up a multitude of possibilities for appropriation by those who have for so long been labeled a "problem" barring Guizhou's entry into the modern world. But, in order to understand just how complicated this new unstable terrain of commodification has become, we need to explore more thoroughly the political economy of tourism in Guizhou. For as tourism introduces the potential for new, liberating subjectivities for non-Han minorities, the promise of freedom is accompanied by a perhaps even greater force of alienation than the state and all its past projects of ethnic assimilation. That force is the logic of commodity exchange, and as we shall see in the following chapter, its rationalizations present a whole new regime of colonization to rural Guizhou.

4 False modern triumphant

Tourism and cultural development in Guizhou

INTRODUCTION

Although Guizhou's colonization has been a process extending back several centuries, it entered a fundamentally new phase in the early twentieth century. Nationalism became the primary source of legitimacy for bringing China's peripheral regions and peoples into the folds of a unified and modernizing Chinese society. While modern nationalism certainly added ideological fuel to the state's agenda of political and economic integration of peripheral territory, it more significantly provided a new justification for *cultural* integration. An integrated nation-state required not only advanced administrative and economic institutions, but also a unified and modernized culture enabling people throughout the territory to communicate, trade, and otherwise interact with one another. As suggested in Chapter 1, however, the project of nation-building and creating a modernized civic culture had simultaneously to invent a placed, museumified, and all-but-lost folk tradition upon which to build a sense of popular solidarity. In Guizhou, therefore, modernization and integration served to produce a foundation of local traditions from which to build a developed culture and economy. Even as the state continued to brand minority culture as "unhealthy" to the development of socialist modernity, it maintained a posture of selectivity, claiming the right to choose particular symbolic aspects of non-Han lifestyles to add to the stew of a (multi)national state. Touristic modernity in Guizhou embodies this seemingly paradoxical aspect of nation building: the simultaneous development of modernity and tradition, or the modernization of tradition.

Tourism's role in the political and economic integration of peripheral regions throughout Asia has been documented by a number of observers. David Zurick (1992, 1995) has written of adventure tourism among Nepal's isolated and subsistence populations as a fundamental component of national and local economic development. Stanley Stevens (1991) has similarly noted that tourism in Nepal has introduced important changes which serve to link peripheral Sherpa populations more closely to a national economy. These changes include new local divisions of labor as tourist-oriented commercial development ensues, the consequent replacement of subsistence with increasingly cash-oriented forms of production, the emigration of male laborers associated with increased local demands for industrial goods and cash incomes, conflicts and/or loss of local control over natural resources, and conflicts over local settlement rights. Jean Michaud has been particularly observant of this process in Ladakh and northern Thailand. He argues that the modern tourism industry offers national governments "an additional opportunity to extend their powers further into these previously isolated communities by means of increasing the minorities' dependency on the national economy, in turn precipitating fuller and irreversible integration with the national identity" (Michaud 1993: 23). While state strategies are promoted as development and modernization for impoverished regions, Michaud (pp. 27–8) interprets national integration as a form of subjugation for previously autonomous local societies:

> Employing rhetoric heavily laced with the concepts currently in vogue at the World Bank and the International Monetary Fund – sustainable development, locally managed agriculture and marketing, consultation and village participation, and so forth – programmes are initiated by the state which in fact accelerate the sedentarisation of nomadic groups, obligate subsistence farmers to shift to cash-cropping, introduce obligatory education in the national language, . . . induce the monetarisation of the local economy, lead to political proportional representation, and thus finally achieve economic, political, and cultural subjugation, which is then carried further by the widespread introduction of the mass media that in all its forms promotes the values of the capital city.

Tourism's role in the state's modernization and development of peripheral regions is particularly important because it costs the state much less to "open" a region to tourism than it does to implement other modernization schemes. A report in the 1980s, advocating tourism as the solution to the problem of modernity in China's "backward" areas by transforming the self-sufficient values of indigenous people, argued thus:

> The consumption patterns of the indigenous population in backward regions can, though emulation and learning, become enriched thus resulting in production for exchange, and from this there emerges the possibility of transforming modes of production. The modern culture and information brought in by tourists from developed regions has, in effect, a similar impact to the personnel from developed regions brought in to backward regions by the industrial strategy for development, and can be a tremendous impetus for change in lifestyles, patterns of consumption and concepts of value among the local inhabitants. The difference is that information comes free with the tourists who at the

same time are contributing enormous amounts of capital accumulation
for the economic development of backward regions.

(Wang and Bai 1991: 171)

The geographical factors that conspire to render such regions remote and
"backward" yet self-sufficient, are the same factors that appear attractive to
tourists. More important, though, is the generally favorable reception
tourism development receives among the local population. In remote regions
confronted with resource scarcity and historical cycles of subsistence crisis,
tourism offers to bring modernity right to villagers' doorsteps, a welcome
alternative to chasing it in far-flung places. Michaud (1993: 34) argues that,

> due to the low density of the population and the absence of any large-
> scale industries, the opportunities for regular employment for unskilled
> work are too scarce to absorb the already available laborers and the ones
> who would willingly decide to sell their labor-force. Thus, when harvests
> are bad, and the villagers are hard-pressed to get by, they are by neces-
> sity very receptive to any local employment opportunities that demand
> little capital and almost no training in new skills (a labor intensive situa-
> tion). The advent of tourism offers such a break.

Even with minimal financial returns to the villagers, tourism helps sustain
the existing village scene in important ways. At the same time, however,
changes are introduced that make villagers increasingly vulnerable to
broader markets and networks of production and consumption. Cash
incomes are used to purchase industrial goods produced outside the region,
new social cleavages are created while those that already exist are often
augmented, and soon the villagers are seen to be flaunting the symbols of
their new found modernity. For many tourists, this translates into the
corruption of "cultural authenticity," and metropolitan agents will respond
by finding new sites not yet despoiled of their cultural purity. According to
Horne (1992: 254), tourism in such situations helps to construct a distinction between self-professed modern tourists and "people of the past who
can't make the present work." Living in the past, they display charming lives
worth gazing upon and vicariously experiencing, "yet if they make the
present work in our terms they are likely to be seen as having degraded
themselves by abandoning their own culture." This attitude itself becomes
part of the national colonizing project, linking villagers to the whims of the
national and international tourist market. Deprived of their cash income,
Michaud argues, but now used to having money around, many in the remote
villages will be forced to leave and seek work elsewhere, becoming an easily
exploited unskilled labor force. Places which have become "too modern" and
lose their tourist site status thus find new ways to further their dependency
on the national economy.

Tourism's colonizing power is great, but not simply because it disrupts customary divisions of labor or introduces new exchange relations that render villagers increasingly dependent on the whims and volatility of external markets. It is the combination of these typical symptoms of capitalist dependency with the culturalist project of nationalism that renders tourism such a havoc-wreaking force. Thus, not only do we need to examine the kinds of political-economic disruptions evidenced by case studies throughout the developing world (Lea 1988; Adams 1990; Connell 1993; Silver 1993; van den Berghe 1992), but we also need to address, critically, the production of culture that accompanies these disruptions. The alienating potential of tourism as a modern project is perhaps most significantly found in its powers of representation rather than its logic of accumulation. Villagers are not just integrated into the broader labor and commodity markets of the state, but are more importantly expected to become willing performers of "folk tradition" in terms that are deemed acceptable to the needs of the abstract nation. This "tradition" is the modern product of a dominant state and the forces of capital, each of which profits from its production in different, though often complementary, ways. Michaud presents the picture of a very tightly coordinated venture between the state and capital in his cases from Ladakh and Thailand. He is thus understandably pessimistic regarding the possibilities for villagers to overcome their objectification at the hands of this newly encountered political economy. In China, however, there remains a considerable amount of tension between the state and capital. The state project of socialist modernity has been a much more significant force in rural people's lives, while capital remains an alluring, though distant, alternative. But appealing to the interests of capital can often be a way of counteracting the more familiar objectifications of the state. Villagers in Guizhou thus attempt in many ways to play these two dominant forces off each other in trying to determine the outcome of tourism's colonization for themselves. That they do so rhetorically requires us, first, to examine the dominant narratives accompanying the political economy of touristic modernity in Guizhou. These narratives articulate what I've termed a "false modern triumphant" in Guizhou, a discourse of modernity based on the misplaced search for authenticity, and derived from the standardizing abstractions introduced by the tourism industry and its state sponsors.

In this chapter, then, we examine both the political-economic mechanisms of tourism development in Guizhou, and the major voices articulating its accompanying narratives of modernity. These voices include those of agents within the tourism industry itself, and the socio-cultural significance they invest in tourism as a modernizing force in the countryside, those of local state officials, who in rural southeast Guizhou are mostly elite minority cadres, and those of tourists themselves, who display a considerable diversity of voices according to their origin. These agents collectively serve to administer the channels of representation through which dominant cultural ideas are produced and conveyed. While detailing the modernizing fragmentations introduced by tourism into rural Guizhou, the chapter argues that the most significant aspect of these disruptions is the representation of *minzu* culture that is meant to repair the damage of modernity. This production, a triumph of misplaced authenticity, seeks to establish that "calming certainty" already encountered in Shenzhen's theme parks. It is a *minzu* culture that is timeless, harmless, and dependable for the needs of the nation-state and capital.

REPRESENTING *MINZU* CULTURE

Early in 1994, *China Daily* (8 January 1994) ran a story on a new theme park being built on the northern bank of East Lake in the city of Wuhan. The park's objective was to recreate the culture of the ancient Chu kingdom, which had been centered around Dongting Lake in the fertile basin of present-day Hunan and Hubei before the Qin unification over 2,000 years ago. Discussing the innovative ideas of the park's architects, the article made a point of distinguishing the Chu gardens in the park from the "more sophisticated" classical gardens of Suzhou, which, in the words of one of the architects, "have too many artificial touches such as rockeries and man-made ponds." Instead, the Chu park would have a more "natural" feel to it. Of course, he admitted, very little was actually known of Chu culture, so they had to improvise somewhat, but felt they had recreated the spirit of the people, their belief in mystical Daoism, their advances in astronomy, their closeness to the natural world, and their entrepreneurial spirit. Entrepreneurial spirit? The Chu people, apparently, were also great consumers and producers of commodities, for at the center of the park was the "Chu Market," full of restaurants, tea houses, wine shops and many souvenir stands bursting with "offerings of Chu flavor." Conveniently, the Chu people had bequeathed to their descendants all the necessary ingredients to build a distinctly Chinese national modernity, one in which age-old tradition and commodification go hand in hand.

The Chu park is only one example among hundreds of touristic landscapes of spectacular consumption – China's "theme park fever" – initiated by the success of Splendid China in Shenzhen. While these spectacle environments help construct a nation-building museum of carefully imaged folklore, they are also fantastic shrines to the consuming urges of post-ideological China. As such, they offer ready-made environments in which one can play at being modern and being Chinese at the same time. But another process is at work here as well. The Chu park is not simply a landscape conveying the "calming certainty" for a Chinese nation; more important, it offers a distinctly localist claim of marketable uniqueness, for Chu is less a Chinese tradition than one based more specifically in the Middle Changjiang region of Hubei and Hunan. Regional comparative advantage has become the ideal model that Chinese localities seek to emulate in their desire to attract investment as the Maoist pattern of centralized economic planning recedes. With the beginning of the 1990s, then, local governments from the province down to the village sought to define and promote their "local flavor" as a means of attracting capital accumulation. More than anything else, this is what has been driving the "theme park fever" in China. The Chu park illustrates most of the important components of this trend: Hubei's version of a distinct local folk tradition setting it apart from the rest of China, a reconstruction of a traditional *minzu* culture which articulates well with the demands of commercial exchange and market integration, and a (multi)national ideology inherent in Chu's contributions (religion, science, technology) to China. In Guizhou, the projects of manufacturing traditional *minzu* culture for the purposes of tourism development and national integration display these components as well. *Minzu* culture is constructed in order to establish Guizhou's local distinctiveness, to encourage commercialism, and to patriotically boast of the links between Guizhou's local folk traditions and the assertive, confident nationalism of modern China.

Such a neat package of outcomes, however, is seldom the only result of the state's enlisting of market forces and its spurring of the people's consumer desires. The state's relationship to capital in China remains suspicious. It therefore supports a sustained moralistic narrative dictating proper behavior in the brash new world of the market (seen, for example, in its sustained campaign of "socialist spiritual civilization"). The state's attempts to maintain its regulatory legitimacy over the social body is also found in its support of cultural development, or *wenhua fazhan*, among "backwards" populations. In Guizhou, then, the desire for a touristic modernity of commodified local tradition is articulated through the discourse of cultural development, as not simply a developmental necessity, but as a moral imperative as well. Local cadres in minority areas have been the chief narrators of this "civilizing mission."

The discourse of cultural development among minority elites

Wenhua fazhan derives from a concept of culture which implies change and improvement toward more civilized, elite forms. This idea of change is inherent in *wenhua*. *Wen* may be translated as "writing" or "language," and as an adjective it means "refined," "civil," or "gentle"; *hua* means to change, melt, or dissolve. Together, they most directly translate as "education" or "civilization," but *wenhua* is also misleadingly translated as "culture." The inherent components of *wenhua* should make it clear that the term is not an equivalent to the contemporary Western anthropological sense of culture as a "way of life," a relativistic concept which is quite the opposite of *wenhua*'s idea of transformation toward a more refined way of life. When *fazhan* ("development") is added, the result is a modernized manifestation of the centuries-old "civilizing project" of imperial China (see Harrell 1995).

As a post-Mao modernization ideology, *wenhua fazhan* implies the attainment of literacy (in standard Chinese), an education in science and technology, understanding of modern commerce, expertise in enterprise management, and even an entrepreneurial spirit. But it also implies the enlisting of selected and invented cultural traditions to be paraded both as markers of progress and as local delegates to the national assembly of symbolic cultural diversity. *Wenhua fazhan* has thus come to celebrate the creative blending of traditional arts and crafts, cuisines, and performances with modern commercialism, that is, the commodification of an invented tradition. Ideally, cultural development enables a sense of local cultural autonomy and preservation, even as economic and social integration proceeds toward the state's desired goals of nation-building.

In Guizhou, *wenhua fazhan* is most commonly used to describe positive developments in minority regions. Any activity which celebrates cultural traditions and "local color" (*difang tese*) while at the same time promoting commercial economic development and further integration into broader markets, is upheld as an example of *wenhua fazhan*. Newspapers are full of such examples. During the 1993 azalea blossom and Huangguoshu famous liquor festivals, *Guizhou Ribao* ran several such stories. One covered the opening of scenic Sajin gorge by Fuquan county, which had invested over RMB 870,000 in developing the site. The new tourist site opened with a three-day "Sajin *Minzu* Song and Dance Festival," coinciding with the Huangguoshu famous liquor festival; according to county officials, the festival would "highlight how modern civilization and traditional customs complement each other in cultural development." A Huangping county crafts factory was also praised in *Guizhou Ribao* (9 August 1993) for making toys to be sold all over China which "combined traditional skills with modern ideas." It was with such a combination, the journalist commented, that minority groups would finally "go to the world."

One particularly striking example of *wenhua fazhan* was Guizhou's first *Minzu* Clothing Fashion Show, held in Anshun on 17 August 1996. A report on the fashion show in Guiyang's *Guizhou Dushi Wanbao* (27 October 1996) proclaimed that changing *minzu* fashions were an indication of progress and modernization among minority groups throughout Guizhou. "The thick and heavy (*houzhong*) clothes of yesterday have become the simple and beautiful clothes of today," the reporter wrote. Clothing was now machine-produced instead of home-spun, and real silk was now used for embroidery. New, bright and vivid color combinations were being adopted. "Under the precondition of preserving the traditional features of their clothing, our province's *minzu* groups have boldly reformed (*gaige*) their clothing styles." Echoing the popular conception of traditional *minzu* culture as a subsis-tence-oriented barrier to modernization until broken free by the prosperity-inducing winds of state reform policies and the commercialism they're meant to inspire, the article pointed out that young people previously had no choice but to wear the old clothes and ornaments passed down from generation to generation. "Now, girls in Miao and Dong villages wear head-dresses that reflect the latest fashions, paying as much as four thousand *yuan* each. Minority *minzu* clothing is blossoming into a hundred flowers with splendid prospects." Going to the modern world of fashion was bringing about the change in attitude necessary for solving the problem of modernity in Guizhou.

As we saw in the previous chapter, "going to the world," became a rallying cry throughout Guizhou in the 1990s. It was heard particularly clearly, though, among scholars and officials promoting the development of Guizhou's minority regions. What is significant about *wenhua fazhan* is not simply that it represents national integration, but that it is celebrated by locals as the means by which they can become modern while retaining the traditions and customs that mark them as distinctive and around which they seek to maintain a sense of *minzu* identity. As Picard (1993) noted of local officials in Bali, state-sponsored integration is enthusiastically embraced by Guizhou's minority elites if it leaves open a space for local cultural autonomy. As one writer claimed, "the question of turning traditional culture into a cultural commodity, and marketing that commodity domestically and internationally, is not simply one of economics, but of the *value* of a particular *minzu* group" (Lei 1992: 33, my emphasis). Ethnic cultural commodification, he continued, is a bridge between *minzu* groups and modernity; the goal is not just to sell *minzu* culture, but to *develop and modernize* it.

In November 1990, the Guizhou *Minzu* Cultural Studies Association held its annual meetings in Kaili, and the theme for the conference was "*Guizhou minzu wenhua zouxiang shijie*" ("aligning Guizhou's *minzu* cultures going to the world"). Papers were delivered on the subjects of preserving traditional *minzu* culture and on how to articulate *minzu* traditions with the needs of modernization (collected in *Guizhou Sheng Minzu Wenhua Xuehui* 1991).[1] A paper by Shi Chaojiang was illustrative of the general tone of the conference. Titled "*Miaozu chuantong wenhua yu shehuizhuyi xiandaihua*" ("Traditional Miao culture and socialist modernization"), the paper first described the various features of traditional Miao culture which were positive attributes for a modernizing society. Because of their history of migration and perseverance in the face of adversity and hostility, the Miao had a "pioneer spirit" (*zhimin jingshen*) of mutual aid and assistance. They were familiar with being cast out into the wilderness and being forced to make it productive. This was precisely the spirit, Shi exclaimed, needed to build socialist modernization. The Miao were also very democratic, and valued social equality. They had a spirit of industriousness and hard work, and they believed, like Deng Xiaoping, in "seeking truth from facts." Yet the Miao also exhibited some conflicts with the spirit of modernity. While their high moral and ethical standards were to be praised, their morality of respect for the natural environment conflicted with modernization's need for exploitation of natural resources. The Miao had for too long been isolated subsistence farmers and harbored a "*xiaonong jingji sixiang*" ("small farming mentality"). Their deep-rooted religious beliefs prevented the popularization of scientific knowledge, and their insistence on marrying locally kept the population from being invigorated by outsiders. Shi concluded that these conflicts with modernity needed to be "put in order" (*qingli*) and discarded. The former aspects of Miao culture that articulated positively with modernization should be supported and promoted.

Added to this message of selective cultural engineering, which was repeated in most of the papers, were accounts of how Guizhou's *minzu* traditions formed the very touchstone of China's socialist modernization. In the essay which introduced the published papers from the conference, it was argued that *minzu* culture was the basis for China's industrialization and modernization, and that it provided China with distinctiveness in the face of "Westernization" and prevented assimilation as China entered the global economy. In fact, *minzu* culture was already more modernized than most people thought. *Minzu* culture in Guizhou, the essay enthusiastically declared, already reflected the world's twenty-first-century desires. "People in the twenty-first century will thirst for the kind of cultural traditions we have in Guizhou." To quench this thirst, Guizhou hospitably offered not only bowl upon bowl of rice wine proffered by jovial villagers, but beautiful batiks and embroidery patterns, reed pipe *lusheng* dancing, the "oriental disco" (*dongfang disikou*) of Fanpai village's famous song and dance troupe, the "oriental choir" of Dong village girls, literature, legends, and more. In this, the papers offered a localist take on what had become an important intellectual trend in China's "culture fever" (*wenhua re*) of the late 1980s. The Kaili conference had reworked a broader culturalist vision – initiated by scholars at the Academy of Chinese Culture under Tang Yijie – that had originally sought to link the reconstruction of (autonomous, non-Western) modern Chinese culture with a reinvented Confucian tradition, one that was, ironically, amenable to capitalism (Zhang 1997: 42–4). In Qiandongnan, however, this idea was being reinterpreted so that minority culture, rather than Confucianism, was regarded as the tradition needed for an alternative Chinese modernity. Like the culturalists, however, the objective was not simply cultural, but economic: the amenability of such a tradition to the needs of commercially generated modernization.

This approach to *wenhua fazhan* not only calls for the selective breeding of symbolic cultural diversity as the captive antidote to modernity's cravings, but enables local leaders to confront, actively, the sense of loss that over four decades of socialist modernization has engendered. The paper delivered by Wu Dehai, an active Miao scholar and former governor of Qiandongnan, openly discussed his discomfort with the "decline" (*shuaitui*) of traditional *minzu* culture in the face of modernization. Wu lamented that traditional festivals and *lusheng* meetings had declined in popularity since the 1950s; there was less diversity in the songs and dances performed. Many instruments which used to be around were no longer played. Fewer and fewer people knew the old myths and legends, new buildings used less traditional architecture, and traditional *minzu* medicine was now rarely practiced.

As a Marxist, he had to admit that this was something of an historical inevitability, and the positive result of progressing to a more advanced stage of history. But he also believed in Marx's claim that we are the makers of our own history, albeit within conditions not of our own choosing. This, he claimed, was why going to the world was so important. The world was increasingly interested in preserving cultural traditions, and Guizhou's *minzu* groups simply needed to link their futures to this larger trend by creating more tourist sites, museums, "cultural departments," and stronger laws preserving people's traditional customs.

The "going to the world" inherent in the *wenhua fazhan* of Guizhou's *minzu* cultures illustrates the ideal patterns of national (indeed, global) integration promoted by the Chinese state. In Guizhou, tourism is envisioned as one of the chief agents of *wenhua fazhan* and (inter)national integration. Tourism has made a significant contribution to the development and integration of certain regions of rural Guizhou. Many villages within or near popular tourist sites have, for example, experienced significant shifts in the means of production and the local division of labor. Economic activities in these villages are increasingly tied to a much broader scale of markets and politics. In many of these cases, villagers have had little say in these changes and have felt clearly alienated by them. Their stories will be explored in greater detail later in the chapter. First, however, we must confront the broader implications of touristic *wenhua fazhan* in Guizhou.

Manufacturing *minzu* culture

Most significant in tourism's spurring of Guizhou's cultural development, modernization, and national integration has been the commodification of *minzu* culture. Promoted as both investment enticement and outright commodity, *minzu* culture is ubiquitous not only in Guizhou's tourism activities, but in nearly all aspects of rural and urban economic development. *Minzu* culture is produced in trade fairs, in festivals promoted for tourism and trade, in tourist villages and theme parks, in performances, on television, in magazines, and in the rationalization of ethnic crafts production. In each of these processes, *minzu* culture becomes increasingly linked to political and economic processes operating on much broader scales. Representations of exotic culture and charming customs have become the heart of marketing Guizhou tourism, and indeed of marketing Guizhou itself as an attractive site for external investment. *Minzu* culture is not only reproduced according to the demands of rationalized commodity production, but is in fact invented and manufactured in order to facilitate the local specializations necessary for economic integration and tourism development, as well as contribute to the cultural construction of an alternative modern China. Guo Laixi, one of China's leading scholars on tourism development, argues that tourism affects three aspects of *minzu* culture; it encourages the revival and continuation of customs and traditions, it "selects" particular customs and traditions appropriate for development, and it "creates new culture" (*chuangzao xin wenhua*) (Guo 1993). According to Guo, the opportunities provided by tourism for groups to invent new culture contribute to their cultural development. Tourism, he believes, is an integral part of China's modernization in that it actively helps people transform their cultures. Yet cultural development also means "aligning" *minzu* culture with the broader world, and the consequences are not always positive. The increased integration inherent in ethnic cultural standardization and commodification brings with it new relations of dependence and vulnerability for Guizhou's cultural producers. It is in this arena, perhaps, that the continuation of Guizhou's internal colonialism is most apparent. Increased integration in the reform era has not only made Guizhou vulnerable to a continuing political-economy of structural unevenness, as argued in the previous chapter, but also conspires to articulate core and peripheral modes economic production and cultural reproduction in a way which precludes an autonomous indigenous modernity in the periphery.

The national project of manufacturing traditional, yet commercialized, *minzu* culture tends to construct folk culture primarily as a performance. For example, the most common feature of Guizhou's ethnic village tourism is the song and dance performance. These performances provide an accessible medium for tourists to recognize *minzu* culture, and have an experience that meets their expectations of village life and customs. Song and dance performances in villages are thus largely modeled on the media extravaganzas which are found on Chinese television featuring professional *minzu* performance troupes. An example of one of these was held in Guiyang in February 1994. Featuring over 200 performers, it was a very professional, nationally televised show with troupes from China's *gaoyuan* (plateau) provinces of Tibet, Qinghai, Yunnan, and Guizhou. The masters of ceremony were from television stations in these provinces and from Beijing, and they presented a theme emphasizing a "spring wind" blowing the "warmth and spirit of the plateau" down to China's "cold east." Underlying this theme of *minzu* vitality invigorating the national spirit of China proper was an implicit message of *wenhua fazhan*. Traditional minority numbers were spaced by contemporary Han pop songs, and even the minority songs and dances were infused with contemporary styles, music, and effects. Even while the announcers made efforts to "do the *minzu* thing" by jokingly trying their hand at some of the songs and dances, or trying on traditional clothing, the performances themselves presented the opposite theme of cultural development toward commercialized modernity. Several numbers were introduced with the comment that this is what results when we combine "traditional spirit" with "modern culture." Although the Han announcer from Beijing was teased throughout the show for knowing so little about the customs of the plateau, the performances themselves left little doubt about who the teachers were supposed to be.

A similar construction of *minzu* culture as performance can be found at all official *minzu* celebrations, such as the Guizhou Provincial Dong Association's celebration of Dong New Year in 1993. This was an invitation-only performance and banquet at Guizhou's most exclusive country resort outside of Guiyang, the same place where China's top leaders stay when visiting the province. Present were the provincial vice-governor, the chair of the provincial people's congress, and the presidents of Guiyang's three major universities. The activities began with a "road-block wine" (*lanlu jiu*) cere-mony, in which everyone lined up to receive a cup of wine from costumed and singing women, followed by a circular dance in which everyone joined hands and marched in a great circle, a dance which has come to symbolize not so much any particular *minzu* group (since all groups seem to perform it) but the national unity of all groups under the paternal leadership of the state. After the dance, everyone filed into an auditorium to hear speeches extolling a new era of modernization and *wenhua fazhan* for the Dong. The 90-year-old head of the Dong Association, for his part, stressed paying attention to developing "socialism with Chinese characteristics" and reading the collected works of Deng Xiaoping. Speeches were followed by a staged song and dance performance and a banquet featuring, curiously, not Dong but Han food. We were also invited to view an exhibit of paintings by Dong artists. These were classical-style (as opposed to peasant-folk style) land-scape paintings featuring drum towers and covered "wind and rain" bridges tucked away amid seas of gnarled karst pillars. One, however, was inspir-ingly titled "Modernization comes to the Dong lands" and featured – in addition to these traditional architectures tucked among the mountains – roads with buses, trains passing through tunnels and over bridges, high-tension power lines passing overhead, and black billows of smoke pouring out of factory stacks.

Throughout this affair, interest in Dong culture was expressed in two dominant ways. One involved discussions, in the speeches, of modernization and *wenhua fazhan*. This interest in progress and development for the Dong was complemented by an official nod to tradition in the form of drinking ceremonies, circle dances, and staged performances. These selected versions of *minzu* tradition were implicitly presented as those aspects of Dong culture which articulated positively with modernity. Like tradition itself, they were the contemporary inventions of Dong culture needed to make sense of and repair modernity.

Beyond these official celebrations and televised performances, though, traditional folk culture was being constructed by Guizhou's local tourism industry as a resource for attracting tourists and investments, and for fostering *wenhua fazhan* and *minzu* unity. Yet, in creating a commercialized national folk tradition for people to purchase, own, and feel attached to, these constructions achieve little more than predictable and standardized exoticism, despite their efforts to enhance local distinctiveness and territorial competitiveness.

The year 1994 was proclaimed China's *Wenwu Guji Lüyounian* ("Historic

Cultural Relics Tourism Year") by the NTA, and throughout China the NTA and local tourism promoters were busy creating new folk cultures to sell to tourists. One of the more ubiquitous of these was "Buddhist culture." The NTA sponsored a "Sichuan Buddha Festival" at Leshan, the site of the giant stone Buddha overlooking the Minjiang River. In Xinchang, the site of Zhejiang's "Grand Buddha Temple," a "China Buddha City" was built with investments of over RMB 10 million. It would include miniaturized versions of the Leshan Buddha, the Longmen and Yungang caves (*China Daily* 2 January 1994). In Guizhou, officials at the Longgong Tourism Administration (LTA) decided to create a Buddhist cultural theme out of a newly opened cave. "Foreigners will really like this," I was told by an LTA officer, "They really like Buddhist culture." Like thousands of others throughout China, Longgong's candidate was known as the "Guanyin Cave," and featured the remains of bodhisattvas sculpted into its walls. These would be restored and visitors to the cave would be received by attendants dressed like Buddhist monks, "just as if they were going to a *real* Buddhist cave."

Wenwu Guji Lüyounian also had the effect of stimulating an explicit focus on Guizhou's colonial past by tourism authorities in Anshun. The general tourism development plan put forth by Anshun (Anshun Tourism Bureau 1993) advocated the construction of *tunbao wenhua* as a local tourist resource. "*Tunbao* culture" refers to the historical *tun tian* garrison culture created by the mixing of soldier-settlers sent to Guizhou, particularly after the province's founding in 1413, with the local people who predated them in the Anshun region. While there is nothing left of these ancient walled garrisons themselves, Anshun's authorities have stumbled on a local cultural practice ideally suited for preservation and marketing as a tourist resource: *dixi*, or "ground opera." Local scholars believe that *dixi*, a type of folk opera performed in over 300 villages throughout western Guizhou, is a remnant of operas brought by Ming soldier-settlers and adapted to local performance customs of the time. Many *dixi* performances, for example, tell stories of famous Ming generals, emperors, and warriors; all emphasize a militarized lifestyle thought to be similar to that lived by soldier-settlers.

Dixi's recognition by local authorities as a valuable cultural resource actually did not come until 1984, when a French scholar was invited by the Chinese government to investigate ancient opera forms. He ended up seeing a *dixi* performance at the village of Caiguan, near Anshun, which resulted in Caiguan's *dixi* troupe being invited to perform at the *Festival D'Automne à Paris* in 1986. The festival that year was featuring ancient Chinese performance art, including, in addition to Caiguan's *dixi*, two kinds of classical opera, teahouse performances in the Chengdu tradition, puppet shows, traditional instrument ensembles, and choral performances (including a Dong group from Qiandongnan). In an apparent fit of rapture, the festival director pronounced *dixi* a "living fossil of Chinese opera," and expressed his hope that this ancient style of performance would be preserved for the future. In Guizhou, the response to his proclamations was very enthusiastic. Caiguan village soon became known as the *Caiguan dixi chenlieguan* ("Caiguan ground opera museum"), and began receiving state funding to maintain the troupe, receive tourists, and build a old-style fort tower overlooking the performance square.

Caiguan's popularity encouraged Anshun's tourism authorities to produce a development plan based on *tunbao* culture. Development plans included emphasizing Anshun's ethnic tourist village of Loujiazhuang as a site of "Miao defense fortification culture." More ambitious was the planned transformation of nearby Panmeng village into the "Guizhou Ancient Han (*Tunbao*) Tourist Village." Ancient-looking structures would be built, water and electricity would be provided to the village, and the environment would be "beautified." A typical *tunbao* person's house would be built, along with a *tunbao wenhua* museum, a folk-clothing photo studio, and a performance arena. Performances would include folk lantern shows, wedding ceremonies, songs and dances, and storytelling. This development would be followed (as long as investment capital could be found) by a "*Tunbao* Culture Villages" theme park situated on a nearby mountainside and consisting of three parts: an ancient Miao village at the foot of the mountain, a walled Han village at the middle of the mountain, and a Buddhist temple on the summit (featuring "Buddhist temple cultural activities"). Tourists would pay for one ticket that would entitle them to wander about the mountain and experience the "mixing of Guizhou's *minzu* folk traditions."

Yet if the popularization and standardization of *dixi* is any indication, Anshun's development plan is simply a formula for a tourist culture which, based solely on the replication and performance of a few selected symbols and markers of *minzu* exoticism, bears little distinction from folk cultures being promoted and standardized throughout China. By 1994 Caiguan's tourist income was actually declining. Locals complained that this was because the *dixi* masks sold to tourists as souvenirs were being mass produced and sold in Guiyang, Shenzhen, and even Taipei. The village could no longer compete in marketing its own masks. In addition, Caiguan had lost tourists to newly opened ethnic villages closer to Guiyang. Travel agencies, it seems, were making no distinctions between Caiguan as a *dixi* village and other villages offering *minzu* songs and dances in settings more exotic than Caiguan's. In Anshun's promotional literature, *dixi* is referred to in the following way: "The ground play, often referred to as a 'fossil drama,' is an ancient folk play popular among the Bouyeis, the Gelos, and the Miaos." While it is true that all groups in the area perform *dixi* in the same fashion as a result of centuries of cultural borrowing, there is no mention that the style has its roots in *Han* tradition, and that Caiguan, its "most characteristic" representative, is in fact a Han village. In an effort to make it commercially marketable, *dixi* is glossed with minority exoticism. *Dixi* is said to be "unsophisticated and unconstrained," and it is perhaps easier to say this about long-dead cultures (like Chu) and still-living minorities than about the Han themselves, the self-professed modern vanguard of China.

Anshun's tourist authorities also actively promote the construction of a local "batik culture." Batik has become canonized as a local *tese* by Anshun's annual batik festival, which features a large, state-sponsored commodities fair for attracting external investment. However, Guizhou's most important example of manufacturing a *minzu* culture according to the demands of commercial exchange and investment is not "batik culture," but "liquor culture" (*jiu wenhua*). This effort has been centered on Zunyi, Guizhou's second largest city, where a "liquor culture museum" has been built to document the various drinking traditions of Guizhou's different *minzu* groups. The region around Zunyi is one of China's premier liquor-producing regions, with the most famous being Maotai, which earned notoriety as the liquor used when Mao Zedong and Richard Nixon toasted each other in 1972. It is difficult to overemphasize the importance of "liquor culture" in Guizhou's promotion efforts. All tourist villages, performances, and official festivities and celebrations feature ritualized drinking as a core component of local *minzu* folk tradition. Liquor is also the most important commodity at Guizhou's various trade fairs. At the 1993 Huangguoshu Scenery and Famous Liquor Festival, 25 per cent of the total reported sales (RMB 450 million) were in liquor. Guizhou's largest distillery, Xijiu, made sales of over RMB 150 million during the festival. In 1993, Guizhou was also able to attract RMB 80 million in external investment for a "China International Liquor Exhibition Center" in Guiyang, which would, of course, feature "*minzu* architecture" in its design. Trade fairs, thus, play a major role in creating these market-ready *minzu* cultures based on batik and liquor, as well as other craft forms, such as embroidery, and bamboo instruments or masks.

Traditional festivals also serve as convenient settings for an injection of "commercial consciousness" through the manufacture of *minzu* folk culture. Two of the most well-known of these festivals – *Zimeifan* ("Sister's Rice Festival") and *Longchuanjie* ("Dragon Boat Festival") – are held in the town of Shidong, on the Qingshui River in Qiandongnan's Taijiang county. Both are multi-day festivals that have been heavily promoted by the local and provincial tourism bureaus; they attract numerous international and domestic tour groups along with the thousands of local villagers who converge on the town for the festival period. *Zimeifan* celebrates the ritualized nature of Miao courtship, and features much public dancing by local women dressed in their festival ornaments. The heart of the festival is supposed to be found in girls offering balls of rice containing items that symbolize their feelings toward the boys to whom they are given. But while few tourists have the opportunity to actually witness these private exchanges (although performances are sometimes arranged), they have plenty of opportunity to buy ethnic commodities. More than anything, *Zimeifan* is a three-day shopping spree for tourists and a big commercial event for entrepreneurs who arrive from throughout Qiandongnan to sell antique textiles and ornaments. During the festival's three days in 1994, the Shidong Hotel's parking lot was covered by the goods of as many as 40 different merchants, all women, who travel the countryside collecting old textiles and crafts from villagers eager to earn some easy cash by selling their old useless heirlooms.

Zimeifan was helping to generate a number of changes important for the construction of commercialized and integrated *minzu* culture. The arrival of hundreds of tourists rivaled the size of the local audience and helped precipitate the development of a clear-cut distinction between public performances where tourist's cameras were tolerated, and rituals that local families tried to keep private. This distinction made it easy to identify those features of local *minzu* tradition that could be enlisted in the forces of *wenhua fazhan*: the public dance performances and the commodification of ethnic crafts gathered from throughout the region. At the same time, the festival's popularity served to help construct an image of the "authentic" Miao traditions upon which festival performances were based. For tourists participating in *Zimeifan*, these traditions were said to have actually died out in Shidong itself, which was too "Hanified" (*Hanhuale*) and "assimilated" (*tonghuale*) to Chinese ways. If one wanted to see the "real" version of *Zimeifan* he or she had to hike high into the hills surrounding Shidong. This was a crucial recognition on the part of the tourists, for it indicated that the promotion and commercialization of Shidong's *Zimeifan* was engendering the invention of tradition that necessarily accompanies modernity.[2] Shidong's *minzu* traditions, it seems, had not only been modernized, but served to construct an unseen reservoir of misplaced authenticity "up in the mountains," which would always provide the imagined benchmark for measuring progress and *wenhua fazhan*. While it was unclear the extent to which townspeople themselves shared this reaction, Chapter 5 provides evidence of this happening in other tourist sites around Qiandongnan.

The other major festival promoted in Shidong is *Longchuanjie*, and, according to Schein (1989), it displays many of the same trends in commodification as *Zimeifan*. Indeed, Taijiang county has officially dubbed it as a festival for "opening *minzu* regions" (*kaifa minzu diqu jieri*), and sponsors a conference, in conjunction with the festival, introducing the county's economic development program and the various projects that are in need of external investment. But *Longchuanjie* is significant for other reasons as well. *Longchuanjie* is Shidong's version of *Duanwujie*, the marking of the fifth day of the fifth lunar month celebrated throughout southern China. *Duanwujie* commemorates the legend of Qu Yuan's drowning, but it seems that local people, especially on China's frontiers, have for centuries come up with their own reasons for holding the festival, which probably existed, according to Hawkes (1985), long before it was appropriated by Confucianists to canonize the memory of Qu Yuan. Thus, *Longchuanjie* has been promoted not simply as a conduit for modernization and development, but, because it provides a clear link between *minzu* tradition in Qiandongnan and dominant Chinese traditions downstream, as an explicit symbol of nation building and modern cultural integration. One of the three functioning exhibition halls in Qiandongnan's *minzu* museum, in Kaili, is devoted to the region's "dragon boat tradition." As this exhibit makes clear, Shidong's Dragon Boat Festival is promoted because it conveniently features a dominant Chinese folk tradition that has been borrowed by the local Miao and made into an exotic and spiritual ritual instead of a boat race. Dragon boat races, in fact, have been a tradition in most of the towns along the main rivers of Qiandongnan, whether Miao, Dong, or Han. They reflect the important influence that river-born trade had on the culture of this hinterland region. While its population is now Miao, Shidong itself has the architecture of a nineteenth-century Han river town, with walled compounds, ancestral temples, and guild halls. Promoting *Longchuanjie* helps Qiandongnan officials emphasize a historical link which becomes the metaphor for current campaigns of modernization and *wenhua fazhan*.

Territorial competition was also on the leaders' minds when they selected the difficult-to-reach Shidong over more accessible dragon boat festivals celebrated in Zhenyuan and Shibing. As dragon boat festivals became increasingly popular throughout southern China during the "culture fever" of the 1980s, Qiandongnan officials needed something to distinguish theirs from all the others being held downriver. The exoticism of Shidong's festival provided the answer. Then, as Shidong's festival became popular there was a rapid revival of dragon boat races throughout the river towns of Qiandongnan. In 1994 alone, four new festivals were initiated, all featuring boat races, parades, and local commodities exhibits. In the town of Rongjiang, the new festival was praised by county leaders for "stimulating the economy through culture and sport" (*Qiandongnan Bao* 14 June 1994). In Chongan the event was promoted by the local elders' association with the goal of stimulating local tourism development.

A final example of manufacturing *minzu* culture can be found in the Guizhou Tourism Bureau's plans for recognizing China's *Minzu Fengqing Lüyounian* ("Ethnic Tourism Year") in 1995. Although Guizhou was not selected as one of the main sites hosting NTA-sponsored activities, as it was in 1993, the GTB planned to promote Guiyang's *Siyueba* festival (the "8th day of the 4th lunar month") as Guizhou's prime ethnic festival. *Siyueba* would become Guizhou's version of Mardis Gras and Oktoberfest. As one GTB official commented,

> *Siyueba* will become Guiyang's own 'carnival' (*kuanghuanjie*). By promoting it we will enable foreigners to better understand and relate to Guizhou's *minzu* festival culture. It's like when we decided to promote the Fanpai drum dance as a "Miao disco"; that was something foreigners could relate to. There are hundreds of festivals in Guizhou

each year, but none are famous because we have not put enough effort into promoting just one.

(Sun 1994)

Siyueba was selected because it is the only minority festival celebrated in Guiyang itself, and because it is actually celebrated by many different Miao groups. Turning it into a commercialized carnival reflected the GTB's belief that tourism can help, as Guo Laixi put it, "create a new culture" which is more developed and modernized while at the same time based on quaint *minzu* traditions.

Minzu culture as commodity

Tourism in Guizhou has encouraged not only the manufacturing of "traditional" *minzu* culture, but the rapid growth of commercial ethnic crafts production as well. The entrepreneurial energy seen at large festivals such as Shidong's *Zimeifan* has been expanding, especially in Qiandongnan, into one of the most important sectors of local rural industry. Yet the process of commercializing and standardizing ethnic crafts production is a project full of paradox and contradiction. For the commodification of ethnic crafts involves not simply their standardized production, but their entry into a new "regime of value" (Appadurai 1986: 15) in which consumption is driven in part by the idea that the tourist purchases not just a souvenir, but a representation of the true folk themselves. Marketing folk crafts must include the construction of an ideal type underlying the concept of "village life" being sold. This is the so-called "subsistence" mode of production thought to mark the authentic cultural economy of the pre-modern folk. While only a general term, usually equated with pre-industrial and pre-capitalist rural production relations, "subsistence" (or its Chinese derivative, "small farmer mentality") remains, as demonstrated in the previous chapter, commonly used in popular, official, and even some scholarly characterizations of the more "backward" regions of China's countryside. Subsistence and semi-subsistence producers are thought to prevent modernization as they persist in their ways of self-sufficiency and *ad hoc* participation in local markets. More important, however, is the charge that such peasants are not sufficiently entrepreneurial, and therefore fail to create conditions in which capital can accumulate. Production relations of subsistence are not oriented toward profit – that is, extracting surplus labor value. Rather, as Chayanov's (1966) work argued, peasants simply try to maximize gross production to meet the demands of population increase or to accommodate any income-earning opportunities which present themselves.

For the Chinese state, such peasant stubbornness is a problem. For those marketing ethnic crafts, however, it is the fragile artifact of a way of life long lost in the industrialized regions of the world. Labor-intensive crafts production – such as ornate batik and embroidery – is felt to only be possible in a non-commercial subsistence-oriented production environment. Changing the subsistence environment of the village would thus destroy the uniqueness (and marketability) of the crafts. While Guizhou's crafts producers are in fact very much tied up in broader structures of commercial exchange, sustained capital accumulation in crafts production necessitates maintaining the myth of a particular "way of life," that is, a production environment dominated by kinship relations, where the household is the production unit, and the production process itself is not regulated by a disciplined regimen of time. "Cultural preservation," in fact, becomes an avenue of capital accumulation, and can result not in the state's ideal of cultural development for "backward" regions, but in their continued subordination and dependence on unequal exchange relations, that is, their continued colonization.

Two dominant ideologies can thus be identified regarding the production and commodification of *minzu* culture in China. On the one hand, preserving "traditional *minzu* culture" has become important for China's projects of nationalism and modernization, since "tradition" forms both the ideological glue to build an imagined national community and the means by which local *minzu* groups can participate in national integration without feeling like they're losing their local cultures. On the other hand, pursuing economic and cultural development in order to combat rural poverty, eradicate subsistence and "small-farmer" mentalities, and otherwise transform the nature of rural production systems, has meant that "*minzu* traditions" are only preserved if they can accommodate commercial production and exchange. Combined, these ideologies have generated an environment in rural Guizhou in which the preservation of authentic *minzu* culture legitimizes a division of labor in which rural labor remains subordinated to urban capital. *Minzu* traditions of producing elaborate crafts, particularly batik and embroidery, are valued for their commercial potential in spurring the development of rural industry and increasing household incomes, as well as for their "museum value," that is, as artifacts of national folk tradition worthy of preservation. The ideology of preservation, in this case, colludes with capital to "fossilize" rural modes of crafts production as a national cultural resource, and as a reservoir of skilled yet cheap exploitable labor.[3]

In rural Guizhou, particularly Qiandongnan, this process can be seen in several ways. The *minzu* groups of Qiandongnan, particularly the Miao, have become well known for the embroidered textiles they produce. Embroidery was a skill acquired by girls at a very early age, and was used to make elaborate clothing to wear at festivals and other important social occasions. Concern among local minority officials that with modernization these skills would die out encouraged the promotion of economic schemes which would convince rural households that traditional skills could in fact be exploited to increase their incomes. This would enable modernization without losing an important resource of *minzu* culture and identity. In Taijiang county, for example, the local minority affairs commission (*minwei*) became involved in attracting a number of coastal trading companies to set up labor-intensive, export-oriented textile factories. By 1994 three of these were operating in Taijiang, along with several more in at least six other county towns throughout Qiandongnan. One of the Taijiang factories was set up by a Jiangsu company to produce tie-dyed silk cloth to be exported to Japan. It employed about 100 women, recruited from the countryside, who sat all day tying up thousands of tiny dot patterns on silk. They were paid RMB 6 for every 10,000 tied dots, and although the manager said they could typically tie 5,000 dots per day, workers on the shop floor indicated that the most anyone earned was between RMB 30 and 40 per month. By comparison, average monthly income in 1992 for wage earners in Taijiang was RMB 165 (GTN 1993). Another Taijiang factory employed a similar number of rural women earning similar wages making embroidered cloth for export to Southeast Asia. Visits to similar factories in Kaili and Congjiang revealed that in all cases women lived in factory-provided dormitories, but were responsible for their own food. Employment averaged about 100 per factory, and wages seldom exceeded RMB 50 per month. Because of special policies developed to attract this kind of economic activity to Qiandongnan, local governments were collecting few tax revenues from these factories.

An officer at the Taijiang *minwei* justified these exploitative ventures by stressing that they only represented a first step in modernization. He likened them to a window through which more coastal companies could see the county's investment potential. He said that Taijiang's rural households still had few opportunities to earn a cash income, and that these factories would help generate a "commercial consciousness" in the countryside. He did not believe that future development might be truncated by using Guizhou's countryside purely as a source of cheap labor and enhancing capital accumulation opportunities for coastal companies dabbling in international trade. Nor did he seem to appreciate that coastal companies might have an incentive to preserve rural Guizhou's peripheral status in order to maintain this supply of cheap labor. By 1996, however, the county's attitude had changed considerably. It had refused to renew any leases for the coastal-run factories, citing insufficient pay and poor working conditions. For Taijiang, the previous goal of attracting external capital at any cost had, as with the province in general, clearly backfired. "We lost money and the workers were treated badly," a *minwei* officer admitted. Furthermore, the county no longer had any funds available for promoting commercial crafts production. As the impacts of fiscal decline continued, the county *minwei*'s annual appropriation of RMB 10,000 had been cut, and what funds they did receive in the form of development grants were being swallowed up by day-to-day administrative expenditures and salaries (Taijiang *Minwei* 1996).

Thus, by 1996, the local state's role in promoting rural "commercial consciousness" had diminished considerably. In Taijiang, all hopes for this were being pinned on private urban entrepreneurs. Clearly Taijiang officials had become aware of the implicit tension between the interests of "development" and those of capital. Nevertheless, the ideology of cultural development remained, and the Miao farmers beyond the county town continued to be portrayed as harboring a "subsistence mentality" from a pre-modern stage of production and culture. This ideology is illustrated in a chapter in a book titled *Zhongguo Qiye Yinghao* ("The Heroes of Chinese Enterprise"). The chapter – about one of Taijiang's most successful ethnic crafts producers – chronicles the history of a Miao villager named Pan Yuzhen in a way which stresses how she was coaxed out of her "pre-modern" thinking to blossom as a successful entrepreneur and culturally developed citizen of "new China." The chapter begins with the following paragraph:

> It used to be that the Miao women living amid the mountains believed in the tradition of making embroidered clothing only for their own use. They would never think of giving it to outsiders, and certainly would never think of selling it. This was the law of tradition. Embroidery was never to be used for anything but making oneself beautiful, especially for marriage. But in 1979, the reforms swept through China like a flood, and in the mountains the pool in which commerce was thought to be shameless started to ripple. The winds of reform were felt by one woman there, who turned against traditional rules, broke the customs, and sold her first piece of embroidery. Since then, she has travelled China from south to north, and has brought the Miao out of the mountains and into the world of commerce. From the point of a needle, they have filled the earth with embroidery, and leapt to earning over 800,000 *yuan*. This is not dream; this is a very true story.
>
> (Zhang 1993)

Passages like this reflect an ideology that explains problems of rural poverty and lack of local capital accumulation not in terms of broader structural mechanisms that perpetuate peripheral status, but as a result of centuries of backward traditions awaiting the arrival of the state's enlightened modernization policies to finally break them down. That this ideology perpetuates a fiction about the Miao was clear to Pan Yuzhen herself. When asked about this passage, she claimed that it misrepresented the Miao. In fact she insisted on taking me to a remote periodic market near Taijiang to prove it. At the market, she pointed out the lively trade going on in silver ornaments, embroidery, and batik, items whose commercial value are thought to only be realized once tourists stumble upon the scene. "These markets have always been busy selling these things," she said. There was no "law of tradition" preventing their sale. For example, she pointed out, it was often the case that women in a large family did not have time to teach or make elaborate embroidery for their children, so they would buy it. Silver ornaments, she said, had always been a specialist's trade, and most embroidery designs were actually purchased from skilled artists who specialized in drawing them.

The state's campaign to commercialize the countryside has involved the mythic construction of a purely subsistence economy in "backward mountain areas" such as Qiandongnan. Peasants are represented as locked within a *xiaonong jingji* ("small farm economy") mentality until "liberated" by the state as it benevolently spreads the winds of reform to even the most tenacious strongholds of custom. To reveal the presence of a thriving "commercial consciousness" among the Miao – independent of state reforms – would be to open up a whole new line of argument concerning the economic backwardness of the mountain areas, one which might point out that exploitative structural forces and insufficient opportunities, not "traditional thinking," are what keep these regions impoverished. More importantly, it would undermine the exoticism which is the commercial attraction of the Miao. That they come from a subsistence, tradition-bound society is what makes Miao embroidery so "authentic." Tourists want things which come from "real villages," not factories. Miao society must be constructed in this way if it is to remain commercially attractive to outsiders. Such is the contemporary pattern of Guizhou's internal colonialism. Ideology and expectations of ethnic remoteness have become part of a process seeking to preserve an idealized subsistence mode of production and, thus, preventing ethnic commodity production from initiating independent rural accumulation.

But if the state seeks to opportunistically encourage such representations as a means of modernization and cultural development, the interests of capital may in fact ultimately undermine this goal. Commercialism begins to develop its own logic of unequal exchange that tends to perpetuate "backwardness" rather than offer the cure hoped for by the state. Taijiang county had already experienced this at the hands of exploitative capital from the China's coastal region. But the logic of commercial exchange exploited and augmented social cleavages in the region in other ways as well. The concerns expressed by distant metropolitan consumers and tourists for preserving the authentic nature of crafts production in Qiandongnan were clearly not lost on local urban entrepreneurs, for example. In Kaili, a number of local shops opened, hoping to take advantage of the tourist market in ethnic craft souvenirs. Shop owners traveled throughout the region collecting crafts, mostly textiles, from villagers, and sold them in Kaili for a profit. They also sold a number of items, such as bamboo masks, produced at local crafts workshops. Increasingly, however, these shops began offering their services to guide tourists to the ethnic villages to buy directly from the peasants. With more and more crafts factories springing up in the region, tourists, it seems, were becoming more interested in insuring that their purchases were authentic village crafts. While on a trip to a nearby village to collect an order of *lusheng* bamboo pipes, one shop owner expressed her exasperation at the behavior of these tourists. Her comments were profoundly ironic. "They don't understand business!" she exclaimed. "I took an Australian woman to a village the other day and she paid 500 *yuan* for a weaving I would have sold for no more than 250. Incredible! 500 *yuan*! Why don't they just buy these things from us? Instead they want to go to the villages and get ripped off!" When I suggested that tourists were perhaps more interested in making sure their money went straight to the producer, rather than getting the cheapest price, she replied that this kind of behavior did not make sense for "developed people." Nevertheless, she had decided to accommodate tourists by offering to take them to villages for a fee.

This desire for authenticity complements well the dominant patterns of capital accumulation in Qiandongnan's growing crafts industry. As ethnic tourism in the region has grown, local entrepreneurs have set up numerous crafts factories, most of which are located in Kaili, with others in Taijiang, Liping, and Huangping counties. With inadequate capital and a very limited market, many of these shut down after only a few months of operation, get combined with other operations, or are acquired by larger state units which can afford to subsidize them, such as timber companies or the army. Those which survive do so only by establishing market links with coastal China and/or Hong Kong and Taiwan. Unlike the examples discussed above, such as the silk tie-dye factory in Taijiang, these factories seek to manufacture marketable products featuring "authentic" ethnic crafts, such as wallets and clothing made with cloth embroidered or batiked in traditional patterns. While they tend to employ a number of rural women on site, mainly to perform final assembly tasks, the majority of production occurs within village households on a contractual basis. The manager of Qiandongnan's largest crafts enterprise, the Miao Embroidery Factory in Taijiang (which is partially funded by UNICEF), estimated that 65 per cent of his factory's income came from the sale of products which have been primarily produced in the countryside. The manager of a smaller factory in Huangping gave an estimate of 70 per cent for this figure. Rural women in Huangping contracting to apply the wax for batik tablecloths were earning about 10 per cent of the factory's wholesale price.[4] At the Taijiang factory, contract producers could earn as much as 20 per cent of the final sale by producing embroidered patches for wallets. With higher value items, however, such as clothing items destined for markets abroad, the proportion would generally be around 1 per cent. Nevertheless, contracts often provided a source of cash income where no commercial opportunities existed.

More important than the extraction of surplus labor value inherent in such contract arrangements was the way they insured that control over production remained in the hands of urban factory managers who not only dictated piece-rates, but provided the "authentic" designs and patterns in order to insure standardization. Managers felt they were contributing to rural development by teaching peasant households the value of money and enabling them to achieve a "commercial consciousness." But they also felt good about convincing peasants to respect the value of their traditions. "If it wasn't for me," one proudly proclaimed, "peasants around here would forget their old patterns." This attitude illustrates the colonial nature of economic development which characterizes touristic modernity in rural Guizhou. It offers the extreme case of false modern triumphant. Contract arrangements were lauded for helping to preserve a pre-modern (that is, pre-commercial and pre-capitalist) mode of production, and for maintaining authentic *minzu* traditions which were important not simply for their museum value, but more significantly for their exchange value. The importance of cultural preservation, here, can be interpreted as an aspect of modernity's misplaced need to construct authentic placed traditions in response to an overwhelming sense of loss and in an effort to repair the inevitable disruptions of modernization. This false modern triumphant can result in a perpetuation of colonial power relations that help insure the subordination of peripheral rural economies.

Two examples serve to illustrate the way metropolitan concerns for cultural preservation and authenticity result in increased subordination and vulnerability for Guizhou's peripheral producers of *minzu* culture. The first takes us back to the town of Shidong, which in addition to its well-known festivals, achieved notoriety during the 1980s as one of Guizhou's most important ethnic crafts-producing sites. Before 1990, Taijiang's Miao Embroidery Factory dealt exclusively with Shidong for its contracted embroidery. As the factory's manager, a Han, explained, "Shidong was much more developed than Taijiang [the county seat], and this legacy is still evident today. The people there are very entrepreneurial, and so it was easiest for us to get started there." Shidong was perfect, he said, because it had developed early as an important river port; craftsmanship had become refined there. Then, after liberation, those traditional crafts were "frozen in time," because Shidong was forgotten. Roads and railroads replaced the river as the region's most important transport network, and state investments went to developing the county town as a government seat. By 1980, he said, Shidong had preserved a rich tradition in isolation while Taijiang town had developed and become "Hanified." This gave Shidong new popularity in the culture fever of the 1980s, and crafts production developed rapidly due to official promotion of Shidong's festivals and contracts with crafts factories.

But recently, the manager said, the Miao Embroidery Factory had been getting less and less of its embroidery from Shidong. "It's getting harder and harder to find authentic work there," he said. "They've become more and more influenced by Han culture, and so the patterns aren't as authentic." Another problem, he said, was that textile production in Shidong was no longer the result of a self-sufficient, enclosed economy, but an increasingly commercial one, and this had also influenced local embroidery styles. His solution to this "contradiction" was to maintain a sort of cultural bank of authentic traditional styles, frozen in time, that would form the basis of sustained future production. "If peasants want a job," he said, "they'll have to produce embroidery according to the styles we require, and these will be the authentic ones." Other managers had come to the same conclusion about

Shidong and the need to counter, actively, the cultural losses incurred by commercial development. The result for Shidong producers was an increased vulnerability to losing lucrative contracts unless they surrendered to the judgment of their outside employers in determining what was authentic and what was not.

At the same time, factory managers clearly saw themselves in the business of "development," and this fueled their attitude that they had helped modernize Shidong and could now move on to more authentic, but less-developed, villages. This appeared to be little more than a justification of the logic of capital accumulation. Profits for urban crafts factories depended on rural women maintaining a high level of craft skill, while at the same time not requiring higher wages, and remaining committed to village lifestyles so that authentic designs and ideas could be passed on. As the manager of a Kaili factory claimed, village contracts helped rural society develop and "open to the world," but what was most important for him was that they made good economic sense. "Village contracts are the best way to increase my economic benefits," he said. Expanding production through contracts was more efficient, more flexible, and cheaper (especially since the household, rather than the factory, assumed the costs for reproducing its labor power).

The second example illustrates how cultural preservation in rural Guizhou is a product not simply of local strategies of capital accumulation, but also of international patterns of consumption. International tourists who visit villages and festivals often express an interest not only in the preservation of authentic traditions, but in questions of "sustainable development" and "empowerment" for villagers, especially village women. Although I conducted no comprehensive surveys of tourists in the region, the Western tourists I met travelling to Qiandongnan were generally elite adventurers who had already visited China numerous times, had developed something of an intellectual interest in China's *minzu* groups, and were actively concerned with questions of development and cultural preservation. A popular story in Taijiang was how the Miao Embroidery Factory's UNICEF aid came about because of a tourist who had influence at the United Nations. Qiandongnan also attracts many textile scholars and artists from Europe and North America, many of whom make repeated collecting trips to the region. One of these was a clothing designer and artist from the United States who, with the assistance and cooperation of tour guides in Guiyang, initiated a development project called "Far Village." The project would involve the design, production, and marketing of fashionable clothing for Japanese, European, and American markets, incorporating traditional weaving, embroidery, and batik work from rural Guizhou.

As stated in the Far Village project proposal (Exley 1994), the designer's objective was to foster economic development and empowerment for village women, while at the same time encouraging the preservation of their craft traditions in the face of modern social transformations. Younger women, she wrote, who "lose these skills as they move away from the village," should "be offered a way of earning money in order to retain their embroidery, weaving, and batik skills." She went on to make it clear that, "Rather than just selling a product we want to sell the concept of Far Village; that the world needs to protect and help these ancient cultures to survive; that things made by hand are valuable and should be honored; and that the market-place will respond to such a selling technique." Thus, not only did the Far Village proposal represent a modern metropolitan need to preserve and fossilize the traditional customs of "ancient cultures," but showed that capital can be enlisted to support such an ideal. This attitude, by itself, did not necessarily present a problem for Qiandongnan's rural producers. Indeed, the proposal called for the inclusion of village women "in the deci-sion making process, as in a cooperative," suggesting that each village have a woman representative for the project, and that women should be shown "where the work is going and how it is being adapted to a marketable product." Although based on the idealistic and misplaced search for moder-nity, the project nevertheless represented the best option for enhancing locally controlled accumulation in the Guizhou countryside, given the prevailing political-economic situation.

Unfortunately, these goals were not being realized as the project got underway in 1994. Instead of empowerment, the proposal's ideals of preser-vation and respecting tradition were used to legitimize an urban entrepreneurial elite's desire to keep rural producers subordinate and vulner-able. Although the project's American designer apparently envisioned a direct link between village producers and the market, Far Village was in fact being pasted onto the existing exploitative structure of commercial crafts production in Guizhou. Four existing workshops throughout the province were selected, including two in Qiandongnan, one of which was Taijiang's Miao Embroidery Factory. Far Village work was being parceled out by these workshops according to the same contractual arrangements that had existed before. At the village level, nothing had changed. In addition, the whole project was shrouded in secrecy, especially the designs themselves. Ostensibly, this was because of intense competition from other factories. The Miao Embroidery Factory was especially sensitive to this since one of its own designers had quit in 1992 to start his own workshop, stealing his previous employer's designs in the process. But there was another, more disturbing reason for all the secrecy. As the manager at the Taijiang factory claimed, "It's necessary to keep the designs and objectives secret so that the idea doesn't get out of control, so that peasants don't start trying to do this kind of thing for themselves. That would influence their traditional designs." It was also important to keep the designs a secret since, according to him, competing crafts factories were less concerned with cultural preservation and long-term benefits and more interested in making quick money. Ultimately, he said, secrecy was in the best interests of the peasant producers themselves, since once they started trying to making modern things themselves they would lose any market potential they might have had and would be unable to develop a commercial crafts industry with a foreign market.

The original Far Village proposal explicitly sought the involvement of village women in the decision-making process, and called for work not to be a burden on their daily lives. It envisioned a cooperative-style approach to ethnic commodity production with the producers in control. But most women involved in contracts worked between 8 and 12 hours a day, and were not even told what their work was being used for. Urban managerial elites, rather than village women, maintained control over the means of production, and retained the right to decide what was authentic, and what was in the best interests of rural producers. Far Village's inherent politics of Western consumer culture, wrapped up in the rhetoric of cultural survival and multiculturalism, was ultimately no different from the more blatantly colonial patterns of capital accumulation represented by commercial crafts factories and coastal-run export-oriented sweatshops. As if to emphasize this point, by 1997 the project was in shambles, most of its working capital having been absconded by one of the Guiyang tour guides entrusted to manage the project.

Colonial patterns of development are evident in the various dimensions of Guizhou's incipient commercial crafts industry. These patterns are a result not simply of some blind logic of capital accumulation, but of combining that logic with uneven social power relations between rural producers and metropolitan consumers and tourists, power relations that carry with them ideologies of authenticity, preservation, and tradition. Metropolitan capital extracts rural surplus labor value not simply via contract relations that lead to household self-exploitation, but also with the help and legitimacy of the state's dominant ideology of traditional folk culture. While this pattern is perhaps most evident in Guizhou's commercial crafts industry, it has parallels in the other aspects of tourism development discussed in the following section. As an agent in the state's projects of national integration and *wenhua fazhan*, tourism is a commercial industry infused with metropolitan values that are ultimately complicit in the economic, political, and cultural subjugation of Guizhou's peripheral societies. While most of the tourists visiting Qiandongnan's villages would be loathe to condone such complicity, few would be willing to believe that it partly stems from their own misplaced desires to construct, idealistically, other traditional worlds worthy of preservation in the face of what they alone have come to think of as modernity's onslaught. Ethnic tourism's complicity in the subjugation of the periphery, in other words, is a consequence of an incomplete understanding of modernity as a cultural experience, one that has been blinded by rationalization and alienation so as to miss the potential for creativity and freedom as the outcome of so much "melting into air."

THE TOURISM INDUSTRY IN GUIZHOU

The production of *minzu* culture is characterized by an important tension between the nation-building agenda of the state and the logic of capital accumulation. While the former seeks to realize a particular version of modernity marked by progressive cultural development, a patriotic sense of national identity invested in the heritage of *minzu* folklore, and the integration of "backward" regions into the national mainstream, the latter both colludes with and diverts from the state's modern project in its exploitation of rural–urban income differentials and the ideology of cultural preservation. Capital works less toward the state's ideal of cultural development than toward its own dynamic of producing and then feeding from geographical inequalities. As a particularly powerful force in the production of *minzu* culture, Guizhou's tourism industry has displayed this same tension between political and economic versions of modernity's unfinished project in China. As with the ethnic crafts industry, we find in the tourism industry a similar cacophony of voices seeking to dominate the discourse of Chinese modernity. As the previous chapter suggested, increasing economic integration throughout China has been accompanied by considerable fiscal decentralization and decline. The above example of Taijiang's crafts projects reveals the resulting consequences for local governments seeking to foster alliances with mobile capital. The patterns of tourism development in Guizhou have been no exception to the contradictions of China's decentralizing and fragmenting political economy. Though for the most part "state-owned," the Guizhou tourism industry does not operate as a bureaucratic extension of the state. Rather, it operates as a diverse set of competing enterprises, driven by profits and the requirements for business survival (see also Xu 1996: 21). The interest of capital are already intimately bound up with the workings of an industry that has been unleashed by the state with the hope of realizing the state's objectives. This raises a two-fold set of problems. On one level, as we've seen, the interests of capital often contradict those of the state (Xu 1996: 122); on another level, tourism can also be deployed – often at cross-purposes – by the central government in its efforts to appropriate revenues and by local governments in their strategies for regional development. But whether propagandized as "poverty alleviation" or legitimized as cultural development, tourism for those most actively involved in its development is simply about making money. As the various interests of the central government, local governments, and entrepreneurs meet and diverge, the tourism industry emerges as an important field in which varying narratives of modernity emerge, circulate, and – ultimately – become appropriated by those whose lives are increasingly wrapped within the industry's dislocating dynamic.

History and geography of tourism development

The most convenient date to ascribe to the initiation of Guizhou's tourism industry is 1982. In that year the provincial tourism bureau was established as a branch of the foreign affairs office, while Guiyang municipality and Zhenning county (where Huangguoshu Falls is located) were opened to foreigners traveling with tourist visas. As recommended by the NTA in Beijing, the GTB began promoting two separate tourist circuits (*lüyouxian*) extending west and east of Guiyang. In 1984, the central government initiated a significant round of deregulation in the tourism industry, resulting in a surge of tourism development initiatives at the regional and local level throughout China (Xu 1996: 23–4). In Guizhou, the response was the opening of six more counties to foreign tourists in 1985, and a new round of investments in the province's two tourist circuits (see Figure 4.1). Yet these developments were for the most part centrally dictated; throughout the 1980s, Guizhou was characteristically regarded as a place rich in (scenic) resources to be developed for the benefit of the nation. Such resources were primarily concentrated on the karst plateau lands of the western circuit: the many waterfalls clustered around Huangguoshu, the caverns and subterranean river of the Dragon Palace (*Longgong*), the spectacular Zhijin Cave (*Dajidong*), and the scenic and recreational opportunities at Hongfeng Lake, the large reservoir built in 1958 just west of Guiyang that submerged the Miao village of Heitu. These all became state-level scenic sites, qualifying them for direct central investments from the NTA (see Table 4.1).

The eastern circuit, focusing on Qiandongnan Miao and Dong Autonomous Prefecture (see Figure 4.2), did have an assortment of scenic attractions as well, including the state-level Wuyang River, the eroded karst canyons of Yuntai Mountain, and the state-level nature reserves of Fanjing and Leigong Mountains. But local officials soon recognized that ethnic customs were the primary attraction in Qiandongnan, and thus began concentrating on developing local festivals and selecting villages to promote as tourist attractions. By 1987 seven villages had been selected as official ethnic tourist sites in Qiandongnan. Unlike scenic sites, however, ethnic villages were not recognized in the central state's funding hierarchy. This fact, combined with Qiandongnan's relative inaccessibility compared to the western circuit, and the reluctance of NTA or GTB authorities to take ethnic tourism seriously, resulted in a much more rapid pace of development for Guizhou's western sites. More important, it contributed to a distinction between the eastern and western circuits, with the latter becoming more enveloped in centralized tourism planning and the former exhibiting tendencies of local autonomy.

By 1987, 14 more counties had been opened and tourist arrivals began increasing steadily each year, with the exception of 1989, which saw a sharp decline in response to the military crackdown on student demonstrations in Tiananmen Square in Beijing (see Figure 4.3 and Table 4.2). Between 1980

Table 4.1 A selection of recognized tourist sites in Guizhou, 1994[a]

	Western circuit	Eastern circuit
State scenic sites	Huangguoshu Falls Longgong (Dragon Palace) Zhijin Cave Hongfeng Lake	Wuyang River
State nature reserves		Fanjing Mountain Libo Karst Forest
Provincial scenic sites	Huaxi Park Baihua Lake Sanfen River Maling Gorge Zhaoti Scenic Area Nidang Stone Forest Lubuge Scenic Area 100-Li Azalea Belt	Jiulong Cave Sajin Gorge Xiaoqikong Scenic Area
Other scenic sites	Tiantai Mountain	Leigong Mtn Nature Reserve Yuntai Mtn Scenic Area
State cultural relics	Puding Chuan Cave	Qinglongdong Temple Liping Meeting Site Cengong Drum Tower
Ethnic and cultural villages[b]	Heitu Changlinggang Loujiazhuang Shitouzhai Huashishao Caiguan Gaopo	Langde Qingman Matang Wengxiang Fanpai Baojing Xijiang Gaozeng Zhaoxing Tonggu Chong'an Shidong

Source: Guizhou Tourism Bureau.

Notes:
[a] Omits a number of sites in northern and northwest Guizhou.
[b] Includes only regularly visited village sites; many more villages are actually recognized as prepared to receive tourists, especially along the eastern circuit.

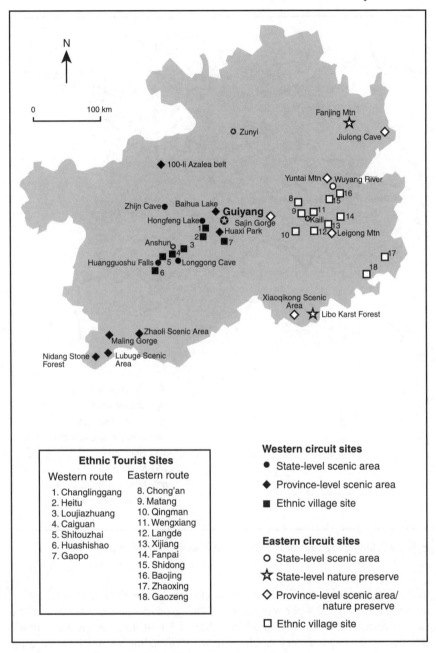

Figure 4.1 Guizhou: eastern and western tourist circuits, 1994

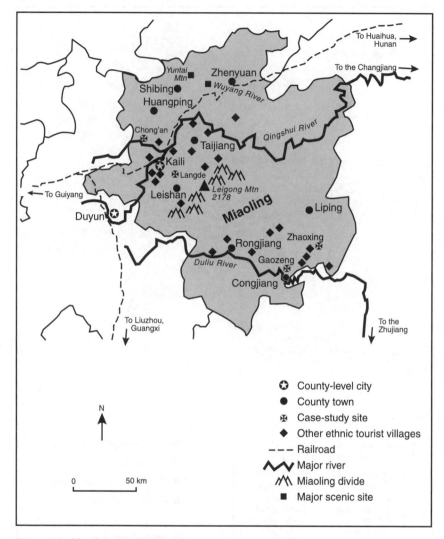

To Huaihua, Hunan

To the Changjiang

Yuntai Mtn Zhenyuan
Shibing *Wuyang River*
Huangping

Chong'an *Qingshui River*
Taijiang

Kaili
Langde
To Guiyang Leishan Leigong Mtn 2178
Miaoling Liping
Duyun

Zhaoxing
Rongjiang Gaozeng
Duliu River
Congjiang

To Liuzhou, Guangxi

To the Zhujiang

N

⊘ County-level city
● County town
✠ Case-study site
◆ Other ethnic tourist villages
- - - Railroad
∿ Major river
/M\ Miaoling divide
■ Major scenic site

0   50 km

Figure 4.2 Qiandongnan Miaozu Dongzu Autonomous Prefecture

and 1990, the number of international arrivals in Guizhou increased by an annual average of 30.4 per cent. Most of this growth was concentrated along the western circuit. As indicated in Tables 4.3 and 4.4, the eastern circuit (Qiandongnan) saw a very small portion of Guizhou's total international arrivals, and received only 5.5 per cent of Guizhou's tourism investments between 1985 and 1990. Tourists, however, tended to stay longer and spend more money in Qiandongnan, and the region soon became known as a destination for elite adventure travelers. As with China in general, international markets were initially the exclusive focus of Guizhou's tourism promotion efforts; tourism was, during this time, advocated simply as a convenient means of generating foreign exchange, rather than as a dynamic economic sector in its own right (Xu 1996: 18). During the 1980s, foreigners made up about 32 per cent of Guizhou's international arrivals. The rest were primarily from Hong Kong and Macau, with some arriving from Taiwan after 1988.[5] Of the foreigners, the Japanese were the largest group, followed by tourists from the United States, Great Britain, France, Sweden, and Germany.

Most of Guizhou's international arrivals during this period, especially those from Hong Kong and Macau, were independent travelers rather than group tourists, reflecting Guizhou's still relatively unknown status among international agents organizing trips to China, and limiting greatly the tourism income earned by the province. Indeed, the focus on international

Table 4.2 International arrivals in Guizhou, 1980–95

Year	Total	Overseas Chinese[a]	Compatriots[b]	Foreigners	% foreign
1980	1,694	13	995	686	40.5
1981	2,339	25	1,714	600	25.7
1982	5,084	61	3,236	1,787	35.1
1983	7,066	48	5,104	1,914	27.1
1984	10,249	23	7,501	2,725	26.6
1985	11,263	402	7,927	2,934	26.0
1986	14,021	196	9,270	4,550	32.5
1987	18,820	337	10,810	7,673	40.8
1988	23,646	1,043	15,060	7,543	31.9
1989	13,666	555	8,377	4,734	34.6
1990	24,112	126	16,542	7,444	30.9
1991	37,462	99	27,001	10,362	27.7
1992	76,293	328	57,259	18,706	24.5
1993	102,483	1,125	58,788	42,570	41.5
1994	120,809	1,622	43,054	76,133	63.0
1995	136,459	1,446	58,177	77,836	57.0

Source: Guizhou Tourism Bureau.

Notes:
[a] Refers to citizens of the PRC who reside abroad.
[b] Refers to citizens of Hong Kong, Taiwan, and Macau.

Table 4.3 International arrivals in Qiandongnan, 1984–95

Year	Number	Share of Guizhou total (%)	Estimated receipts[a] (US$)
1984	71	0.69	
1985	206	1.83	
1986	430	3.07	8,000
1987	864	4.59	9,900
1988	1,071	4.53	20,700
1989	920	6.73	9,950
1990	1,174	4.87	20,930
1991	1,414	3.77	38,100
1992	2,096	2.75	53,000
1993	3,951	3.86	80,500
1994	9,849	8.15	n/a
1995	13,178	9.65	n/a

Sources: Qiandongnan Tourism Bureau, Guizhou Tourism Bureau.

Note:
[a] Revenues based on food, lodging, and official fees for tour groups only.

Table 4.4 Comparison of eastern and western tourist circuits, 1984–9

	Eastern	Western
Average length of stay		
Foreign tourists	2.84 days	0.76 days
Hong Kong, Taiwan tourists	6.06 days	1.22 days
Average expenditures per foreign tourist[a]	RMB¥ 106.53	RMB¥ 11.94
Tourism investments (to 1989)	RMB¥ 500,000	RMB¥ 8,550,000

Source: Yang (1991: 60).

Note:
[a] Revenues based on food, lodging, and official fees for tour groups only.

tourists was a poor strategy for local capital accumulation in the first place, since the central government was able to retain the majority of foreign exchange generated from tourism (Xu 1996: 156–7).

The 1990s brought a new phase to Guizhou tourism in a number of ways.

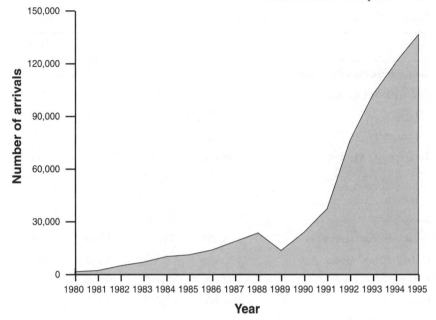

Figure 4.3 Guizhou: international arrivals, 1980–95

Economic liberalization and fiscal decentralization resulted in increased incentive for local governments to promote tourism development (see Xu 1996: 14–21). At the same time, tourism was being regarded as an important economic sector in its own right, with a potential for contributing to Guizhou's own modernization. By 1992, 44 counties had been opened, making over half of the province accessible to foreign tourists, with many more "closed" counties accessible with special permission. As part of a general trend throughout southwest China, international arrivals began to increase sharply, and, as indicated in Table 4.5, group tourism began to increase significantly, especially among foreigners (see also Figure 4.4), indicating an intensification of marketing efforts by both the NTA and GTB. Most of this new growth in foreign group tourists initially came not from Western sources, but from Taiwan and Southeast Asia – the nouveaux riches of "Greater China."

In 1992, over 55 per cent of Guizhou's international tourists were from Taiwan (Figure 4.5), and by 1993 three out of the top four foreign markets for Guizhou tourists were in Southeast Asia. Singapore alone accounted for over 41 per cent of all foreigners arriving in 1993, although that year represented a peak in Southeast Asian tourists coming to Guizhou (Table 4.6). Many of these tourists were taking advantage of new direct flights between Kunming and Singapore and Bangkok, and were coming into

Table 4.5 Characteristic of Guizhou tourism, 1991–4

	1991	1992	1993	1994
Total international receptions	37,462	76,293	102,483	120,809
• Hong Kong, Macau	8,634	14,854	13,087	22,998
• Taiwan	18,367	42,405	45,701	20,065
• Foreigners	10,362	18,706	42,570	76,133
Total group receptions	19,402	43,682	70,117	n/a
• Hong Kong, Macau	n/a	6,334	7,925	n/a
• Taiwan	n/a	25,947	25,612	n/a
• Foreigners	n/a	11,401	35,791	n/a
Total individual receptions	18,050	32,611	32,366	n/a
• Hong Kong, Macau	n/a	8,520	5,162	n/a
• Taiwan	n/a	16,458	20,089	n/a
• Foreigners	n/a	7,300	6,977	n/a
Length of stay (days)				
• Total average	1.80	1.72	1.93	1.69
• Foreigners	2.24	2.19	2.06	n/a
Foreign receipts (US $ × 1,000)	3,038	6,861	10,495	21,096
Per tourist (US $)	81	90	102	175
Domestic receipts (RMB¥ × 1,000)	91,750	271,899	n/a	601,796

Source: Guizhou Tourism Bureau.

Guizhou from Yunnan for a quick tour of western circuit scenic attractions. This trend precipitated some important consequences within Guizhou.

First, the concentration of tourism along the western circuit helped reinforce the dominance of Guiyang and Anshun as the primary conduits of tourism revenue for both the province and the central government. In 1992, Guiyang accounted for 72.4 per cent of Guizhou's receptions and 94.1 per cent of its revenues, while Anshun accounted for 21.4 per cent and 4.6 per cent respectively (ZLN 1993: 217). Second, and more significant for our purposes, a number of ethnic tourist villages were developed along the western circuit in order to present more efficiently Guizhou's scenic and ethnic qualities to western circuit tourists who tended to spend no more than one night in the province. As will be discussed below, this was a response to the growing popularity of locally initiated ethnic tourism in Qiandongnan,

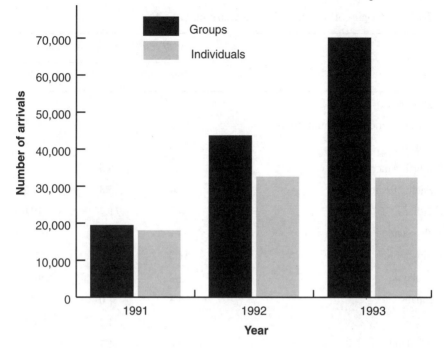

Figure 4.4 Guizhou: international group and individual arrivals, 1991–3

while at the same time, it helped further solidify Qiandongnan's status as the domain of Guizhou's more "authentic" ethnic villages. As one guide in Guiyang put it, "Those villages [along the western circuit] are way too commercial, too close to the city; they don't have very traditional lives, and their values are oriented toward money, they always want money for every-thing." She said she preferred taking tour groups to the villages in Qiandongnan, which were "much less spoiled, more traditional." Whether a village satisfied Western tourists, apparently, was seen as the best indicator of authenticity. Travel agencies in Guiyang were thus more likely to take Western tour groups to Qiandongnan because Westerners were known to appreciate "more traditional villages."

By 1995, the Southeast Asian Chinese market had seemingly peaked and began to decline the following year. Although Qiandongnan – being domi-nated by Western tourists – remained largely unaffected by this (see Table 4.3), the western circuit sites were more affected. The GTB offered three reasons for this decline. First, Guizhou was too dependent on Yunnan for the majority of its international arrivals – since most came from Southeast Asia via Kunming – and the Yunnan travel agencies that hosted most of these tourists were no longer including Guizhou sites on their itineraries, in part because conditions and services in Guizhou remained poor in comparison to

Table 4.6 Origins of foreign arrivals in Guizhou, 1992–4

Origin	% of total foreigners received		
	1992	1993	1994
By region			
Asia (not including compatriots)	63.5	77.8	65.9
Europe	14.8	9.2	9.9
North America	8.4	5.5	9.2
Pacific Region	4.4	5.8	2.1
Other	8.7	1.7	10.0
By country (top 6)			
Singapore	31.2	41.2	30.9
Malaysia	5.8	9.3	16.8
Japan	16.4	7.0	10.4
USA	6.6	4.2	6.8
Thailand	4.8	4.7	3.9
France	n/a	2.9	3.7

Source: Guizhou Tourism Bureau.

Yunnan. Second, the Yunnan tourism industry had kept its prices very low, making it impossible for Guizhou to compete. Third, Guizhou's tourism industry was plagued with management problems and poor regulation – one problem being intense price competition among local agencies resulting in a reduced quality of service. Others in the industry, however, confidentially spoke of the rampant nepotism and incompetence within the GTB itself as the real reason for the decline, with most of the talented personnel leaving in disgust for the private sector after being passed over for promotion.

Ethnic tourism in Qiandongnan

The attitude of Guiyang tour guides regarding Western tourists and the authenticity of Qiandongnan's ethnic villages underscores a compelling role played by that region in Guizhou's tourism development. That Qiandongnan was regarded as more authentic according to Western sensibilities implies that the western circuit sites more closely reflected the theme park version of a triumphant Chinese modernity. The western circuit received the more consistent focus of the GTB's development efforts, and it was the western sites that

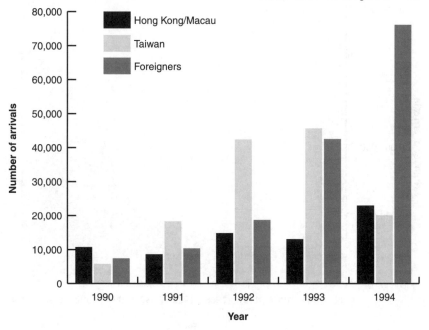

Figure 4.5 Guizhou: international arrivals by category, 1990–4

were increasingly visited not by Western tourists, but Chinese. The rising number of visitors in Guizhou came to be increasingly dominated by Chinese tourists. Domestic tourism has risen steadily since 1990 (Figure 4.6), while most of the new markets in Southeast Asia were also being driven by ethnic Chinese. The majority of these Chinese tourists are primarily interested in seeing Guizhou's major scenic attractions. While they may be willing to visit an ethnic village if it is conveniently located along their two-day itinerary, only a few would travel to Qiandongnan just to see ethnic customs. On the other hand, according to officials at China International Travel Service (CITS) in Guiyang and in Kaili, almost all Westerners who come to Guizhou visit Qiandongnan, and Westerners (including Japanese) make up the majority of Qiandongnan's international tourists. Most of these Westerners are interested in seeing remote ethnic villages, primitive customs, and examples of "uncorrupted" or "pre-modern" culture. In Qiandongnan, this trend was initiated by the Japanese, who made up roughly 60 per cent of the region's international visitors between 1985 and 1990. The idea that the Miao and the Japanese came from the same origins had become popular in Japan after teams of Japanese ethnographers visited Qiandongnan in the early 1980s and published books on the Miao. The books commented on Miao customs and dress which were similar to those found in ancient feudal Japan. Soon many Japanese tourists were coming to Qiandongnan to look for their roots.

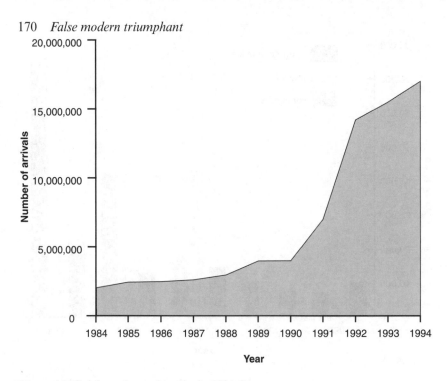

Figure 4.6 Guizhou: domestic arrivals, 1984–94

Thus, whereas the western circuit developed into an efficient string of scenic sites interspersed with highly standardized and performance-oriented ethnic villages to meet the demands of Chinese tourists on tight schedules, Qiandongnan emerged as a contemporary reincarnation of the *Miaojiang*. But the resurrection of the "Miao borderlands" and their exotic primitiveness was at the behest of a wholly new narrative of modernity, that of the capitalist West and its misplaced search for authenticity. Qiandongnan came to be marked as the authentic source of unique and exotic traditions by the most significant judges of touristic modernity: "developed" Western tourists themselves. In many ways, Qiandongnan was a pioneer region for Guizhou's touristic modernity. Ethnic tourism as a force of cultural development emerged there first, and initially due to the demands of Western tourists. It was only later that the nation-building and income-generating potential inherent in ethnic tourism began to be exploited by the broader state and tourism industry in the more commercialized tourist villages of the western circuit. It was there, along the western circuit, that the misplaced search for authenticity reached its rationalized and alienating height, as the innovative approaches of Qiandongnan came to be increasingly standardized and pointed toward the state's unfinished project of modernizing China. Qiandongnan's local initiative in the promotion of ethnic tourism also anticipated a general shift in tourism throughout the province as Guizhou entered the 1990s. As mentioned in the previous chapter, tourism came to be envisioned not simply as a local duty to the foreign exchange needs of the central government, but as a strategy that could be geared to local development needs. In Qiandongnan, it was clearly the perceived need for *wenhua fazhan* that encouraged local leaders to focus on ethnic tourism.

Ethnic tourism in Qiandongnan began when officials in Kaili, in particular the then-governor Wu Dehai, a Miao, and his appointed tourism bureau director – a Han from Shanghai who had been exiled to manual labor among the Miao during the Cultural Revolution – quickly recognized ethnic minorities as the main attraction to the increasing numbers of Japanese tourists arriving in Qiandongnan. During his enforced rustication in a Miao village, the Shanghai exile had been so taken by the local culture and customs that he chose to stay and promote the region for tourism, and it was primarily through his agency, with Wu's political support, that Qiandongnan became an ethnic tourist destination. Established in 1985, the Qiandongnan prefectural tourism bureau (QTB), began devoting itself to establishing a number of ethnic tourist villages around Kaili. By 1987, seven villages – all Miao but one – had been selected where tour groups could be treated to elaborate welcoming ceremonies, song and dance performances, and crafts demonstrations.

Other than the role played by foreign tourist demand, especially from the Japanese, there were two important reasons for Qiandongnan's locally initiated emphasis on ethnic tourism. First was the issue of local control over tourist resources and returns on investments. The QTB director said he had no interest in investing precious capital in yet another cave, waterfall, or canyon. "Developing scenic sites," he said, "requires much more money than developing an ethnic village; it takes a long time to realize any returns. And now, with so many scenic sites already being developed in western Guizhou, there's no point in trying to compete." More importantly, the prefectural tourism bureau had virtually no say in the development of Qiandongnan's major scenic sites, since they fell under the jurisdiction of state organs that had the capital necessary to develop them. Yuntai Mountain was being developed by the ministries of construction and forestry, while most of the money for the Wuyang River came from the hydroelectric bureau. These were large state-level units that bypassed Qiandongnan's local tourism authorities. In the decentralized economic environment in which local units were expected to be fiscally responsible, and in which Qiandongnan's tourism bureau was expected to fund its own projects by expanding tourist revenues, there was little incentive for the QTB to encourage tourists to visit scenic areas. Indeed, the director actively *discouraged* trips to the Wuyang River, claiming it was a boring trip in a noisy motor boat on a man-made reservoir that was usually not filled to capacity anyway. "The hydroelectric bureau – what do they know about tourism?" he exclaimed. Ethnic tourist villages, on the other hand, were directly administered by the prefectural tourism bureau, which set the fees to be paid to the villages. Although most of the investments for these villages actually came from the Prefectural *Minzu* Affairs Commission (*minwei*), the tourism bureau administered their use and distribution. The *minwei*, claimed the director, didn't know anything about tourism, "so they just let us take care of it." Thus, the tourism bureau and the local branch of CITS realized direct returns from ethnic village tourism.

Second, ethnic tourism was much more explicitly a project of modernization, and as such fit better the development needs of Qiandongnan, a region of much greater ethnic concentration than western Guizhou. According to the QTB director, ethnic tourism offered locals the chance to benefit directly in ways they couldn't from scenic tourism. Although scenic sites offered places for locals to sell souvenirs and other services, they also locked up large amounts of land in areas where land is the precious source of one's livelihood. As will be discussed below, this was certainly true at the large cave and waterfall sites along the western circuit. In Qiandongnan, at the Wuyang River and Yuntai Mountain, local peasants were prevented from cutting trees for firewood. But they did so anyway, especially on the steep slopes of the canyon where erosion defaces the hillsides and muddies the river. This put them in direct conflict with the government and alienated them from the potential benefits of tourism. Such environmental conflicts with the state were not likely to happen in ethnic tourist villages, the director said. More important, while rural incomes derived from tourism remained rather limited (that is, beyond the actual tourist villages), tourism was regarded by officials in Kaili as a force which could break through the isolation that still pervaded the contemporary *Miaojiang*. The director explained it in these terms:

> It all has to do with transportation. Rivers, roads, or railroads, it's all the same; this area has always been extremely difficult to get to and get around in. Why don't the Han have the hundreds of festivals which people in this region take part in each year? Because they've never had to come up with an excuse to bring people in neighboring areas together. Here, because of the difficulty of transport, local villages have always kept to themselves; but they need occasions for trade, social interaction, and particularly, opportunities to get their youth married. That is the main purpose of the local festivals. Why have minority people here been getting shorter and shorter? Because they never go more than a few kilometers to get married. And this kind of local breeding causes other shortcomings as well; they have little ambition to broaden the horizons of their world. The most important thing tourism is doing here is changing everyone's perspective. It's not important they learn about America or France or even Hong Kong and Taiwan; but what they *are* learning about is what the people in the next valley over are doing, and particularly, what's going on in the towns and in the city of Kaili.

Echoing the principles of cultural development and nationalist integration, the director believed that the most important change tourism was capable of bringing to Qiandongnan involved broadening local horizons and strengthening the people. Committed, as he was, to the overall development of the region, he saw the encouragement of ethnic tourism as the most effective approach. His chief supporter, Wu Dehai, was also known for his commitment to tourism as a form of cultural development. As documented in an account by Liu (1994: 34–8), tourism development under Wu's guidance helped villagers cast off ancient superstitions and create a healthier scientific and modern culture:

> In Qingman village, customs dictated that the *lusheng* [a bamboo pipe] couldn't be played, nor could drums be beaten, between spring planting and autumn harvest. To violate this custom, it was said, was to risk some great natural calamity. Wu Dehai himself is a Miao, and wanted to respect the customs of his own people. But he also wanted to adapt to the new environment of reform and openness. So he himself went to the Miao village, found the village elders and cadres, spoke to them in rational and scientific terms, opened their thinking, and reached an agreement to establish an ethnic tourist site. After this, when tourists came, villagers performed, playing the *lusheng* at any time of the year, enabling locals to receive an enlightening education and increase their enthusiasm for tourism.

The approach to ethnic tourism in Qiandongnan, however, reflected not only a concern for local cultural development and "scientific rationalism," but an awareness of how the concept of authenticity drives the Western tourist market as well. The QTB director, for example, believed that the tourists who appreciated Qiandongnan the most were Westerners. "Chinese are only interested in staying in big fancy hotels, seeing famous scenic spots," he said, "but here, you can really learn about Chinese history. The Han are too developed; they've lost their history. Because of their isolation in mountain areas, the minorities have preserved their culture and traditions."[6] Most significant, though, was the fact that in Qiandongnan the idea of authenticity itself had become a contributing factor to the ultimate project of integration and cultural development. After the initial selection of seven tourist villages in 1987, the number grew to over 40 by 1994.[7] Only about half of these were regularly receiving tourists, but the QTB's strategy was to maintain a list of villages in order to cater to the particular needs of a tour group. According to the QTB, those needs were increasingly characterized by the desire for unmediated authenticity. Tourists wanted to visit villages other tourists had not yet reached, and to see "unstaged" versions of everyday village life. Whereas the original tourist villages featured elaborate on-demand receptions and performances for tourists, newer selections were being featured as sites where tourists could enjoy an unmediated experience.

As far as the director was concerned, the more tourists seeking authentic villages the better, since this would push the wave of tourism-inspired cultural development further into the stubborn remnants of the *Miaojiang*. He regularly told visitors to these villages that they were the first foreigners the locals had ever seen, a remarkably effective selling point among Westerners whose imaginations remain filled with a China shrouded in isolation and mystery.

The director pointed out that the expected cycle of development for these newly selected villages could already be seen in the original seven villages. Each of these villages went through a particular phase of relatively intense popularity, a *"lüyoure"* ("tourist fever"), followed by a slackening off of visitors as newer villages began to open up. Several factors contributed to this eventual decline in each village. The most important, probably, was the attitude among guides from Guiyang that the village had become "too commercial," and "too touristy." Another is the fact that, as a village grew popular and became increasingly linked to a web of outside connections, many of the village's more talented youth left to pursue new opportunities: jobs in Kaili or Guiyang (at hotels, song and dance troupes, crafts workshops), or in ethnic theme parks in Shenzhen, Beijing, Kunming, or Guilin. Rather than joining the mass of *liudong renkou* ("floating population") migrating to Guangdong and looking for work, like so many of their rural neighbors, these youth were actively recruited by agents seeking representatives of authentic *minzu* culture to serve in the metropolitan tourism sector. With many of the village's most talented youth gone, the quality of reception and performance activities declined, and tourists were ushered on to new sites.

The most illustrative case of this cycle was Fanpai, a Miao village in the region where the QTB director had been rusticated during the Cultural Revolution. During that time, he became familiar with the unique customs of Fanpai, which is tucked deep into the folds of the *Miaoling*, as the mountains of Qiandongnan are called. When he became the director of tourism for the prefecture, Fanpai was one of the first villages on his list as a place whose traditions would help cast off its poverty. He helped organize the Fanpai Song and Dance Troupe, whose performances were soon dubbed *dongfang disikou* ("oriental disco"). Through its tourist connections, Fanpai's troupe ultimately traveled as far as the United States and France to give performances, and many villagers were recruited into performance jobs throughout China. As more and more village youth left, fewer and fewer tourists were taken to Fanpai; for Guiyang tour guides, the *dongfang disikou* had apparently lost its charm. But the director did not regard this as an unfortunate turn of events for Fanpai. On the contrary, he regarded the *"lüyoure"* as a kind of jump-start phase for Fanpai's modernization. Now, he claimed, with so many youth earning money and learning about the outside world with their jobs, and with the villagers more accustomed to a commercial economy, the wheels of cultural development had been set in motion in Fanpai, and would continue to turn on their own. Tourism, he triumphantly declared, had broken the *Miaoling*'s grip on Fanpai. Tourism had wrapped the earth-bound Fanpai in a glistening cocoon, from which emerged a beautiful butterfly poised to take flight.

Not only was the misplaced desire for authenticity important in fueling the expansion of tourist villages in Qiandongnan – thereby spreading modernity and development – but also in helping to preserve and convey to the modern world what the QTB director thought of as the "true" customs and culture of the villagers, and, by extension, of China as distinct from the West. This was very important to him, for modernization would paradoxically have to be founded upon a celebration of and respect for traditional *minzu* culture. In this view he sought to link Qiandongnan's tourism development to the broader desire for an indigenous, organic modernity for China, a move we have already seen expressed among minority elites in their calls for *wenhua fazhan*. Echoing the culturalist trend in intellectual thought that pervaded China during the "culture fever" (*wenhua re*) of the mid- to late-1980s, he saw Qiandongnan's ethnic culture as a vital resource to be mined for a confident modern Chinese identity. The director regarded Qiandongnan as a vast storehouse of traditional resources, ready for exploitation, but also needing careful cultivation and conservation. There were limits, therefore, to what could be "staged" in tourist villages. He was increasingly convinced that the most authentic understanding of village culture came through spontaneous interaction and discovery. Traditional festivals, of course, provided attractive settings for this. But he felt festivals presented problems because they started too late in the day, were unpredictable, and were seeing traditional activities increasingly being replaced by modern ones, such as basketball tournaments. He therefore advocated the establishment of trekking in Qiandongnan, and of home-stays for tourists. He said this distinguished Qiandongnan from the newly established tourist villages of Guizhou's western circuit, which excelled in their ability to receive guests in a systematic and professional way, but which were also too "performance-oriented" and staged. He had come to believe that tourists should be free to go and mingle, discover, and learn about other people's lives, while villagers should be given the opportunity to learn from the tourists about the outside world.

Decentralization and localism within the tourism industry

An important theme emerging out of this discussion is not simply the issue of tourism-inspired integration, modernization, and *wenhua fazhan*, but the initiative and agency displayed by local officials, such as the QTB director, as well. Since the mid-1980s, local initiative has been enhanced by the continuing decentralization of the tourism industry and the subsequent increase in competition among local agencies (Oudiette 1990).

One of the driving forces of competition within the industry is the demand for foreign exchange. All international tour groups coming to China must be assigned a host agency, which charges a set fee in foreign exchange, for arranging transportation, lodging, and activities within China. During the early years of Chinese tourism, all tourist services were centralized at China Travel Service (CTS) in Beijing, of which CITS was the branch responsible for hosting international tourists. Each major city had its own CITS branch office, but these did not operate independently. Beginning in 1985, the system began to decentralize, with branch offices in popular cities such as Suzhou and Xi'an leading the way in demanding more autonomy. At the same time, local branches themselves began to fragment into several different independent agencies. By 1994, all local CITS branches operated on independent accounts, and a host of new agencies had been created. This process occurred rather late in Guizhou. It wasn't until 1993 that Guizhou CITS was divided up into three separate agencies, each of which was a financially independent entity. In addition, the CITS branches beyond Guiyang – in Kaili (Qiandongnan) and Anshun – became independent. Along with decentralization came a classification scheme determining those agencies that could be licensed to host international tourists and receive foreign exchange (Class A, or *zhutuansi*), those that could arrange travel for international arrivals but not host them (Class B, or *jietuansi*), and those that could only host domestic Chinese tourists (Class C).

With decentralization, it thus became possible for local agencies (that is, those given Class A status) to earn foreign exchange. Before this, all foreign exchange earnings had been retained by CTS in Beijing. While Beijing still plays the dominant role in hosting international tourists, earning the majority of their foreign exchange receipts, local agencies actively cultivate direct relationships with foreign agents in order to bypass Beijing and collect (as well as set) the host's fee themselves. Guizhou agencies, however, have had a difficult time in establishing such direct and profitable connections. In 1993, Guizhou's two Class A agencies, CITS Guiyang and Overseas Travel Company (OTC), hosted only 15.6 per cent and 5.6 per cent, respectively, of their total tourists received. Hosting groups can be extremely profitable. Agencies receiving tourists hosted by other agencies receive set payments to cover their costs and little more. But host agencies are free to set a price they feel the market will bear, or may choose to undercut other agencies with cheaper prices in order to increase business. The impetus to establish direct ties with foreign agents increased even more with the 1994 abolishment of Foreign Exchange Certificates (FEC). Whereas before 1994 the *jietuansi* would receive some FEC to cover its costs, after the abolishment of FEC it would only receive domestic currency (RMB), which can not be traded for foreign currency. By 1997, however, the share of international tourists hosted by Guizhou travel agencies had not increased. As indicated above, GTB officials stressed that they were loosing their meager market share to larger Yunnan agencies that were able to offer cheaper prices because of their higher volumes (Interview with GTB official, 4 November 1996).

The expectation that travel agents be fiscally independent, while at the same time officially restricted in their markets, created a rapid growth in "informal" deals among Class B and Class C agencies. In the early 1990s, Qiandongnan CITS was a Class B travel agency, officially prevented from acting as a *zhutuansi*. As the vice-manager at CITS Guiyang said, "Strictly speaking, Qiandongnan cannot host foreign tour groups. But, in fact, it sometimes happens by virtue of close ties forged between them and agencies in foreign countries. Many 'informal' arrangements can be made." Thus, the QTB director had travelled to Hong Kong, Singapore, Bangkok, and even Paris in order to promote Qiandongnan *minzu* culture and establish connections with foreign agencies. Increasing the profitability of Qiandongnan CITS was a major concern of his, since state investments for tourism development along the eastern circuit remained so limited, and since Guiyang agencies were increasingly unable to develop new tourist markets. Convinced he could no longer rely on the state, or even on Guiyang, the director began to stress developing his own connections with the major tourist center of Guilin, a half-day's drive from Qiandongnan's southern border. While developments in Guilin indicated that local tourism authorities had already instituted a significant ethnic tourism plan including an ethnic theme park and trips to nearby Yao and Dong villages, the QTB believed there was room for Qiandongnan as a more authentic hinterland to the "more developed" villages around Guilin. Indeed, by 1997 the villages of southern Qiandongnan were primarily seeing tourists arriving from Guilin, rather than Kaili or Guiyang. This represented an active alignment away from Guiyang and its increasing dominance of Guizhou tourism. By forging direct ties outside of the province, the QTB director believed that he could create more opportunities to "informally" host foreign groups coming to Guizhou. He claimed the Class B distinction didn't mean much anyway. "What's to stop me from receiving their fax, buying their tickets, and making their reservations? There is no reason why I can't do this." He pointed out that when a Guiyang-hosted tour group came through Qiandongnan, there were specific contracts governing how much local agencies could receive to cover their costs. "We make very little profit by doing this," he said. It would be better, he said, if he could tap into tourists in Guilin seeking to travel through Guizhou on their way to Yunnan or Sichuan.

Hosting more groups would generate more profits for Qiandongnan, which could then be reinvested into further tourism development. Guiyang agencies had already provided a clear illustration of the benefits of this arrangement. The early 1990s growth of ethnic tourist villages along the western circuit was in many ways enabled by Guiyang's dominance in retaining most of Guizhou's tourism revenues and foreign exchange. The two most visited of these western circuit villages – Heitu and Changlinggang – were set up with funds largely provided by OTC in Guiyang, which was looking for villages to develop along the route to Huangguoshu Falls and the Dragon Palace. In short, not only had decentralization generated increased interregional competition, but it became a factor in encouraging local agents to distinguish their "local color" from the competing region's. The QTB director thus saw western circuit villages as "too staged," and believed he could use his profits to promote a more authentic version of ethnic culture in Guizhou.

Waiting for butterflies? Wrapping villages in the cocoon of tourism

There was no master plan in Guizhou governing the use of tourism to commercially integrate village economies with regional, national, and international markets. While it seems apparent that central authorities in Beijing viewed tourism as a modernizing force from the start, local officials in Guizhou were rather slow to exploit tourism in ethnic villages for the purposes of economic development. Unlike some of the more recently established western circuit villages, such as Heitu and Changlinggang, the earliest sites in Guizhou's fledgling ethnic tourist industry were opened as "living museums" primarily for research, educational, and propaganda purposes. Instead of cultural development and modernization, the main goal in identifying and promoting these sites was more explicitly one of cultural preservation. The active preservation of historic and cultural sites became a state goal during the 1980s, and can be seen as part of the general cultural revival which followed in the wake of economic reform and official condemnation of the "leftist" excesses of the Cultural Revolution.

The administrative bodies most involved in preservation have been the Cultural Relics Division (*wenwuchu*) of the Ministry of Culture (*wenhuabu*), and, in minority regions, the *Minzu* Affairs Commission (*minwei*). Whereas the *minwei* is concerned with all aspects of *minzu* affairs and is the major source of funding in the promotion of ethnic tourism in Guizhou, the *wenwuchu* is more specifically responsible for selecting and preserving cultural artifacts. These include temples and pavilions, houses and guild halls, tombs and graves, bridges, city walls, and revolutionary sites. Like all administrative units in China, *wenwuchu* selections are governed by a spatial hierarchy. Protected relics may be selected as county-, province-, or state-level units, with the distinction determining where their funding will come from. In Guizhou there are some 1,200 recognized county-level sites, most of which receive virtually no funding for their maintenance and care. The 237 province-level and 9 state-level sites are only slightly better cared for.

As early as 1982, local *minwei* and *wenwuchu* officials in Guizhou began informally selecting for recognition entire villages that represented well-preserved examples of typical *minzu* architecture and customs. Although not an officially recognized *wenwuchu* category, *minwei* funds were made available for renovation and "beautification" at five "preserved cultural relic villages" (*wenwu baohu cunzhai*) during the mid-1980s. Qualifying for funds to maintain the traditional character of *minzu* villages obliged locals to abide by a code preventing new "modern" buildings from being built, or traditional buildings from being altered or modified. In such cases, state cultural preservation sought to fossilize certain aspects of *minzu* cultural tradition, drawing distinct boundaries around local customs, fixing them in time and space and insuring that they remain encased as exhibits for the modern metropolitan world to observe and appreciate. Two of these – Huashishao and Shitouzhai – were Bouyei villages near Huangguoshu Falls, and the other three – Langde (Miao), Gaozeng, and Jitang (both Dong) – were in Qiandongnan. In addition, other villages earned informal recognition as "open-air museums" by local administrative units, in particular Guizhou's *Minzu* Institute (*minzu xueyuan*), to serve as sites for research field trips and propaganda excursions for official visitors and journalists. Perhaps the most popular of these sites were the Miao village of Xijiang, on the slopes of Leigong Mountain in Qiandongnan, and Gaopo, high on a karst plateau south of Guiyang.

Of these early recognized villages, only Langde, largely through the efforts of the QTB, emerged as a major ethnic tourist village in the 1990s. The other Qiandongnan villages remained too far off the more well-travelled tourist routes. More conveniently located, the western circuit villages of Huashishao, Shitouzhai, and Gaopo all received significant numbers of visitors during the mid- to late-1980s, but then declined as newer, more "professional," sites were opened by Guiyang travel agencies such as OTC. Between 1990 and 1993, for example, international visitors to Gaopo declined from 352 to 66. When asked to explain this decline, the local officer in charge of tourism in Gaopo said that the village leadership had not, in the past, thought of tourism as an industry, and had not been encouraged to view their customs as a product that could enhance their incomes. He said that he felt it was simply part of his job to display Gaopo for outsiders who were interested in learning about Guizhou's *minzu* traditions. He never kept a record of how much money was made from these visitors. Besides, he said, few of them paid the village anyway; the money went to the leaders who brought the visitors. It wasn't until 1993 that he began to question whether this was a good arrangement, and even in 1994 was hesitant to challenge the paternalistic relationship between Gaopo and the Guiyang units hosting the village's visitors. Similar stories were told by leaders at Huashishao and Shitouzhai. Initially opened as "living museums," these villages were not encouraged to develop a systematic means of earning a tourist income; preservation, rather than commercial transformation, was the goal of their recognition. But as the "culture fever" of the 1980s began to dissipate in the more cynical and money-conscious post-Tiananmen era, development and modernization through commercialism came to be the dominant theme in Guizhou's ethnic village tourism. As mentioned above, Qiandongnan, under Wu Dehai and the QTB director, had emerged as the pioneer in promoting tourism as a force of cultural development. Along the western circuit, instead of using the existing set of "preserved" villages, new sites that better

matched the logistical needs of travel agencies were established for principally commercial reasons – both in terms of earning profits for the tourism
industry and encouraging the lucky inhabitants of these newly selected
villages to adopt a new "commercial conscience."

By 1993, Guizhou's most visited ethnic village sites were Langde in
Qiandongnan, and the western circuit villages of Heitu and Changlinggang in
Qingzhen municipality bordering Guiyang to the west (see Table 4.7).
According to a combination of village initiative and organization, and the
nature of the local tourism administration, different systems of economic
compensation were developed in these villages. Langde is one of the oldest
and most successful of Guizhou's tourist villages. Qiandongnan CITS
initially paid the village a reception fee (*jiedaifei*) of between RMB 40 and 50
per group visit. Success and village demands resulted in raising the *jiedaifei*
first to RMB 150 and then, by 1994, to 320. This money went to the village
collective; about 20 per cent was used to cover the costs of putting on receptions (for example, buying firecrackers and wine), while the rest was
portioned out to villagers who participated in welcoming and performing for
guests.[8] Actual revenues distributed to villagers in 1993 worked out to an
average of RMB 268 per household. According to villagers, this represented
roughly two-thirds of their household tourism income, the remainder coming
from the vigorous sale of souvenirs. Collective officers estimated an average
annual household income of RMB 2,000, meaning tourism accounted for
between forty and fifty per cent of household earnings in Langde.

Changlinggang and Heitu earned substantially more from tourism in
1993. Unlike Qiandongnan CITS's flat-rate *jiedaifei*, these villages received
fees directly proportional to the number of tourists in each group.[9] The
result was a much higher income from reception fees, and less need among
villagers to sell souvenirs aggressively, as was the case with their counterparts in Langde. Guides at OTC recognized this as a positive result of their
strategy to present more "professional" village sites for the larger numbers of
western circuit tourists. Unlike Langde, tourists in Heitu and Changlinggang
were rarely pestered by crafts hawkers.

By 1994 Guizhou had at least 15 villages earning their primary income
directly from receiving tourists. Tourism income had, in turn, helped alter
village economic patterns. As evidenced by the production and marketing of
village crafts, tourism had certainly engendered a "commercial consciousness" among villagers. One village near Anshun, in fact, had itself
established contracts with hotels and shops as far away as Kunming and
Guilin to sell its crafts. The commodification of village crafts had also
resulted in a gendered division of labor. Selling souvenirs in these villages
was almost exclusively regarded as "woman's work," as was their manufacture. Often village women became local distributors more than producers.
They would visit nearby villages buying old textiles, bamboo instruments,
masks, and silver ornaments to be resold in their own tourist villages for a
profit. New cash income, from tourism and from village youth who had been

Table 4.7 Comparison of three ethnic tourist villages in Guizhou, 1993

	Western circuit		Eastern circuit
	Changlinggang	*Heitu*	*Langde*
Total tourists received	4,063	1,343	3,945
Foreign	2,324	801	530
Domestic	1,739	542	3,415
Fees paid to village (RMB¥)	68,090	22,878	43,103
Fees per tourist (RMB¥)	16.76	17.03	10.67
Fees per village household (RMB¥)[a]	1,745.89	571.95	399.10
Fees per villager (RMB¥)[a]	362.18	103.99	81.33
Net peasant income in county (RMB¥ per capita, 1990)	528	528	209

Sources: *Guizhou Xianqing* (1992); Qingzhen *minwei*, village secretaries.

Note:

[a] Actual figures will vary since not all the fees are distributed to households and not all households participate in tourist receptions. Some housholds will earn substantially more (up to 150% of the basic per household fees) by selling handicraft souvenirs to tourists.

hired to work in China's metropolitan ethnic tourist industry, meant that some households could capitalize on other money-making schemes, such as raising pigs. Most of it, however, was spent on luxuries previously out of reach to villagers: televisions, tape-players, bicycles, and other conspicuous symbols of modernity. In Langde, the local director of tourism bought himself a pool table, which quickly became the most popular place in the village for young men to socialize.

While villagers regarded these as positive developments, they also recognized that tourism had brought increased vulnerability and dependence as it linked their economies more directly with the broader world. As villagers grew more conscious of their role in the larger tourism industry, they began to seek a larger share of travel agency revenues, as well as more independence in managing their tourist activities and developments. In 1994, Langde could expect to receive between 10 and 20 per cent of the fees paid by foreign tourists to the travel agency. Changlinggang would receive between 5 and 15 per cent.[10] Village leaders in Langde had repeatedly requested that the QTB increase the *jiedaifei* to at least RMB 500, but were wary of pushing their demands too far for fear that the QTB would retaliate by taking tourists to other villages. Referring to the QTB, one villager exclaimed in anger, "*Tamen yidian dou buzhichi women! Tamen shi zhuaqian le! Diao de hen! Hua de hen!*" ("They don't support us one bit; they're greedy!

Very tricky, very cunning!"). The QTB, he fumed, was very clever in preventing the village from getting the money it deserved. Instead, the villagers were scolded for not doing a good enough job. Indeed, members of the QTB said that Langde's performances had definitely declined in quality. The QTB director, as indicated above, fully expected this as the consequences of a modernizing culture. According to the QTB and villagers alike, this was because too many talented village youth had left for jobs in Guiyang, Guangzhou, Shenzhen, and Beijing. The younger generation did not know the songs and dances as well. But for villagers, the key problem was not declining talent, but lack of control over their own "resources." Village leaders realized that it would be best if Langde could somehow bypass the QTB altogether, but felt powerless to really do this. "They won't let us do it," one told me.

> They say that if we receive tourists without going through them we'll be punished, and will have to pay a fine. They do this so they can charge tourists more money and keep it for themselves. They even bring independent tourists themselves to come and photograph the village, have some of our women dress up in traditional clothes. We don't get one cent from it! The tourism bureau keeps all the money.

Langde's collective members had also come up with their own plans for enhancing the village's tourism development, but were dependent on the QTB and the *minwei* for funding. The *jiedaifei* was enough to keep village households interested in participating in tourist receptions, but it was not enough for the collective to accumulate its own capital for investment in future projects. Petitions to the QTB and *minwei* were met with repeated rejection. The QTB, for its part, was not willing to relinquish its hold on coordinating the region's ethnic tourism development. In a particularly ironic twist, QTB leaders feared that putting tourism development in the hands of villagers would compromise the village's "authenticity" as a site of *minzu* traditions. Langde's proposals of building a parking lot, and requiring tourists to buy a ticket (*menpiao*) to enter the village, would, according to the QTB director, turn Langde into little more than another ethnic theme park. "Qiandongnan is not a theme park," he said, "*it's the real thing.*" Thus, not only had tourism tied Langde's economic fortunes to a broader world over which it had no control, but it also wrapped and stifled local initiatives in the tight cocoon of modern ideas about authenticity and tradition. Interestingly, Langde's plans to emulate the theme park version of Chinese touristic modernity was derived from the same force of cultural development praised by the QTB itself: the migration of village youths to more developed regions. Langde's village youth who had spent time working in the ethnic theme parks of Shenzhen, Beijing, and other metropolitan centers returned with the goal of appropriating the success of attractions such as China Folk Culture Villages for their own village. That the QTB saw this as a threat reveals the ironic contradictions of modernity's misplaced search for authenticity.

Langde's dependence on paternalistic higher authorities was an experience shared by Guizhou's other recognized ethnic tourist villages. In all cases, tourism had brought with it a taste of potential wealth accompanied by increased dependency. The most extreme examples of this were found in Huashishao and Shitouzhai, both Bouyei villages within the Huangguoshu Falls state-level scenic area. As two of Guizhou's earliest recognized "preserved relics," both were promoted as repositories of "typical" (*dianxing*) Bouyei culture and were featured throughout the province's tourist literature, in television documentaries, and even as settings for nationally distributed films. Both villages, however, had been unable to take control of their own incipient commodification and realize a consistent income from tourism, despite their proximity to Guizhou's most popular tourist site and single most lucrative tourist resource: Huangguoshu Falls (the falls was visited by 650,000 tourists in 1993 alone and collected revenues of RMB 7.2 million).

For Huashishao, the problem was a combination of poor rocky land (which made subsistence itself difficult), land alienation, and authoritarian control of tourism development on the part of the Huangguoshu Tourism Administration (HTA). Between 1981 and 1984, 38 per cent of Huashishao's land holdings were appropriated by the HTA for tourism development (in the form of restaurants, shops, parking lots, and roads). Of the remainder, 60 per cent was rocky slope-land classified in the lowest of China's three productivity categories. This forced the village to rely on Huangguoshu tourists to generate enough income to survive on. Villagers earned money from tourists by selling fruit and sugarcane (for which it devoted 15 per cent of its slope-land), by village women hawking embroidery and batik textiles, and by some households operating restaurants and souvenir shops at nearby parking lots. These households rented spaces for RMB 600 per year on land they previously farmed. According to the village head, about 20 per cent of household incomes came from sales to tourists.

If tourism was meant to be an impetus for the commercialization of the village economy, the HTA's appropriation of village land had certainly stimulated an understanding among villagers of the importance of a cash income. Yet by seeking to maintain control over all aspects of tourism development at Huangguoshu, the HTA had also prevented Huashishao from realizing commercialism's full potential. The villagers themselves wanted to "open" Huashishao, and start charging tourists money for a stroll through the village's scenery, quaint stone houses, and ancient banyan trees. They wanted to build a new path directly from the parking lot and put up signs advertising the village. But despite the fact that villagers were not asking the HTA for any funding, their requests were consistently denied. The HTA, it seems, had its own plans to eventually open the village as an on-demand cultural spectacle. HTA officials tended to see Huashishao's lack of economic benefits from tourism as the village's own problem. "It's because they're farmers," one official said. "They don't understand how to develop tourism, don't understand how it should be managed. If they open their village by themselves it will be a mess, tourists won't be happy, and it makes the whole place look bad. They'll have to wait for us to do it for them." When asked what the HTA had in mind for Huashishao's development, he became very excited. "Look," he said, "have you been to Shenzhen? The China Folk Cultures Park? You go there, you buy a ticket, you go in and you get to see all sorts of activities, song and dance performances, at any time. When we open Huashishao, it'll be like Shenzhen. They want to build a new path? When we open it, you won't even have to walk there; we'll build a road. It will be very convenient." And would the villagers collect the fees? "Well," he replied, "it will be our investment, so we should collect the income. But the village will get a cut." His suggestion of a "cut" was on the order of 10 per cent. Although villagers themselves imagined a theme-park future for Huashishao, they did so with the hope of being the gatekeepers themselves.

But, the approach of the HTA also represented something of a paradox, claiming, in effect, that tourism in Huashishao could not be promoted because not enough tourists went there. "Look what happened to their museum," the officer said, implying the villagers' ignorance in running a tourist business. In 1986, the prefectural cultural bureau invested RMB 50,000 to improve the village path, build benches around the great banyan tree, and build a traditional-style "museum" in the village. The plan, at the time, was for tourist income to pay for filling the museum with displays. Since Huashishao was never given the opportunity to accumulate a tourist income, the building fell into disrepair; the roof fell in and the insides were a mess. With an initial investment which paid for the building and nothing else, it never became a museum and village children took to trashing the place. It subsequently became a symbolic argument for the HTA in preventing Huashishao from initiating its own tourism developments.

A similar situation existed somewhat further away in Shitouzhai, Guizhou's so-called "home of batik" (*laran zhi xiang*). While Shitouzhai's subsistence situation was not as desperate, it too had no regular means of accumulating a tourist income other than the informal sale of crafts to tourists who came to enjoy the scenery as a side trip on the way to the falls (Shitouzhai can be reached by road). The village leaders decided they should build their own batik factory, and even attracted a couple of potential investors from Guangdong. But the investors pulled out, and the village was refused a loan. Nor would the local *minwei* offer them a grant. The village head thought that this was because the government had no money, and the conditions in Shitouzhai were "just too poor for a factory." It would make more sense, he admitted, for it to be built in the nearby county town (which, in fact, already had a batik factory; probably the main reason Shitouzhai's requests were denied). Indeed, with all the batik being produced in the

Anshun region, it is arguable whether a factory at Shitouzhai would have been a good idea. But it is ironic that the "home of batik" could not scrape together the capital to build its own batik factory. Instead, it remained Shitouzhai's role to be the quaint, hand-made handicraft village seen in postcards.

While the pressures brought to bear by tourism created an increased sense of vulnerability among villagers, the changes were lauded by provincial leaders as examples of tourism's ability to help villagers cast off their poverty and "develop culturally." The best example of this can be found in Longtan, a mixed Han and Bouyei village located at Guizhou's second most popular tourist attraction, the Dragon Palace (visited in 1993 by 314,572 tourists who spent over RMB 3.2 million on tickets to take a boat ride through the cave). Along with the Miao village of Heitu, Longtan was featured in numerous official accounts of the successes of tourism development in Guizhou, most of which noted its rise from a net peasant per capita income (*chunshouru*) of RMB 114 in 1982 to over 700 in 1992, village savings of over RMB 1 million, the employment of over 30 village youth in the tourism industry (mostly as boatmen), and the establishment of some 25 specialized households and over 100 individual enterprises (*getihu*).[11]

But along with the rising incomes has come a less equal distribution and access to wealth in Longtan. In 1994 Longtan's villagers farmed 53 per cent of the land they tilled in 1984. Grain production per capita had decreased by 38 per cent. Farmers were compensated for state-appropriated land, but these one-time payments in fact went to the village collective which, in turn, distributed a portion to the affected households and kept the rest for development projects.[12] Because of the state's policy preventing the redistribution of land for 20 to 30 years following decollectivization, households that lost land had no choice but to find alternative sources of income. Land holding thus became less equal, and all the villagers expressed resentment about the "no-change" (*bu bian*) policy – meant to encourage long-term investment in agriculture – which prevented those who had lost their plots from acquiring new land. Selling souvenirs was no substitute for farming, they said, and only a few households in the village were actually becoming rich. Although official accounts made much of village youth employment at the scenic area, Longtan villagers in fact made up only 15 per cent of the Longgong Tourism Administration's employees in 1994. Despite its success on paper, Longtan only marginally benefited from the area's tourism development. While the village has enjoyed RMB 300,000 in *minwei* investments, this was a small figure compared to the RMB 12 million that was pumped into developing the area's scenery. Few tourists actually stayed in Longtan, since it was only an hour from Anshun, and if they did stay, the two hotels were both run by state units that kept the revenues for themselves. The village itself could only earn money by collecting parking lot and toilet fees from tourists, and by selling food and souvenirs. The village head said that they had tried running a hotel but had to shut it down because of competition from the higher quality state hotels.

False modern triumphant?

While it may be ironic that villagers themselves advocated a theme park style of tourism development, this fact remains a testimony to the powers of representation inherent in touristic modernity. It is representation, more than anything else, that conditions the political economy of tourism in Guizhou. Lack of control on the part of villagers – whether it be in realizing tourist income, directing future plans, or developing crafts production – was primarily the result of their encounter with the ideological power of misplaced authenticity. The ideal of authenticity, as a repair for modernity's fragmentations, was deployed by both the state and capital in Guizhou, with the result being increased disempowerment for those expected to play the part of the folk. For the state, the project of *wenhua fazhan* sought to standardize *minzu* culture into an exploitable resource for modernization, thus necessitating the production, preservation, and representation of "authentic" folk heritage that contributed to nation building regardless of the actual needs of the villagers concerned. Thus, local state officials drew on the discourse of cultural development itself in order to alienate villagers from the tourism development decision-making process. Similarly, within the commercial tourism and crafts industries, the authentic representation of villages and crafts came to be recognized as a key avenue of accumulation. These representations appealed to the misplaced needs of metropolitan tourists, rather than villagers seeking to define for themselves a modern future.

Yet, there remains a subtext to this chapter's discussion in that, although the development of tourism in Guizhou is certainly one infused with the objectifying and alienating logic so characteristic of a state/capital dominated modernization project, touristic modernity nevertheless needs to be viewed as an open-ended and contradictory experience. The desire on the part of villagers to appropriate for themselves a theme park version of development is the most obvious evidence of this. Chinese modernity is not just another project of standardized rationality implemented on a national scale, as has been the common depiction of modernity in the West. It is also recognized as an unfinished, crisis-ridden, and open-ended project requiring distinction from, rather than simple emulation of, the colonizing West. Thus, modern projects of tourism development and *wenhua fazhan* are fueled by representations of tradition and authenticity as much as progress and development. The promoters of change in rural Guizhou, such as tourism officials and local *minzu* leaders, display considerable ambivalence about what has been lost in the face of modern socialist transformation, and regard modernization as an important opportunity to develop local comparative advantage, as well as to contribute to China's alternative modernity.

Indeed, as this chapter reveals, ethnic tourism itself began in Guizhou under the auspices of cultural preservation rather than a more straightforward project of economic development. The contradictions inherent in the modernity's misplaced search for authenticity have been shown in this chapter to increase the subordination and vulnerability of rural producers in Guizhou's tourism industry. Yet it should also be obvious that these contradictions necessarily leave a space open to local cultural appropriation, and that local villagers themselves act as significant players in claiming a sense of agency over the forces of change which swirl around them. The case studies in the following chapter are devoted to illustrating this cultural appropriation on the part of villagers in Guizhou's ethnic tourist sites.

5 Reclaiming the tourist landscape

Struggles for an authentic subjectivity in Guizhou

INTRODUCTION

We sat with our backs against the warm stone walls of the Caiguan village head's house, facing the winter sun of central Guizhou's plateau country, each of us dazed from too much mid-day rice wine. I was, nonetheless, determined to complete the interview before sleep overtook us, or before another altercation at the gambling table inside the house – where the wine still flowed freely – interrupted us. I kept pressing the village head and *dixi* troupe leader with questions about income from tourists and economic benefits for villagers, trying to assess the extent of Caiguan's cocoonment in tourism's colonial web. My informants were very unsure about income and such things. They fished around for figures which might make me happy, but none of the numbers they came up with made sense. We grew increasingly exasperated with each other. The troupe leader, finally, was fed up. "Look," he blurted out, "what do we care about economic benefits? We're just farmers, and China is a communist country, isn't it? We don't do this to make money. *It's our culture!* We do it to promote China."

His tone was defensive and proud, as if to say, "Your questions don't make sense to us, because this is not a business, it's our cultural contribution to China's national development, and our own way of life." Indeed, my informants had both been to Paris, representing and promoting China at a prestigious international arts festival. They had been praised, wondered at, treated to three weeks in the City of Light, for no reason beyond their art and "ancient culture." More than being incomprehensible, my questions were probably insulting to them. Yes, they were paid when a bus load of tourists from Taiwan, Singapore, or Switzerland showed up demanding entertainment, but there was a different, more important reality enveloping *dixi*. It was, for my informants, the heart of Caiguan's identity; it marked Caiguan as a distinct place, and symbolized a landscape that villagers claimed as their own. Yet tourism actually had much to do with this ennobling of *dixi* as the crystal of Caiguan's place-identity. Villagers did not elect it on their own. They had help, for example, from the Paris festival's director who proclaimed *dixi* a "living fossil" worthy of preservation, from

Anshun officials who arranged funding for the troupe, a new performance square, and a replica fifteenth-century garrison turret, and from the tourists themselves who came from so far away just to see farmers dance around with masks and costumes on.

The gap between my questions about income – my prying for signs of exploitation – and my informants' insistence that the issue was not economic but cultural, reflects a crucial tension at the heart of Guizhou's touristic pursuit of modernity. Indeed, it is the same tension that lies at the very heart of the experience of modernity in China. It is the same tension that defines the paradox of modernity, between creativity and freedom on the one hand and rationality and standardization on the other. As the previous chapter illustrated, tourism in Guizhou is driven by the standardizing and often alienating logic of commercialism and nationalist integration. Indeed, that tourism is capable of spurring new, more "commercially developed" culture, leads us to think that control over the means of cultural production has been taken away from those groups who serve as the primary tourist attraction in Guizhou, and upon whose commodified exoticism the province hopes to build a new economy: *lüyou tatai, jingmao changxi*, economic trade performing on a stage built by tourism. But the villagers who have become objects of the tourist gaze are also participants in a dynamic process of local cultural change that is on-going, and which, rather than being snuffed out by the onerous forces of market integration, actively engages these broader forces. The broader forces marshaled by the tourism experience presents villagers with tremendous opportunities for articulating in new ways the importance of place, tradition, and identity. These local cultural features are not so much "revived" by tourism as they are reconstructed and reinvented according to the new conditions brought to bear by a broader political-economic and cultural order.

One interpretation of the Caiguan troupe leader's outburst might simply point out that this is precisely the kind of cultural development the state wants in its nation-building project, and that his attitude represents less a claim for Caiguan's identity than a capitulation to the power of the state in dictating the kind of modernity envisioned by its subjects. Given the discussion in the previous chapter, this could simply be another confirmation of the false modern triumphant in Guizhou. But to leave it at that not only condemns villagers to subjugation, but denies them the very possibility of an authentic modernity. Indeed, it denies modernity its only truly liberating potential: the possibility of defining one's own subjectivity. The paradox of modernity, however, is that this potential emancipation is brought about only through an experience of profound social dislocation and fragmentation. It is not by turning away from this experience and seeking refuge in tradition and custom, but by embracing it, that a truly authentic modern subjectivity may be attempted. What the Caiguan troupe leader was articulating was not simply a capitulation to a state/capital-dominated touristic modernity, but also the only hope for claiming subjectivity over that modernity by appropriating and redefining it. Understanding the geography underlying this move helps reveal, I believe, its significance. For at the heart of his claim was the importance of place as the terrain upon which an authentic identity could be realized.

Villagers at tourist sites in Guizhou, such as Caiguan, participate in a web of linkages that fundamentally condition their place-identity. It is the same web woven by the state's projects of nationalist integration, modernization, and commercial economic development, the same web that, as Jean Michaud argues, draws peripheral villagers into increasingly vulnerable and subjugated relations with the nation and the world. But to see in it only these political-economic dimensions is to miss the point my Caiguan informants insisted on making: that the web is woven with culturalist ideologies, and that villagers themselves help weave it no less than state elites pursuing *wenhua fazhan* or the tourism industry's metropolitan agents pursuing capital's accumulating logic. This chapter seeks to establish this claim by examining four tourist sites in Qiandongnan, exploring the broader web conditioning place-identity in each, and focusing on the perspectives of particular villagers who maintain access to the various linkages which form the web. Before exploring the cases in detail, however, I will attempt to sketch out a brief model of the web: the broader geography of identity in Guizhou's ethnic tourist villages.

The cocoon is a web: mapping identity in Guizhou's ethnic tourist villages

Figure 5.1 offers a schematic version of the broader web of linkages conditioning the construction of place-identity in Guizhou's ethnic tourist villages. Three broad forces have been identified in an effort to separate the linkages into distinct spheres of activity: the tourism industry, state ethnic and cultural policy, and economic development policies of commercialization and "market socialism." Together, they make up the most important components of the state and capital in relation to the lives of villagers. Most of these linkages have already been discussed in the previous chapter, but this model represents an effort to map them in a systematic fashion. Whereas the previous chapter concentrated on how relations of subjugation and vulnerability – fueled by the ideology of misplaced authenticity – flow along these linkages, the goal of this chapter is to illustrate how they also carry the ideas and meanings that villagers appropriate for their own narratives of modernity and place-based identity. It is also important to note that the arrows are not simply one-way. The model rejects the conceptualization of these broader forces simply "impacting" village communities in a one-way fashion. Rather, villagers actively "move about" the web, and thus display their own agency as participants in what is a very dynamic and ever-changing system of connections.

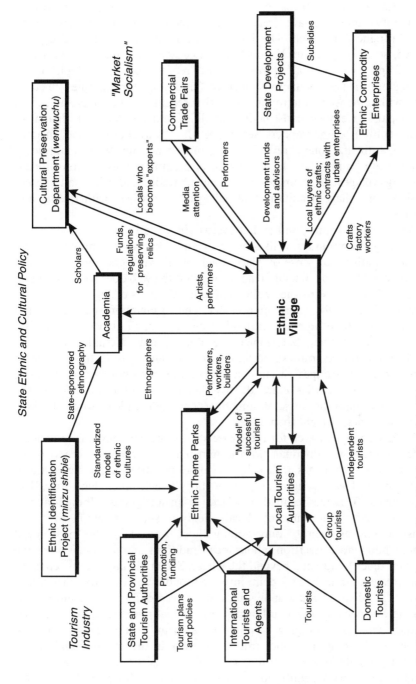

Figure 5.1 The field of place identity in Guizhou tourist villages

An important point, conceptually, is that for the villagers the web represents the overall process of modernization. Dominant narratives of modernity – those we have already encountered in previous chapters – circulate throughout the web. The ideas of local tradition and local culture, indeed, sense of place itself, constitute discourses that are not confined to the village itself, but are produced and reproduced by multiple actors throughout the web. Numerous ideals of "tradition," for example, are circulated within the web – metropolitan tourists seeking the uncanny and exotic, theme park developers constructing simplified and standardized versions of *minzu* culture, ethnographers separating out "authentic" *minzu* customs from "inauthentic" ones, crafts factory managers deciding which embroidery patterns are "authentic," local tourism and cultural preservation officials selecting villages as examples of "typical" traditional life – all present versions of village tradition that villagers themselves gather, sift, and process.

Another important point is that tourist villages do not necessarily represent a single community of like-minded people sharing a common memory of local tradition or sense of place. Each of the villagers who gather, sift, and process the ideas that circulate throughout the web does so according to the specific linkages that he or she maintains. Villagers of high social status, such as village heads, cadres, and elders, tend to maintain such access to a greater extent than others. Men tend to be more connected to the tourism industry than women, but women are more linked to ethnic commodity production. Village youth often have their own links due to their travels in song and dance troupes, or stints as workers in metropolitan theme parks, hotels, or crafts factories. Place-identity, therefore, is not a simple fact of the community, but a discourse of sometimes contending ideas, some of which carry more social weight than others.

In conducting research for these case studies, my strategy was to concentrate on the few individuals who dominated each village's access to the broader field of linkages, rather than trying to produce a complete portrayal of the many local versions of place-identity which might have existed in each village. This has resulted, I believe, in an intriguing – though admittedly limited – account of local identity, since it emphasizes the constructions of identity only among those who claim the most social capital, and whose assertions about local traditions and meanings carry the most currency within and beyond the village. Such individuals thus represent their village's primary entry point into the broader web of forces that condition local identity. Such individuals were responsible, for example, for dealing with local tourism authorities, organizing tourist reception activities in their villages, arranging with particular families for village youth to participate in song and dance troupes or work in theme parks and hotels, enforcing regulations concerning cultural preservation, and maintaining good relations with county government officials. Such dealings gave these individuals many opportunities to not only express who they were and what they represented, but also to hear what others thought they represented as traditional *minzu* villagers. In turn, they became the dominant voice in articulating a new modern subjectivity for villagers that appropriated the representations of modernity, tradition, and authenticity that circulated throughout the web.

This method of focusing on village "gatekeepers" is also important in linking these case studies to the conception of place explored in Chapter 2. That chapter suggested that place be conceived, paradoxically, as a terrain expressing the radical displacements of modernity itself, rather than the imagined opposite of those displacements. The village gatekeepers introduced in the following sections are active agents in articulating place-identity in these terms. They do so by reworking the dominant narratives of misplaced authenticity circulated throughout the web, and claiming these for themselves. In doing so, they display the kind of ambivalent creativity one would expect of people trying to balance the need to maintain an authentic sense of place with a desire to benefit from the broader forces of change. Such an approach implicitly challenges the notion of place as a cohesive community. Rather, as a process of change reflecting modernity's inherent tensions, place must be conceived in terms of social stratifications and contested meanings. The villagers discussed below provide an entry point into understanding their places in these terms.

It should be noted, however, that the following case studies are not meant to convey a comprehensive account of the various "contested meanings" that no doubt are present within each site. The absence of diverse village voices, beyond those of the influential "gatekeepers," will have to be remedied in future studies. The method employed here, though, did not seek to establish a complete accounting of subjectivities within each site. Rather, the purpose was to focus on the most apparent examples of process and linkage in the articulation of local subjectivity in relation to broader political-economic processes. The emphasis, therefore, is on verticle linkages throughout the web's implicit hierarchy, rather than horizontal connections among the villagers themselves.

LANGDE: HOME OF REBELS AND THE "TRUE MIAO"

Unlike much of the rest of Guizhou, Qiandongnan is not a karst landscape of eroded limestone mounds, but rather a rumpled mass of folded clastic mountains incised by deep river valleys. The mountains, which reach their peak at the 2,178 meter summit of Leigong Mountain, are locally known as the *Miaoling*, and form the watershed dividing the drainages of the Changjiang and Zhujiang river systems. Thus straddling the frontier between China's two most important traditional transportation networks, Leigong Mountain was the geographical peak of the *Miaojiang*'s remoteness. The tattered remains of dozens of rebel armies made Leigong's hidden valleys and plateaus their final retreat, and the villages around the mountain's slopes remained some of the least accessible in Guizhou. Lying deep in the valley of the Bala River, draining the northwest slopes of Leigong, Upper Langde was actually one of the region's more easily reached villages. Like others who lived in the valleys, tilling narrow flood plain fields, the people of Upper Langde were more likely than their slope-dwelling neighbors to meet the forces of taxation and conscription as imperial authority – implementing *gai tu gui liu* – gradually seeped up the rivers into the *Miaojiang* during the eighteenth and nineteenth centuries.

Contact with imperial authority brought household registration for Langde's villagers and a gradual erosion of local rights and privileges, along with an increasing number of fees and hidden taxes. By 1855, such administrative abuses had grown severe, primarily due to financial and military pressures caused by the Taiping Rebellion. When a garrison official from Danjiang (now Leishan county town) was killed by a villager from Langde, it sparked a local revolt that quickly spread throughout the region, linking up with other spontaneous uprisings to coalesce under the rebel leadership of Zhang Xiumei. Within months most of the region's "encirclement garrisons" had been captured. Some were held for as many as 18 years before the Qing government finally mustered the resources to retake them in 1872. The Langde villager who helped initiate what many in the region still think of as the Miao's proudest moment, was named Chen Shalue, and as a leader in the *Xiantong* rebellion, he adopted the name Yang Daliu. It was the PRC's canonization of Miao rebels, such as Yang, as proto-Bolsheviks, that initially aimed the spotlight of outside officials and scholars at Langde. Rebellion, and the ideological representation of rebellion, initiated Langde's entry into a broader geography of place-identity.

Official interest in turning Yang Daliu's legacy into a propaganda device and his home village into a tourist attraction led to Langde's eventual selection as one of Qiandongnan's first ethnic tourist villages. It was recognized by prefectural and provincial *wenwuchu* authorities as a *lutian bowuguan* ("open-air museum") in 1985. In 1995, 4,669 tourists visited Langde, earning villagers over RMB 76,000 in fees and probably twice that amount in souvenirs (Leishan Tourism Bureau 1996). Langde has been featured in nationally televised programs on minority customs, and has become Guizhou's most well-known tourist village. The NTA's internationally distributed poster advertising China Ethnic Tourism Year (*Zhongguo Minzu Fengqing Lüyounian*) in 1995, featured the Langde Party Secretary's daughter dressed in festival ornaments with the village as a backdrop behind her. The vast majority of Langde's visitors come in groups whose visits have been arranged ahead of time. They are treated to an elaborate welcoming ceremony of singing, along with *mangtong* and *lusheng* music. As they make their way up a rice-paddy-lined path to the village's main gate, tourists are offered bowl upon bowl of rice wine by women bedecked in festival costumes and ornamented in silver headdresses. Having braved this intoxicating gauntlet, tourists make their way to the village's *tongguchang* ("bronze-drum square"), where they are treated to a song and dance performance and, to the dismay of many, more wine. The square's flagstones have been arranged to represent two regal horses, the symbol of the NTA, illustrating Langde's nationally recognized status in China's tourism industry. The villagers' performance ends with a circle dance in which the guests are encouraged to join as a sign of unity and friendship. The circle quickly dissolves, however, as village women rush to grab their baskets of souvenirs which they aggressively thrust upon the visitors as they make their way through the village. Within minutes, most of the tourists have retreated to the safety of their tour van, soon to make their escape with the basket-laden village women looking on. Most visits last about two hours.

In 1994, Upper Langde had a population of 530 in 108 registered households. Village collective officers estimated an average RMB 2,000 household income, with up to a half of this generated by tourism revenues. Their houses crowding a hillside along the clear-flowing Wangfeng River, two kilometers upstream from where it empties into the Bala, the villagers tilled 250 *mu* of scattered paddies; they also claimed about 700 *mu* of dry slope and forest land. Many villagers enjoyed telling the story of how Langde was once one of the poorest villages in the valley. Poor leadership and carelessness resulted in so many fires that it earned the name of "Pumpkin Village" because its houses spewed orange flames so often and resembled pumpkins. Between 1950 and 1965 Langde burned to the ground on no fewer than three occasions. But by 1980, the story goes, things began looking up for Langde, in part due to the village party secretary's enthusiasm for the reform-era's ideology of modernization. In 1983 Langde became the first village in the area to adopt Green Revolution techniques (*kexue zhongtian*) in rice production. Within a couple years grain output had increased substantially, far beyond other villages in the area. Soon, scholars and tourists were arriving to see this new-found museum of Miao tradition which had – as local officials liked to put it – adapted so well to the progressive and rational ideals of science and technology.

Yet, along with Langde's "going to the world," represented by the embracing of Green Revolution techniques, villagers maintained a strong sense of remoteness and hardship defined by the mountains that rose around them in all directions, cutting off the sky, locking them in a fastness once called home by rebel armies. On the first day of my stay in Langde, my host agreed to take me to the upper fields to see some of the surrounding countryside. That he did this only after much pleading on my part said something itself about village sensibilities. He was convinced that I could not hike up a mountain since, being from a "developed country," I could only be familiar with flat land. For him, wealth and development were directly related to topography: mountains meant poverty, backwardness, and isolation. When we reached a high point along the trail, he waved his arm at the view, as if to prove his point. "See?" he said with satisfaction, "nothing but mountains." Indeed, as far as one could see, there was nothing but ridge upon ridge of mountains. Terraces, interrupted by hillside villages, cascaded into the deep valley of the Bala River. Through the haze I could barely make out the long summit ridge of Leigong Mountain, now marked by radio towers. Below, Langde's land was scattered about the hillsides on either side of the Wangfeng River. Some of the plots were at least an hour's hike from the village. My host's land was located in four different sites, including a paddy in front of his house, and one high on the opposite side of the river, an hour's climb away.

Gazing down at the landscape, my immediate impression of quiet and solitude soon gave way to the sounds of farmers driving their beasts back and forth, plowing up the paddy mud in their plots. The hillside was alive with work. Langde as a lived-place was much more than the charming village of tightly packed houses and cobbled lanes visited by tourists. I thought of a comment made in Raymond Williams's *Border Country* (1960) of how visitors to Matthew's home valley seldom appreciated it as a *working* landscape. In seeing only the village, Langde's tourists perhaps lost a sense of the extensiveness of the place, defined not by the quaint village, but by the land, the fields and paths, the views, the time it takes to get from home to plot, and the long hours spent digging, tilling, and weeding far from home. For the village children, the place was also defined by the lower village, along the county road, where they went every day to attend school. Indeed, the villagers' sense of Langde as a place went well beyond just this. As with the old mountain paths before it – paths taken to Leishan or Kaili on market and festival days – the county road, built in 1957, linked Langde to a much broader urban world of officials, scholars, and tourists. Langde as a place cannot be conceived without considering the surrounding land from which people eke out a living, nor can it be simply limited to this. The place-identities constructed by villagers were built not only by the paths to their fields, but by the road that led to Leishan, Kaili, Guiyang, and on to Beijing, Hong Kong, and the world.

The linkages that flowed along this road carried ideas and values which helped shape the ways villagers in Langde expressed who they were to themselves and to their visitors. I have already mentioned the role of Yang Daliu's legacy in creating a name for the village among Marxist historians and propagandists promoting the "Miao Rebellion" as an example, like the Taiping, of class-conscious revolt against feudal control over the means of production. With state funding, Langde made a museum out of what they called "Yang Daliu's former residence." They named the bridge that crosses the Wangfeng River in front of the village "Yang Daliu Bridge." My host spoke of the rebellious legacy of Yang Daliu with a great sense of pride. He would preface his comments with a deferential disclaimer: "It's not very nice to say (*buhaoting de hua*), but in the past, the Miao fought against the Han." Then he would launch into engrossing and exaggerated tales of Yang's exploits with great zeal. "Yang took Guiyang," he would tell me, getting carried away with himself, "and Zunyi! He marched *all the way to the Yellow River* before having to retreat back to Leigong Mountain."

State encouragement had helped enshrine Yang Daliu's story as a kernel of Langde's identity, giving villagers a historical figure that affirmed their autonomous identity as a (rebellious) Miao village while at the same time maintaining legitimation and alignment with the Chinese state. A broader network of scholars and officials was thus actively engaged in helping Langde villagers articulate their place-identity. The same network was also involved in the construction of Langde's other museum, on Miao customs and rituals. The photographs and text which made up this museum's displays were all created by outside intellectuals, and yet were regarded by villagers as a repository of all that defined them as Miao, and marked their place as distinctive. In telling the village's story for tourists, outside ethnographers and cadres who worked on the museum were telling a story to the villagers themselves, one which was reinforced every time the museum was opened to visitors.

As one of Guizhou's earliest preserved villages and ethnic tourist sites, Langde was frequently visited by officials who made efforts to impress upon villagers the importance of their identity as keepers of a specific, state-selected tradition. During my stay, there were two instances of this happening. The first was a visit by officials from the NTA on an inspection tour of Qiandongnan. Accompanying them were provincial, prefectural, and county tourism and government officials, most of whom had already visited Langde on many occasions. During the performance arranged for this delegation, the former head of the NTA talked to me about the importance of Langde. "You see the way they wear their hair up like that, with flowers and little silver leaves?" he asked, pointing to the dancing girls in front of us. "That was China's hair style during the Tang Dynasty. The Miao have preserved it. That's the kind of thing that is so interesting about these people, and such a curiosity to tourists. In the countries where capitalism developed early, all the cultural diversity has been lost already; everyone has been assimilated. That's why tourists from those countries like coming here." He pointed to the green ridge to the east of the village, where Yang Daliu had once built fortifications against Han armies. "Nature is still pure here," he said. "It should be preserved for tourists; all this should be preserved, the customs, the traditions of the minority nationalities." He then stood and made a speech to the villagers, expressing just these sentiments, impressing upon them the importance of keeping their environment pristine and preserving their traditions. Preservation, he told them, would be their path to prosperity.

The other official delegation was a group from the State Cultural Bureau, accompanied by prefectural and provincial cultural bureau officials. Their visit was regarded as an opportunity for Qiandongnan's tourism authorities to promote their plan of preserving certain villages for scholarly and touristic posterity. Two days before the delegation's arrival, the head of the prefectural cultural bureau arrived to give villagers instructions regarding the type of reception these special visitors should receive. The group included a number of Miao from Hunan and Guizhou who had become officials in central and provincial cultural bureaus. After the welcoming ceremony and performance, the delegation was given a feast of local specialties; they even spent the night in Langde's guest house. All of Langde's collective officers, along with several village women proffering wine and song, attended the feast. As the evening wore on, jugs of wine having been liberally passed around, the urban Miao visitors made numerous requests for old songs from the women, praising their vocal skills profusely. As one of the visitors told me, "Only in a village like this can you hear the traditional Miao songs; in the cities they've been changed by modern styles." He made sure the villagers understood this point in the numerous toasts he offered his hosts. For him and the other Miao visitors, coming to Langde seemed to affirm his sense of identity as Miao; likewise, it helped reinforce the perception among the villagers that outsiders place a great deal of value on Langde's role as a living museum and keeper of tradition.

During my stay, artists and intellectuals made up a significant portion of Langde's independent visitors. Some would stay for several days, either in the village guest house or a private household, which was easily arranged through the village collective. One visitor, an artist from Shaanxi, made numerous sketches, many of which he gave to the villagers. Like the others who came, he was welcomed by villagers as someone who was interested enough in Miao culture to "endure hardships" of living in the village for a few days. Although these visitors would pay a nominal fee to their hosts or to the collective, their arrival was much more important simply for legitimizing the village as a site worthy of investigation.

Aside from artists and intellectuals, there was another type of visitor to Langde who influenced the way villagers constructed their sense of place. Entrepreneurs, developers, county officials, and other village heads often used Langde as a model for their own ethnic tourism projects. Usually this simply meant coming and watching an arranged tourist reception. Others came with specific projects in mind. For example, one visitor was from a village just outside the county town, along a section of the Bala River which had been dammed for hydroelectric purposes. The army was turning the reservoir into a fishing and recreation area, and wanted to promote ethnic tourist activities in the village. The man had come to Langde to learn about building village gates and stone cobbled lanes, since his village had none of these. The army was paying him to make his village "look more like a traditional Miao village, more like Langde." There was also a visitor from Beijing, who had in fact stayed in Langde for over six months during 1993. He divided his time between Langde, Kaili, and Beijing, working on various enterprise schemes, mostly having to do with the sale of Qiandongnan wood products to associates in Beijing. He told me he had originally come to learn about Miao traditions, but he became convinced that he could help the people of Langde take control of their own modernization. He was trying to convince villagers that they could earn money by selling the wood they gather for fuel instead of burning it. He also helped one household set up a business raising pigs. His most significant contribution, however, was convincing the villagers they needed to build a souvenir shop. This, he told them, would increase their revenues by making tourists feel more comfortable about buying things. "Modern people," he told them, "like to buy their things in a shop, not from a woman carrying a basket."[1]

Langde's linkages to an outside world that valued the idea of Miao tradition were also maintained by the 45 youth who had left the village for performance, service, or crafts jobs throughout China. One village girl had even been part of a province-wide troupe that attended the 1989 "Four Nations Arts Festival" in Spokane, Washington. In the village museum were dozens of enlarged color photographs from the festival, many of them featuring Langde's sole representative. Although she was still working in Guiyang, her household had become famous in the village for having "gone to America." Many of the youth who remained in Langde regarded this as the ultimate goal in their prospective careers as Miao performers. Several of the villagers most involved in performances during my stay had at one time been employed in performance troupes in Kaili, Guiyang, Shenzhen, and Beijing. They had finished their contracts and returned to the village to marry, take over the family plots, and take a leading role in Langde's continuing tourism activities. Of all the villagers I spoke with, they were some of the most articulate in expressing the importance of preserving village traditions for future economic development.

This last comment suggests that it would be difficult to generalize a single "community identity" conditioned by the linkages discussed in the examples above. Some villagers were more articulate than others in discussing what all this outside attention meant for Langde's identity. As mentioned earlier, these were generally the ones who maintained closer access to the broader web of linkages. During my stay in Langde, I concentrated on the gate-keepers who were the most connected of the villagers, in order to learn how their connections translated into ideas about place-identity in Langde. One was Langde's traditional shaman healer and elected director of tourism activities. The other was the village party secretary. Like everyone in the village, they were both named Chen.

Secretary Chen credited himself for bringing green revolution technology to Langde, for making it the "most scientific village in the area." He also claimed to be the village's earliest supporter of tourism development. Early visits to Langde by Japanese tourists, he told me, convinced him that tourism could have a positive effect on the village. "They were so interested in our Miao lifestyle and customs, *and* they bought things; they paid us money." For Secretary Chen, tourism was primarily a business and an avenue toward rational progress and modernization. When asked about the importance of tourism for Langde, he responded by citing the fact that over

60 per cent of the households now had televisions, all as a result of money they earned from tourism. What could be a better symbol of scientific modernity than a television? The ideals of progress and modernization clearly swayed Secretary Chen. He believed that innovation and change were the keys to Langde's future success as a tourist site. It was important, he told me, for the village to keep changing its reception program, for its tourist services to be innovative, for songs and dances to be updated and changed. "We don't have any culture (*wenhua*) here, but we're developing," he said. Thus, tourism was important as a business, but Secretary Chen believed it also carried with it the benefits of modern *wenhua fazhan*, of change, scientific progress, and innovation. More than anything, tourism helped define Langde as a modern, progressive place. Secretary Chen had adopted wholeheartedly the state ideology of cultural development.

Shaman Chen, on the other hand, saw in tourism not so much the ideals of progress, innovation, and change, but a reinforcement of tradition and a distinct Miao identity in contradistinction to the modern outsiders who visited the village. This perspective made sense given his role as village *jishi*, the healer and master of rituals. Before tourism, Shaman Chen was already recognized as Langde's "keeper of tradition." It was he who knew the most about Yang Daliu, the locations of his crumbling fortifications, the stories of his heroism. When outside scholars and propagandists sought to canonize Yang's memory, it was Shaman Chen who became recognized as the "local expert." It made sense, then, that the village would elect him to organize tourist receptions. He had already gained the respect of important outsiders, and he knew all the rituals, all the songs and dances which could be adapted for tourist performances. It was perhaps largely due to Shaman Chen that tourism had so easily become a way of life in Langde, for he already played an important role in keeping the social fabric of the village stitched together; his direction of tourism was perhaps simply regarded as a natural extension of this role.[2]

Shaman Chen thought that the most positive aspect of the village's tourism business was that it brought the world to Langde. It made him very happy, he said over and over again, to see all these foreign people coming to see his village and learn about the Miao. In the past, he said, this remote, mountain-locked part of China had no chance to be visited by outsiders. "We used to be afraid of foreigners," he said. "Now we shake hands!" In the past, Miao people in these parts neither spoke Chinese, nor knew anything about the outside world. "Now, because of tourism, we're learning more and more." They were also discovering other Miao from Japan and America, which also made him very happy. He told me about Miao tourists coming from America, people who could not speak Chinese, but could speak Miao and English. This was a great thing for him to see: Miao who had not bothered to learn Chinese but could speak fluent English. He was happy for the opportunities to see "developed" Miao people, and to show them the old ways that they forgot. Tourism, of course, was a positive development simply because it allowed them to perform dances, and supported their festivals. "Back in the Cultural Revolution, we were not allowed to do this," he said. "We still did it, you know, but it had to be kept secret, so few people came to the festivals; everyone was afraid. These days, thousands come to the festivals; some even come from foreign countries!"

Unlike Secretary Chen, Shaman Chen felt that the key to Langde's success as a tourist site was in preserving the traditional forms and styles valued by the "developed" world. This, however, was important to Shaman Chen not simply for securing tourism revenues, but more importantly for Langde's identity as a true Miao village. He had gained a special perspective on this by spending a year in Beijing in 1992, accompanying six village youth in performances sponsored by the Central Nationalities Fair. The year in China's capital convinced him of two things, he told me. He did not like living in a "modern place," and he learned that "developed people" are willing to pay a great deal of money to see Miao traditions. Despite not liking Beijing, he said he considered spending another year, but the villagers requested that he return since they felt that Langde's reception program had suffered in his absence. Shaman Chen returned to Langde with a seemingly clearer picture of the village's role in the broader tourism field. As a result, he was often upset with what he felt to be a lack of support on the part of Qiandongnan's tourism authorities:

I've been to Beijing. I know how much they charge tourists for things there. A show at the arena (*tiyuguan*) costs 20 *yuan* per person. 20 *yuan*! You go to a holiday village there and pay 10, 15 *yuan* just to get in the gate; that doesn't even include food, activities, lodging. Just the ticket. But whenever we ask the tourism bureau for more money, they just criticize us, curse us. They keep telling us, "*Nimen gaode buhao! Nimen gaode buhao!*" ("You're not doing it well!"). They never give us any money. All they do is curse us. We do everything ourselves, build our paths, make our buildings look nice, put in our own water system; we're going to build our own parking lot this summer, all with no help from them. They don't help us at all.[3] People come here, they're always very happy, very satisfied. We wear our old clothes for them, show them our old Miao traditions and customs, show them how we live; our clothes are all hand made, the embroidery is all traditional. But all the tourism bureau says is, "*Nimen gaode buhao! Nimen gaode buhao!*" If we raise the price, they threaten us, say they'll take the tourists to other villages. But we're not afraid. Langde is Guizhou's most famous village. Everyone else is happy with us, the province, the county; only the prefecture [QTB] scolds us. We've built these traditional houses, made our village look nice. The province was happy with us, made us a *wenwucun*, a *wenmingcun*, a *lutian bowuguan* ("relic village, civilized village, open-air museum"). So the tourism bureau decided to start bringing visitors, and began telling us how we weren't doing anything right. But we don't listen any more. All through its history, since the time of the rebellion, since Yang Daliu, this village has been very unified; we're all Chens. We're not afraid of the tourism bureau.

What Shaman Chen could not understand, what made him so exasperated, was the QTB's apparent lack of satisfaction. Over the years, he had learned that all Langde had to do was "be Miao," or "be old-fashioned," and the tourists would be happy. How could anything more be expected of them?

We wear our traditional Miao clothes, the embroidery, the long robes. We don't wear Han clothes when receiving guests. All the clothes are hand made, hand dyed; we grow the cotton ourselves, spin the thread. We build these traditional houses. How can they not be happy with that? All the foreigners who come are happy, they like our clothing very much. I know. They tell me. We play the *lusheng*; the Han play the *erhu*. We use different rhythms and sounds with our drumming than the Han, different dances. It's our tradition; we've always been different from the Han. How can they say, "*Nimen gaode buhao*"?

It is clear that the QTB's lack of satisfaction was more an issue of opposing not Miao traditions *per se*, but future development plans that had been initiated by village collective officers, plans the QTB thought compromised Langde's authenticity. But for Shaman Chen, this was a meaningless distinction. More important, though, is the way Shaman Chen appropriated the dominant narratives of tradition, preservation, and even commercialism in articulating his complaints about Langde's dependent relationship with the QTB. For him, those ideas had already become key components of Langde's identity, ideas that could be deployed as Langde staked its own claims on Guizhou's incipient touristic modernity.

Shaman Chen's attitude contrasted sharply with that expressed by Secretary Chen, to the point where the former was convinced that nearly all the money for the village's development came from the village itself. Secretary Chen was more willing to acknowledge the role of outside assistance and support. Shaman Chen saw the village more on its own than Secretary Chen, who was more formally linked to the hierarchy of political control due to his role as party secretary. For Shaman Chen, it seemed much more fundamentally a question of the essence of Miao identity. Simply being an authentic Miao village gave Langde the right to demand more money from the QTB. At one point, I asked Shaman Chen why Langde didn't have a big "*lusheng* meeting" around Spring Festival, like so many other villages in the area, such as Zhouxi? He responded by going straight to the heart of the matter. "We're the *true* Miao (*Women zhen Miao*)," he said. "We don't celebrate Spring Festival or any other Han festival. Zhouxi has its *lusheng* meeting during Spring Festival because they're not true Miao;

they've been Hanified (*Hanhuale*). Here, we only celebrate true Miao festivals, such as *chixinjie, popojie, Miaonian*, and *jizujie*, the grandest of them all."

Each in his own way, the secretary and the shaman had made tourism a fundamental component of what they felt to be Langde's identity. Although Secretary Chen's attitude more closely aligned with that of the state, while Shaman Chen used state categories and rhetoric against the state itself, the point is less one of finding instances of resistance than of appropriation, of how village leaders formulate a sense of place from a much broader set of discourses. Both of them developed a sense of place for Langde based on the dominant narratives made available to them, and in order to assert their village's own modernity in its own terms. While they were the village's chief representatives to the outside institutions of the tourism industry, the state, and academia, their visions of tourism's role in Langde's place-identity were not necessarily shared by all the villagers. Whereas they both shared an attitude regarding Langde's tourism which was basically "the busier the better," other villagers, especially those who did most of the dancing and reception work, seemed to regard tourism as more of a job than anything. At times, it was a job that many wished was not so demanding.

My stay in Langde coincided with the spring transplanting season. With Langde's paddy fields spread out up and down the surrounding mountain slopes, this was a time-consuming and tiresome task. The pressure to get young rice sprouts transferred to the upper fields at the right time was bad enough without having to put on receptions for bus-loads of tourists. During my stay, Langde averaged nearly one reception per day. On days when groups were booked for both morning and afternoon receptions, villagers rose earlier than usual to get a few hours of work in before returning for the morning reception. Then they would return to the fields until the afternoon group arrived. In the evening they would be in the fields again, usually until just after dark. As one woman told me, while offering wine from an ox horn to some Japanese tourists, "I'm tired! This is too much! I don't like being so busy." Even Shaman Chen was forced to admit that he was getting exhausted, and that his work arranging tourist activities was forcing him to deny his services as *jishi* to neighboring villages. He was the only traditional healer in the area, and his services were in great demand, but insuring the success of Langde's tourism had become his chief priority. The demands of tourism also resulted in nobody showing up for one of Langde's three annual hill-climbing festivals, which occurred during my stay. Villagers told me that they were too far behind on their transplanting to take a day off for the festival.

Whether or not villagers viewed their participation in tourist activities as "just a job," it had no doubt become a fundamental part of the way they thought of themselves and the place in which they lived. I have tried to draw attention to the fact that the village leadership's articulations of Langde's place-identity, conditioned significantly by their links to broader tourism, state, and academic institutions, were not necessarily representative of the village as a whole. However, their position as leaders gave them license to make what they felt were claims their fellow villagers would support. This was especially true in Shaman Chen's case, who was elected by villagers to direct their tourism activities and represent them to the QTB and other outside tourism authorities. It was clear that he interpreted this role as one empowering him to stake claims about Langde as an authentic Miao village, a home of the "true" Miao, as opposed to so many other villages which had become "Hanified." This claim of being the most authentic representative of a particular state-sanctioned *minzu* category is a theme we will see developed more explicitly in the following two cases.

GAOZENG AND ZHAOXING: PLACE AND THE COMMERCE OF AUTHENTICITY

Forty per cent of Qiandongnan's population is made up of those who are officially classified as Miao. Another 35 per cent are Dong. The *Miaoling* tends to divide the region into two different cultural landscapes. The Miao are mostly concentrated in the upper elevations of the mountains and throughout the valleys draining northward into the Qingshui River. South of the divide, the topography loses elevation quickly and deep gorges give way to the broad valleys of the Duliu River. This region, considerably lower and warmer than the rest of Qiandongnan, is dominated by the Dong, a *minzu* group belonging to the Tai language family (the Miao belong to the Sino-Tibetan family). Historically favoring settled valley rice cultivation, the Dong in this region were perhaps less at odds with encroaching Chinese culture as the Han established outposts along the Duliu. Perhaps because of their similar cultural economies, and because of the area's greater accessibility via the broad placid Duliu, the Dong were less subject to repressive Chinese efforts to assimilate "uncooked" tribespeople like the Miao. Whereas the Miao to the north were divided into a great diversity of socio-economic and cultural groups with little interconnection between them, the Dong of the Duliu basin maintained a tight social organization based on a representative system of traditional law and order known as the *kuan*, and political administrative units of territory known as *dong*. Chinese references to *dong* regions date to the Yuan Dynasty, and it is perhaps from this term that the Chinese began to refer to these people as "Dong" (they refer to themselves with a variety of names, most of which sound something like "*gaeml*").

The Duliu River basin is the most sparsely populated region in Guizhou. It also contains the least amount of cultivated land, only 4.3 per cent.[4] But the vast majority of this land is irrigated paddy and grain yields tend to be some of the highest in the province. The region is still relatively well forested and timber is the primary industry. Large log rafts can still be seen floating down the Duliu to be processed at mills downstream in Guangxi. Though land in the subtropical valleys can be quite productive, it is extremely scarce and significant capital investments are required to put it into production. All three counties in the region are officially classified as "impoverished counties" (*pinkunxian*), qualifying them for state assistance. This comes mostly in the form of low-interest loans or grants for land engineering projects or diversification schemes, such as planting fruit orchards on marginal slopeland.

The two case studies in this region – Gaozeng and Zhaoxing – are both Dong villages situated in the Duliu basin, not far from the Guangxi border. Both are recognized by provincial and county officials as important centers of Dong culture; each has been a *dong* seat for hundreds of years. They also serve as administrative village seats (*xiang*) representing the lowest level of state bureaucracy in the rural administrative hierarchy. Unlike Langde, they thus maintain a formalized link to the governments in their respective counties. Historically, both were relatively prosperous agricultural communities, enjoying a subtropical climate, abundant rain, and convenient transportation nearby along the Duliu. Today, however, they are regarded as two of the least accessible tourist sites in the province. Once the railroad and major highways (which pass through the northern part of Qiandongnan only) rendered river transport relatively obsolete, Qiandongnan's Miao regions became, ironically, the most accessible in the prefecture. As will be discussed below, this reversed the historical situation and enabled Guizhou's tourism industry to construct an image of these Dong villages as the most remote, mysterious, and authentic in the province. As we will also see, this distinction has not been lost on the villagers themselves as they begin to adjust their senses of place in light of their new situation.

The QTB's interest in developing a viable tourist link to Guilin (in neighboring Guangxi province) had much to do with the promotion of Gaozeng and Zhaoxing as tourist sites. They would be the tourist's first taste of the traditional *minzu* villages that the QTB was trying to promote as authentic counterparts to the more developed and "Hanified" villages in Guangxi. Moreover, the villages had already been selected as "preserved cultural relics" by the *wenwuchu*. That this became a source of some tension between the prefectural *wenwuchu* and the tourism bureau reflected the broader conflict between the state and capital in realizing a particular vision of modernity. The head of the prefectural cultural bureau said he resented how the QTB always took advantage of *wenwuchu* "discoveries," capitalizing on *minwei* and *wenwuchu* investments, and reaping all the benefits. He didn't appreciate that the *wenwuchu*'s efforts to protect cultural relics for future posterity were sometimes undermined by the tourism industry. "The needs of tourism development," he said, "often puts the *wenwuchu* at odds with the tourism bureau over what changes should be allowed to occur in a protected village."

Villagers occupied an ambiguous space between these broader contending forces of state preservation of nationalistic folklore and commercial tourism development. The state has established a framework in which both market-oriented economic development and the preservation of symbolic cultural diversity are encouraged. Indeed, they are supposed to harmoniously reinforce one another in the project of *wenhua fazhan*. Because the idea of ethnic authenticity based on cultural distance from the Han has been sanctioned and institutionalized by the state's ethnic identification (*minzu shibie*) project, agencies like the *wenwuchu*, metropolitan tour guides, and many tourists themselves, are likely to see a contradiction between commercialism and the preservation of ethnic cultural authenticity. As the case of Langde makes clear, villagers were not unaware of the need to meet the expectations of their visitors, but the idea of a contradiction between authenticity and economic development was generally incomprehensible to them. What was important to them was achieving modernity, and this they would do with whatever tools – material and rhetorical – that were made available to them. Villagers thus tended to promote their own commercial tourism development quite vigorously. In Langde, this was seen in the collective's proposals for a parking lot, souvenir shop, and a new path leading to the village, with several viewing pavilions. These schemes have been resisted by both the QTB and the *wenwuchu* (which see the plans as compromising the village's authenticity). As documented above, this had led to a considerable degree of frustration for Shaman Chen.

If the villagers attempt to initiate their own commercial tourism ventures they run into conflicts with the *wenwuchu* over the protected status of their village. The loss of protected status, however, can dramatically alter a village's tourism prospects. This is not simply because of the lost access to state investments which help develop the village's tourist resources, but more importantly because in the eyes of the broader industry – the county and prefectural tourism authorities and the tourist agencies in Guiyang – the village has also lost its authenticity as a true *minzu* village.

The cases of Gaozeng and Zhaoxing represent two different versions of how villagers occupy and appropriate this space between state-sanctioned expectations of cultural authenticity and the state-encouraged development of a commercially viable tourist industry. The two villages have had contrasting experiences: one lost its status as a "protected relic" and has subsequently sought to reclaim its authenticity, while the other has effectively exploited its status as an authentic village by maintaining key linkages with the broader tourism industry. Both, however, display similarities in that villagers are clearly articulating local tradition with extra-local processes as they reproduce their senses of place-identity.

Gaozeng: defending the authenticity of place

Gaozeng is a large village situated at the upper end of a narrow plain of good paddy land extending south to the Duliu River and bordered by mountains which rise 800 meters above the valley floor. Formerly a *dong*, the seat of Gaozeng commune, and now an administrative *xiang*, the village has a history of at least 600 years. The village itself had a 1993 population of 1,825, but is also the administrative and economic center for an area that includes 38 natural villages and some 14,000 people, about 90 per cent of which are Dong. Incomes are derived almost entirely from rice cultivation and timber. Villagers throughout the region produce household wood products and sell them in the county town, only 8 kilometers from Gaozeng. The village actually consists of three clan-based natural villages, each with its own drum tower. Historically, drum towers served as gathering sites for village defense, clan meetings, and festival events. Because of its collection of three towers, hundreds of *diaojiaolou* houses, and a picturesque setting, Gaozeng was designated a "preserved cultural relic" (*wenwu baohu cunzhai*) in 1982, the first village in Qiandongnan to be granted such status. In 1984 Gaozeng received a grant from the *minwei* to renovate the drum towers, repair houses and bridges, and otherwise "beautify" the village. Although the Duliu basin wasn't officially open to foreign tourists until 1993, a few tour groups were being granted special permission to go there as early as 1982. By 1988 the village was seeing a regular flow of about 20 tour groups a year, most of them Japanese.

Gaozeng's early rise in Qiandongnan's ethnic tourist industry was partly due to the efforts of Wang Shengxian, who grew up in the village and became a Dong scholar at the Qiandongnan Nationalities Research Institute in Kaili. During the 1980s he wrote eight books on various aspects of Dong culture, and through his positions in different prefectural propaganda and research organs promoted Gaozeng as an example of ancient Dong culture and civilization. On Wang's initiative, groups of *minzu* scholars began to visit the village. Because of Wang's influence, many of Gaozeng's youth received jobs in performance troupes in Guiyang and other parts of China. Many of the tour groups who came during the 1980s were personally led by Wang and stayed in his family's house, which subsequently became the wealthiest in the village.

Gaozeng's prospects as a center of Dong ethnic tourism were dramatically altered in 1988, however, when a fire destroyed two-thirds of the village and two of the three drum towers. With the fire, Gaozeng's privileged position in the hierarchy of state recognition and cultural preservation was lost. As the director of the prefectural cultural bureau said, "That village is now ruined (*pohuaile*). The villagers may rebuild the drum towers, but they will no longer be authentic cultural relics (*zhenshi wenwu*)." Though the towers were protected relics, once they were destroyed the state saw no point in providing funds to rebuild them since they would have no value as traditional antiques. Although the county canceled Gaozeng's taxes and grain quotas, no relief funds were distributed to help rebuild the village; the drum towers themselves were regarded as a clan responsibility. But wood had grown scarce and the old-growth logs necessary to build new towers would have to be purchased from a neighboring village. By 1996, the money raised was only enough to rebuild one of the towers.

It was somewhat difficult for villagers to raise money, however, because tourism quickly dwindled to three or four groups per year. The QTB and travel agencies such as CITS and OTC no longer promoted the village, and attention began to focus, instead, on nearby Zhaoxing. Meanwhile, the Gaozeng's advocate, Wang Shengxian, had given up on scholarship to become an entrepreneur, investing in local timber and mining schemes. Wang became less concerned with promoting the village as an authentic spectacle and started funding development projects, such as a new school, to get the people on their feet again. Within the tourism industry, it became common to refer to Gaozeng as *pohuaile*. Along with this, the village earned the label of being too "Hanified": it was no longer an authentic Dong village. At the county government, the official in charge of tourism said that if one really wanted to learn about the "true Dong," he shouldn't stay at Gaozeng but would be better off at the more remote village of Xiaohuang, tucked up in the mountains three hours by foot from Gaozeng. Guides in Kaili and Guiyang said the same thing. Besides the absence of two drum towers, the loss of authenticity was visible, to outsiders, in the fact that many of the houses were rebuilt with brick instead of wood; wood was scarce and expensive, and brick had the advantage of being fireproof. Wang Shengxian's family, for their part, built a new cement house, the largest in the village. But the loss of authenticity was especially visible in the new Rural Credit Association building, a large incongruous white cement structure built just outside the village gate. Such a building would never have been permitted if the village had remained a *wenwu baohu cunzhai*.

County officials and leaders in the *xiang* government (most of whom were not actually from Gaozeng but had been assigned there) claimed that such changes were inevitable in Gaozeng, which was, after all, only 8 kilometers from the county town. "Gaozeng is becoming modern," the *xiang* secretary said. He referred to the fact that billiards and smoking cigarettes had replaced music and singing as the main activities of village youth. "Most of the village girls no longer learn how to weave; they want to buy modern clothes in town." But he also claimed that the villagers liked the new credit association building, that it symbolized modernity and progress for them. If tourists wanted to see the authentic Dong, he said, they could hire a jeep to take them to Xiaohuang, but it was important and desirable for Gaozeng to become a developed, modern village. According to him, such a development necessarily entailed "Hanification."

Among other villagers, however, there was a great deal of ambivalence about Gaozeng's loss of protected status and consequent "modernization." Many villagers could not understand why tourists would want to go to Xiaohuang instead of Gaozeng. "Those people," one said, referring to Xiaohuang, "they're not clean (*tamen bujiang weisheng*), they're uncivilized; Gaozeng is over six hundred years old! Why would tourists want to go there instead of here?" Most were acutely aware that after the fire Gaozeng had lost something in the eyes of the *guojia*, the state. The villagers referred to Gaozeng not just as a protected cultural relic (*wenwu baohu*), but also a civilized village (*wenming cunzhai*), and this status, enjoyed during the 1980s, had become an important aspect of their place-identity, and "modernity" was a poor substitute for the loss of that status. "This place is becoming just like the county town," one woman said, "the new buildings, the restaurants, the pool tables; these aren't Dong." In 1984, the county had erected two tablets in the village, declaring it a *wenming baohu cunzhai* (civilized protected village). These were destroyed in the fire and, where the drum towers had once stood, villagers defiantly made their own signs with little white rocks set in the hard ground: *wenming gulao cun*, "ancient civilized village."

For villagers, the loss of identity as a civilized place was symbolically found not only in the absence of the two drum towers, but also in the fact that the village had never rebuilt its splendid covered bridge, which had actually burned down in 1911. Rebuilding these and initiating a new era of tourism was thus seen as the key to reclaiming their status as a civilized place in the eyes of the *guojia* and outside visitors. The campaign to rebuild the drum towers and bridge was being spearheaded by the village elders' association (*laonian xiehui*). As the leader of the association said, "It is now up to the villagers themselves to promote Gaozeng." In 1993, the association petitioned the provincial government for RMB 200,000 to fund a tourism development project that included rebuilding the bridge, rebuilding the road into the village, and developing a scenic waterfall nearby. As the petition made clear, rebuilding the bridge was the "most pressing need" of the villagers: "The hearts of the masses of Gaozeng all want to restore the covered bridge to their lives, to preserve their heritage." Gaozeng, the petition went on to claim, "has been the cultural hearth of the Dong people since ancient times." Its early status as a "village of ancient civilization" was a recognition of this tradition. The association has also been the primary fundraiser for the drum towers, and has organized singing and dancing lessons for village youth so that they will be prepared when tour groups return. To the association's leader, the 1988 fire initiated Gaozeng's decline. After the fire, village youth started playing pool, people no longer built traditional houses, and didn't care what the village looked like. The new credit association building, a *yangfangzi* ("Western building"), was a "disgrace" to the village. The association's petition thus proposed re-routeing the road into the village, and building a whole new gate, so that tourists wouldn't have to see the *yangfangzi* as they entered Gaozeng.

The activities of the elders' association represented an effort by villagers to reclaim the ingredient of authenticity that had previously been such an important aspect of their place-identity. Their sense of place had been conditioned by the broader processes of state cultural policy and commercial tourism, processes in which the ideal of (misplaced) authenticity was highly valued. When Gaozeng's links to those processes was jeopardized by the fire, villagers began taking initiatives to reclaim it. The issue was not tourist dollars, for these had never been significant, but identity as a civilized place, a traditional hearth of Dong culture. Modernity was regarded as a threat only after the village's secure place-identity was lost in the fire, and tourism, which didn't even exist officially until 1993, was already regarded as the necessary medium with which to re-establish Gaozeng's place as a "village of ancient civilization." With drum towers and covered bridges promoted as the "crystals of the Dong people" (Wang 1989) – valuable capital in China's new cultural economy – tourism development became the clearest means by which Gaozeng could reclaim its cultural heritage and express its identity to the outside world. To further illustrate the importance of those links to the commerce of authenticity afforded by tourism, we turn to the next case, the village of Zhaoxing.

Zhaoxing: "the heart of Dong culture"

Like Gaozeng, Zhaoxing has long been an established political and cultural center. Now a *xiang* seat administering a region of 29 natural villages and just over 10,000 people, it occupies a position identical to Gaozeng in China's rural administrative hierarchy. But with a population of over 3,500 (1993) the village of Zhaoxing proper is nearly twice the size of Gaozeng, and boasts not three clans but twelve. It is recognized by county and prefectural officials as the "largest and most ancient" Dong village in China. The village itself sits at the bottom of a deep three-sided basin, with the surrounding ridges rising nearly 1,000 meters above, giving the place an enclosed and hidden quality. It has five drum towers (some of the smaller clans share a drum tower) and five covered bridges (one, washed away in a flood in July 1994, was recently rebuilt). The drum towers were all destroyed during the Cultural Revolution, but since being rebuilt they have been given county-level protected status. Three hundred meters up the mountainside in the village of Jitang – a half-hour's walk from Zhaoxing (still within Zhaoxing *xiang*) – there are another three drum towers, each at least 150 years old. Two of these were given provincial-level protected status in 1982, and by 1985 all of Jitang was recognized as a protected village – an "open-air museum" (*lutian bowuguan*).

Although during the 1980s Zhaoxing was not promoted as a place of authentic culture to the same extent as Gaozeng, it nevertheless developed important connections with the broader commercial industry of ethnic tourism. Because of the density of drum towers and covered bridges in the area, peasants from Zhaoxing were recruited to build replica drum towers for attracting tourists in the county town and in Kaili. They were also recruited to build entire replica villages (complete with drum towers, waterwheels, covered bridges and *diaojiaolou* houses) in the ethnic theme parks in Shenzhen, Guilin, and Beijing. Perhaps more than any other factor, the theme park industry helped secure Zhaoxing's eventual status as a place of authentic Dong tradition. The local builders who traveled to these large cosmopolitan cities gained status as the bearers of an ancient architectural art. They learned that tourists would pay as much as 150 *yuan* per ticket to see their structures. They returned to Zhaoxing with the knowledge that their village was the "most representative" (*zuiyou daibiaoxingde*) of all the Dong villages.

Song and dance troupes recruited to put on performances at the Dong villages in these ethnic theme parks were sent to Zhaoxing to learn "authentic" Dong songs and dances. While I stayed in Zhaoxing, such a troupe from Guilin spent three weeks there. The members of the troupe, all Dong, were mostly from villages closer to Guilin, in Guangxi. Each brought the distinctive clothing and styles of his or her native village. But they had come to Zhaoxing to learn the kinds of songs and dances performed in this, the most authentic of Dong villages. When I asked villagers why they thought Zhaoxing had become so well known for its cultural traditions, most simply answered that it was "the most cultured and civilized" (*zui you wenhuade, zui you wenmingde*) of the Dong villages. Several times I was told the story of a professor from Beijing who came to study the Dong. He had first gone to Guangxi, because "Guangxi is more developed and they're better at propaganda (*xuanchuan*) than Guizhou." When he was about to return to Beijing it was suggested that he visit Zhaoxing. He did, and was so overcome that he exclaimed to the leader of the local cultural bureau, "The Dong of Zhaoxing are the true Dong; the Dong of Guangxi are fake (*jiade*)."

Through a combination of broader industry and local initiatives, the pattern of tourism development in Zhaoxing has been clearly driven by this ideal of misplaced authenticity. In 1994 the NTA sent an investigative team to Qiandongnan to formulate a new comprehensive tourism development plan (the same team which visited Langde during my stay). Although the team visited Gaozeng, its tour of the Duliu basin emphasized Zhaoxing as the comprehensive site of Dong ethnic tourism. Plans called for nearby Jitang to be maintained as an "open-air museum," where tourists could be treated to an authentic Dong experience. The jeep trail to the village was to be improved, a reception house in traditional style would be built, and home-stays for tourists arranged. In Zhaoxing proper, the several *yangfangzi* which had already been built (the bank, theater, school, and old guesthouse) were to be given facelifts to resemble the traditional architectural style of the *diaojiaolou*. While it was recognized that Zhaoxing itself had become more "modern" and somewhat "Hanified," state funds would help restore a traditional look to the place, while the nearby village of Jitang would be promoted as the "authentic Dong village." The head of the Zhaoxing cultural bureau told me that locals also planned to promote other villages in the area, for tourists who were "looking for an even more authentic village." These villages required several hours of hiking to reach. "Those who want to see the *real* Dong," he said, "will be willing to endure some hardship." He also expressed his confidence that if the state failed to supply the funding for the plan, locals would pay for it somehow, since "everyone recognizes how important this is for Zhaoxing's future."

Tourism, though just getting underway in Zhaoxing, was already encouraging locals to express a sense of place that incorporated this ideal of misplaced authenticity – an ideal conditioned by Zhaoxing's links to the broader commercial tourism and culture industries. One result of this was a popular confidence that the Dong of Qiandongnan were more civilized than the Miao. Zhaoxing villagers, like those in Langde, had appropriated the culturalist rhetoric of authenticity and civility to make identity claims *vis-à-vis* others in the region. A retired cadre, living in one of Zhaoxing's outlying villages, illustrated this quite lucidly:

> It's because of history. If you don't understand history, you can't understand the differences between the Dong and the Miao. It all has to do with transportation. Back when there were no roads or railroads, only rivers, transportation to the Dong areas was more convenient than in the Miao areas. The Duliu River was our link to Guangxi and Guangdong. And even though it was hard to get to a place like Zhaoxing, it was easier than getting to Kaili or any of the other Miao places. That's why the Dong are still more civilized than the Miao. It's funny (*qiguai*), because now the situation is reversed. Now transportation to the Miao areas is more convenient, because of roads and railroads. Kaili has become a big, culturally developed city. But in the countryside, the Miao are still uncivilized because of their history.

Not only had this cadre's attitude been supported by state ideology that defines *minzu* categories according to cultural distance from the Han, but also by the tourism industry which legitimized Zhaoxing's claim as a civilized place.

Tourism had also become a factor in building a sense of place that set itself apart from other Dong villages in the region. Several villagers said, for example, that in terms of customs and traditions, there wasn't much difference between Zhaoxing and Gaozeng, but that since the fire in 1988 Gaozeng had become "more like the Han." One went further, saying that Gaozeng was culturally "backward" compared to Zhaoxing. He claimed that many of Gaozeng's musicians and dancers had learned their art in Zhaoxing. "Historically, it has always been this way," he said, "so it makes sense that Zhaoxing has become the more important tourist site. Zhaoxing is the true heart of Dong culture."

Most importantly, however, tourism had given village leaders a way to embrace modernity without losing their identity as keepers of *minzu* traditions, a way to insure that Zhaoxing remain an authentically Dong place even as it "aligned with the world." I asked the head of the cultural bureau whether village youth were becoming less interested in traditional songs and dances. He was emphatic that this was not the case and, if anything, "it's more popular now than it ever was." He went on to say that,

> As this place progresses and becomes more developed, people learn the value of their traditions, and they work harder to support them. There is no contradiction between progress and preserving tradition. On the contrary, modernization will help us keep our *minzu* customs, because our development plan is now based on our traditions. Tourism is a very big part of this. It has encouraged us to work with the elders in the village, the elders' association, to learn again the old ways which were almost forgotten. This makes the elders very happy; they support this kind of development. They support the tourism plan for Zhaoxing.

And did the youth support it? Aren't they itching for change? He said that although this was true in many places "like Gaozeng," tourism had taught the youth of Zhaoxing to respect their traditions. Although I noticed a certain degree of ambivalence regarding this last point among the young people with whom I spoke, they at least seemed more conscious of the issue than their counterparts in Gaozeng.

CHONGAN: "TOURISM EATS THE FOOD PREPARED BY OUR ANCESTORS"

The idea of tradition is obviously of fundamental importance in linking tourism development and place-identity in these cases studies. We should not forget, however, that tradition is being reinterpreted and redefined in these situations, refashioned by locals according to the conditions provided by the broader political-economic system in which they now find themselves. The point is that villagers have been staking claims on a space of autonomous local identity by appealing to an idea of tradition whose origins go beyond that local space. While the broader state, commercial tourism industry, and academic institutions all engage in selecting and sifting aspects of *minzu* culture to produce an "authentic tradition" acceptable to the needs of commercial development, geopolitical stability, and national integration, locals do their own sifting and sorting to create the most meaningful tradition that expresses their uniqueness while not forsaking their connection to the broader world. What has been a misplaced authenticity, a falsification of calming certainty for metropolitans, has, paradoxically, become the raw material for an authentic claim of modern subjectivity. In the final case study, we find this issue clearly illustrated. Here, competing visions of tourism development reflect different senses of place and identity among different *minzu* groups within the township of Chongan. In articulating their visions of future development, competing promoters were involved in very different processes of inventing tradition, based on a combination of contrasting local social status and sense of connectedness to the outside world.

Chongan township (*zhen*) sits along the banks of the Chongan River, a major tributary to the Qingshui. The town occupies the upper end of a fertile floodplain, between the high rocky outcrops of Yuling and Jinfeng mountains, just where the river emerges from a spectacular narrow gorge. The river flows lazily past the town, shaded by bamboo groves, and over a weir, where its waters are diverted to power a number of stone mills. The township's 1990 population was just over 14,000; 61 per cent of which were Miao, 30 per cent Han, and 9 per cent Ge, a group whose classification status remains "undetermined," yet who staunchly insist on a identity separate from the Miao with whom the *minzu shibie* project has been inclined to lump them. Sixteen per cent of the population was registered in non-agricultural households, most of them Han. Locals tended to view Chongan's mixed ethnicity in spatial terms: the Han lived in the town, the Miao occupied the rest of the valley, and the Ge lived in peripheral mountainside villages tilling the township's most marginal land.

In late-imperial times, Chongan was one of Guizhou's most active river ports. It was one of the most western ports for traders coming upriver from Hunan, and became an important transshipment point for Guiyang and Yunnan bound goods. During the late nineteenth and early twentieth centuries, Chongan was one of Guizhou's two major opium ports. Opium was carried on foot from the province's chief growing regions in the west, and put on junks bound for Hunan and the Changjiang corridor. As a merchant town, Chongan's population was composed of migrants from far-away places. Entrepreneurs came from Jiangxi, Sichuan, Hunan, Hubei, Guangxi, and Guangdong to set up shop, forming one of the largest concentrations of Han merchants in southeastern Guizhou. They established elaborate regional guild halls, one of which, the Wanshou Gong, still stands in the town. Dating to 1755, this hall for Jiangxi merchants is now a deteriorating county-level protected cultural relic. Vigorous trade also contributed to one of the most stable local political regimes in the region. The Yanmen *tusi*, just east of Chongan, was established in 1468 by a general from Chongqing and was not disbanded until 1935. The *tusi* for Chongan itself, also established in the fifteenth century, was not disbanded until 1928 (*Huangping Xianzhi* 1992).

Chongan was thus something of a foreign outpost in an indigenous sea of contrasting cultural economies. The townspeople are descendants of traders, all of whom came from other places, from downstream China. Unlike the three cases discussed above, the sense of tradition evoked by Chongan is unambiguously Han Chinese. Much of the town still resembles a nineteenth-century river port, and such an identity carries considerable cultural weight in China, where rivers and canals were the medium of nearly all interregional trade, communication, and interaction. Tourism development plans initiated by townspeople appropriately sought to nurture this enclave sense of river-culture tradition and recreate Chongan's historic role as a portal through which locals could view the "civilization" of downstream China. In 1994, this vision of Chongan's tourism-based economic development was just beginning to focus, aided significantly by the town's elders' association. This group was staunchly proud of Chongan's past, and they seemed to draw their pride as much from a conservative and patriotic commitment to the "great tradition" of downstream China as from Chongan as a distinctive place itself. The head of the association, for example, was a graduate of China's prestigious Huangpu (Whampoa) Military Academy, the same Russian-built school that trained many Communist Party and KMT revolutionaries, including Chiang Kai Shek himself. He was immensely proud of this background and took pains to point it out to his numerous visitors.

The elders' association was supporting a tourism development plan for Chongan that included establishing an annual dragon boat competition, memorializing a nineteenth-century chain-link bridge across the river, and rebuilding a local temple. The overall objective of the plan was to develop Chongan's link with history and, in particular, reinforce the town's connection to the dominant traditions of China proper. The point of developing the old bridge, for example, was to emphasize the different stages of Chongan's history. Pavilions were built on either end of the bridge, each containing a stone tablet. One memorialized those who contributed to the project, while the other told the story of the bridge. It also directed the attentions of visitors to the bridge next to its late-imperial iron-chain predecessor. Built in the 1930s, this second bridge served as a rusting, one-lane reminder of Chongan's "KMT period" of history and, next to it, a third highway bridge had also been built. As the memorial tablet pointed out, this newest of the three bridges symbolized China's era of "socialist modernity." The three dominant phases of history over the past century would thus be neatly laid out next to each other in the form of three different bridges, each crossing the timeless river as it emerged from the untrampled wilderness of the Chongan gorge. The symbolic value of the site was truly astonishing, and townspeople had grasped the importance of exploiting it to its full potential.

Formalizing Chongan's dragon boat festival into an annual competition was also an explicit move by the elders' association to reclaim the town's links with the dominant traditions of downstream China. The association's leader said that, with China's economy growing and with tourism becoming a major industry, promoting the festival would be a good way to help develop Chongan's economy. He added that many of the elders wanted to create "something traditional" that would be carried on after they died, and would insure modern Chongan's link to the past. Shidong's dragon boat festival, he told me, was the only one in the region that had been maintained over the past decades of tumultuous change. Dragon boat traditions in Chongan, Shibing, and Zhenyuan – all Han towns – had died out as they became modernized. Only the minorities in the region, the Miao, had, ironically, preserved what had originally been a Han tradition. "The Miao have kept their link to the past," he said, "and we need to do this as well." Apparently, this was important not simply because Shidong's festival had become a very successful commercial event, but because it helped reinforce a place's links with a particular history and tradition.

While the Chongan elders' association represented the town's collective support for tourism development, much of the group's inspiration and many of its ideas came from the dominant figure in Chong'an tourism, Jun Mingyu. Jun was Chongan's most famous entrepreneur, its wealthiest household, the owner of a small riverside inn and restaurant called *Xiaojiangnan*. Jun's inn had been featured in no less than two *People's Daily* articles, which were proudly framed on the restaurant's wall, and Jun himself was the only private entrepreneur featured in a recently published book (Liu 1994) on leading figures in Guizhou's tourism development. Jun was happy to tell his story to anyone who hadn't yet heard it, and I repeat it here because it gives an important perspective on Jun's particular vision of Chongan's future tourism development, a vision that contrasts significantly with that of the township's Miao villagers, who have devised their own tourism development scheme. Their differences, as we will see, illustrate the ways in which contesting versions of tradition get worked into the place-identities being expressed through the local appropriation of touristic modernity's misplaced search for authenticity.

In August 1984, Jun Mingyu opened the *Xiaojiangnan*. Money came from several local share-holding investors, and a big loan from the construction bank. It was like a dream come true, and Jun set about expanding his business as fast as he could, expecting an onslaught of tourists as China and Guizhou modernized and opened to the world. Jun had always loved to travel. When he graduated from middle school in the late 1950s, he left Chongan and traveled all over China. He had no money but supported himself haphazardly by selling rat poison and carrying luggage for tourist-pilgrims up and down China's sacred mountain sites. It was at one such site, Sichuan's Emei Mountain, that he became inspired to make the tourist experience something all people should benefit from, whether they have money or not. In one week, he said, he carried luggage up and down the mountain five times. In a state of exhausted delirium, he became convinced that the Buddha did not distinguish between the rich and poor, that all could benefit from this kind of worldly experience. He also became convinced that Chongan scenery was unrivaled in China, and that it was his responsibility to promote and develop it. This became his "mad love" (*fengkuang de ailian*), his obsession.

Back in Chongan, he ended up working in the township enterprise bureau (later to become the TVE office). He became active in promoting Chongan's Ge batik by helping to establish the Chongan Batik Factory in 1978. He was also involved in promoting all sorts of events, such as water sports gatherings, which showed off Chongan's scenery and special flavor. Even then, before the reforms, he had dreams of developing these kinds of tourist spectaculars, and from the beginning he believed that tourism was the only real choice for Chongan's modern development. As he watched downstream China break out in "culture fever" he expected armies of delirious tourists searching for roots. After all, the Japanese had been coming for just this reason since the early 1980s.

For most Chinese, however, Guizhou was just an impoverished backwater without culture; the hordes of tourists did not come. Jun had over-extended himself. At one point he had over 60 people working for him. He had built several facilities, in addition to the *Xiaojiangnan*, all designed by himself. But Huangping county was still closed to foreigners without special permission, and Guizhou was still unheard of. Between 1985 and 1986 everything fell apart. Impatient investors forced him to buy back their shares, the bank demanded repayment on its loan, and to top it off, Jun's wife died, leaving him with three children to support and a restaurant to run. He sold off almost the entire business: buildings, beds, tables, chairs, everything except the *Xiaojiangnan* itself. "This is another reason it's a 'mad love'," he said. "It was crazy to keep the restaurant. I had no money, the children had to go to school. But I would never sell it. Without the *Xiaojiangnan* there is no Chongan tourism." The *Xiaojiangnan* was the heart of his dream, not only the heart of Chongan tourism, in his eyes, but a civilizing beacon, a repose of downstream culture in the uncultured wilderness of Qiandongnan.

Gradually, Jun rebuilt the business. In 1988 he remarried, expanding his family to seven children. He attached a guest house to the restaurant, overlooking the river, and then added a new set of buildings – a kind of local "conference center" – including a batik exhibit hall. In 1990 he began offering ethnic tourist services. He contracted with three villages to provide receptions for tourists who want a guided, day-long hike to an isolated minority village (one Miao, one Ge, one Mulao). Jun became an astute packager of place. He was quick to recognize, for example, the need to promote local Ge batik as something unique and special in Guizhou's batik-saturated crafts market. In marketing local batik, Jun emphasized that when Guizhou's largest batik enterprise opened in Anshun in 1958 Ge women from Chongan were hired as the initial training staff. Chongan should thus be recognized, Jun claimed, as the true home of Guizhou batik. Guests at the *Xiaojiangnan* were shown a video, produced in Shanghai with Jun as local organizer, which confirmed the authenticity of Ge batik as "Guizhou's finest," "most ancient," and "primitive."[5]

Jun developed something of an irreverent style in marketing Chongan batik. At the 1992 batik festival in Anshun, Jun opened an exhibit. Realizing he could not really compete with the larger companies represented there, he decided on an innovative approach in advertising his crafts. The advertisement at his exhibit pointed out that his batik products were "backward," "out-dated," "over-priced," and were "one-of-a-kind," in that they could not be reproduced in a standardized way. In addition, production was "unscientific," and the craftsmanship was "not modern." Instead, his products were created solely with "imagination" and "enthusiasm." Although an approach like this would not necessarily turn many heads in the innovative marketing environment of Western consumerism, Jun's was a creative strategy for a China transfixed by the rationality of scientific modernity. More important, it acknowledged Jun's appropriation of misplaced authenticity as a tool for carving his own space within the state's modernization rhetoric. It also revealed part of his broader vision for packaging Chongan as a place. The Ge and their crafts complemented all that was ancient and primeval about Chongan. Their culture, for Jun, helped define something of the area's mystery and spirit, a counterpoint to the state's progressive categories of socialist modernity and civilization.

But while Jun is happy to include Chongan's ethnic diversity as part of his overall, packaged version of the place's attractions, his primary vision of local tourism development drew not from local culture, but from scenery. In other words, it would be foolish to ignore the marketing potential of frontier exoticism; but what really inspired Jun was a humanized version of nature derived from the classical aesthetic traditions of downstream China. In this, Jun turned his attentions to the Chongan gorge. In developing the narrow chasm of the Chongan gorge Jun sought to evoke not untamed wilderness, but a garden of civilized aesthetics, a classical Chinese landscape painting. Indeed, Jun's long-term vision for developing Chongan gorge as a tourist attraction was inspired by the fifteenth-century landscape paintings of Tang Yin.[6] Here, in these 500-year-old paintings of gnarled cliffs, twisted trees, waterfalls, quiet pools, contemplative thatched cottages, pavilions, and bridges, was Jun's vision of Chongan's future. He wanted to create a "return to the past" (*fangu lüyou*) resort in the gorge.

Using the paintings as inspiration, Jun would build a small lodge in the gorge, and a number of resting stations along the river, where tea and wine would be served. At the lodge, everything would be "authentically traditional." A teahouse would offer evening concerts of traditional Chinese music. There would also be pleasant trails along the cliffs, up side canyons, all inspiring the kind of feeling one gets from Tang Yin's paintings. Guests and workers alike would wear traditional robes (the guests would put them on before boarding the boats which would take them into this dream world). Jun would recreate a completely ancient landscape, straight from Tang or Song times. "The gorge would be perfect for it," he exclaimed. "It has never been lived in, a completely untouched landscape." Unlike the "fake" Tang and Song dynasty theme parks popping up around China, Jun's venture would be completely separated from the contemporary world, that separation reinforced by entering a primeval landscape within the gorge, cut off from the outside by steep cliffs and dense jungle. Exiting the gorge, guests would re-enter the modern world by passing beneath the three bridges, first

the late-imperial iron-chain bridge, then the 1930s KMT bridge, followed by
the modern highway bridge.

Jun's sense of touristic history, borrowed from places far from Chongan,
was meant to reinforce Chongan's own legacy as an outpost of migrants.
The town was inhabited by the descendants of people who had brought their
traditions from somewhere else. "Tourism eats the food prepared by our
ancestors," he said. This was also a distinctly local claim, a proud expression
of place-identity. Chongan's tourist resources – the temple, bridges, dragon
boat races, a fantasyland within the gorge – would be the work of the local
people, he said, not the state (*guojia*):

> All the temples, all the ancient culture, all of it comes from our ances-
> tors; they have laid the foundation for me to build on. The state has
> never given me a single cent for tourism. I pay taxes, I help develop the
> economy, and they've never given me anything. It is the ancestors who
> will help me succeed, not the state. The state only gives money to places
> like Huangguoshu and Longgong; it builds big expensive hotels. But in
> Chongan it will be different. Our tourism will depend on the ancestors,
> not the government. The ancestors will see us through.

Thus, Jun had appropriated the discourse of touristic modernity to make
distinctly local claims about Chongan's identity and its impending
modernity.

Significantly, there was no real place for ethnic tourism in all of this.
Certainly Jun had plans for developing Chongan's ethnic tourism resources,
but they were clearly of only secondary concern. Jun was not interested in
serving up for tourists the present-day realities of Chongan. Instead, his
ideas were based on what he himself termed "imagination" (*xiangxiang*).
Tang Yin created the perfect landscape, a perfect model which could be
reconstructed in the gorge. Jun's tourism plan presented an imagined tradition expressing what modern Chongan *might be*, culturally, as a beacon of
civilized light in dark and backward Guizhou. While Jun's plan completely
escaped Guizhou's historical and present social realities, it also presented his
appropriated reworking of *wenhua fazhan*; inspired by no less than the
Buddha on Emei Mountain, tourism was his own civilizing mission. His was
a vision born not of the frontier but of *Jiangnan*, the Changjiang Delta, the
heart of China's civilizing traditions. It was for this reason that his restaurant, named the "Small *Jiangnan*," represented the heart of his dream to
bring culture to his corner of Guizhou, to "transform society from barbarity
to civilization." Minority culture, for Jun, was primitive and uncivilized:
"They hold bull fights; they used to hang the heads of their enemies on their
walls. They have a barbaric tradition. *Tamen meiyou wenhua* (They have no
culture)." *Xiaojiangnan*, designed and built by Jun himself, incorporated
features which reminded the visitor not of the borderlands, but of Suzhou,
Hangzhou, and Wuxi, including a moon gate, traditional lamps, and

traditional calligraphy, written by Jun, adorning the sides of doorways. Indeed, one of these reminds visitors of a state official's inspired exclamation upon lunching at *Xiaojiangnan*. He told Jun: "A *Jiangnan* native, missing the food of his native land, comes to *Xiaojiangnan*, and finds the flavors of his home."

The irony is that while the Chongan gorge represents the climax of Jun's vision, it runs through land controlled by Miao and Ge villagers. Chong'an town remains an outpost in this corner of Guizhou where Miao and Ge outnumber Han by more than two to one. With his tourist vision, Jun reinforced Chongan's link with dominant China, essentially ignoring the "undeveloped" culture of the minorities; they became a temporary side show. Jun's plan did nothing to remind visitors that the iron-chain bridge under which they would pass in boats, dressed like Tang poets and scholars, was built by the Hunan army after it brutally crushed Zhang Xiumei's rebellion, took land from indigenous villagers, and gave it to militarists from Sichuan and Hunan. Chongan's local Miao and Ge villagers are not unaware of the gorge's potential as a tourist resource, but in *their* vision of its development they would be loathe to construct of fantasy of what has for so long been an oppressive downstream culture. Rather, they see developing the gorge as a straightforward path toward economic self-reliance.

By 1994, a plan for the development of Chongan gorge had already been mapped out by the villagers of Huangjin (which controls much of the land through which the gorge passes), with the cooperation of Huangping's county tourism bureau. Jun Mingyu had not even been consulted, and was understandably upset by this. Villagers had already constructed a path from the iron-chain bridge upstream to a waterfall, and had started charging tourists to use the path. They had already spent RMB 30,000 of village collective funds. According to Jun, this was a complete waste of money. "Tourists won't be interested in hiking along a path," he said, "they'll want to take boats into the gorge, just like the boatmen of ancient China." What the villagers should have done, he said, was simply develop the area around the waterfall itself and then charge boats a small fee for docking there. It was just another example of villagers blindly investing their money. "They're Miao; they don't understand business and they don't understand tourism. *Tamen meiyou wenhua.*"

When I spoke with the village head, however, it became clear that exploiting the gorge was simply part of a general development plan for the village. He said they planned to complete a path all the way through the gorge, and to hold ethnic-style receptions for tourists hiking through. He expected the village to invest an additional RMB 100,000 in the project. Huangjin, he said, had actually accumulated quite a lot of cash during the 1980s by specializing in tobacco production. By intensive monocropping they had earned a great deal of money in a short time. But they also learned the importance of diversification, for the tobacco depleted their soil, and now they were forced to return to a traditional rotation of staple crops.

Tourism development was the first of a three-part economic development plan drawn up by the Huangjin village collective. Tourism, it was hoped, would increase the number of outsiders coming to the area, and increase village incomes. This would enable the second part to go into operation: an open market in which local agricultural products and crafts would be sold wholesale or retail to outsiders. They would locate the market near the iron-chain bridge, at the beginning of the path. As income increased, villagers would then build a food-processing plant, so they themselves could earn the value-added on their own agricultural products. The village head said that the rural economy in Huangjin had been getting worse over the past decade. It was becoming more difficult to have a decent life based on grain income alone. Farmers, he said, would have to take the initiative themselves if they wanted to get out of this rut, and the only way was to commercialize their economy.

Whether or not the Huangjin plan was feasible or was simply, as Jun asserted, a waste of capital, it clearly represented a different vision of the relationship between landscape, local culture, and the broader culture and political economy of China. Whereas Jun sought to invest the landscape with the symbolic markers of an imagined downstream tradition of civility, the Huangjin villagers were simply concerned with achieving economic self-determination. The only symbolism Huangjin's plan invested in the Chongan gorge was a walking path toward modernization. Articulating Chongan's place-identity in terms of an imagined downstream tradition only served to remind the Miao of their marginal status; it defined a place where they themselves were the outsiders. The importance of developing the gorge thus lay in "improving" it with cement paths, charging tourists fees to see it, encouraging them to buy village products; the landscape of the gorge would reinforce Huangjin's independence and control over a landscape in which, historically, they had always maintained only tenuous control. The food Jun's ancestors left for Huangjin to eat was bitter. It was their duty not simply to reheat this ancient broth, but make it taste better. A tourism-funded food-processing plant was, symbolically, an appropriate response.

Conclusion

What are we to make of these case studies? In what way can we call the practices described in the previous chapter articulations of a potentially "authentic" modern subjectivity? Is it enough to argue that villagers are eager to exploit their own touristic potential because of their intense desire for modernity, and that they willingly reproduce state-sanctioned categories of culture and identity in order to further their own modernization agenda? Throughout Guizhou, hundreds of village heads journey each year to tourist bureaus in Anshun, Kaili, and Guiyang. They bring with them "portfolios" of their villages: recordings of songs, photographs of architecture and scenery, petitions signed by thousands of villagers. They look with envy upon the dozen or so villages in Guizhou that have been developed as tourist attractions. While no doubt naive about the exploitative machinations of the tourism industry, they very clearly understand both the high stakes of their pursuit of modernity and the misplaced desire for authenticity and tradition among metropolitan tourists. They believe that, beyond tourism, there is very little else on the immediate horizon for their communities as they attempt to escape the trap of rural poverty and continued dependence upon an increasingly degraded resource base. The state's charge of commercializing the rural economy makes tourism one of the most apparent and most desired routes toward this goal for many rural villagers in Guizhou.

While it is arguable whether tourism in Guizhou will ever become a "pillar" industry, and doubtful that the relatively meager tourist market could really become a significant source of income for many of Guizhou's rural poor, the willingness on the part of villagers to *xia hai*, to "jump into commerce," by marketing themselves and commodifying their culture is significant and deserves careful attention. In one respect, the hopeful village heads making their cases to the tourism bureaus are clearly walking in step with the Chinese state and its project of national integration and modernization. They are displaying a "commercial conscience" that will eventually benefit the needs of capital accumulation as profit-minded investors look more and more to interior regions such as Guizhou where poverty will drive people to sell their labor for almost nothing. They are also displaying a kind of patriotic duty in volunteering to help build the (multi)national mosaic of the Chinese nation-state.

They will willingly accommodate the expectations of the state and metropolitan tourists in upholding a mythical construction of "the folk," as long as it promises to increase their incomes. They will even appropriate and internalize the state's cultural and ethnic categories, and reproduce these in the discourse of their daily lives.

It is in these terms that Gramsci would speak of cultural hegemony, or Foucault of subjectivization as a result of the technologies of power. If the subjectivity of villagers is limited to their desire and willingness to "sell themselves" in exchange for the trappings of a more modern lifestyle, then we must conclude with Foucault that the powers of subjugation in modern (and modernizing) societies are exquisitely reproduced by the subjugated themselves, and that power is normalized through the everyday cultural practices of society. The march of hopeful village heads becomes a pathetic gesture of submission and tribute to the irresistible normalizing powers of the state and capital. If this is the case, the "false modern" is not only triumphant but remains the only meaningful characterization of the modern experience, reducing the potential for an "authentic" modern subjectivity to a naive illusion. Yet, in "selling themselves," villagers are also negotiating a complex process of change that is not simply about increasing incomes or pursuing the utopian dreams of a technological and rational paradise. They are engaging in the process of carving a new space of identity and meaning from the ever-shifting world in which they now live. The significance of their doing so lies not in its reproduction of dominant power relations – for these relations are often intentionally subverted – but in the struggle to become the subjects, rather than objects, of an unfinished modernity.

Interpreting the practices of villagers in Guizhou's ethnic tourism industry from the perspective of authentic subjectivity – rather than subjectivization – requires a definition of modernity that is not limited to the objectifications of instrumental rationality. Modernity, in these terms, is a dynamic process in which two opposing forces maintain a tense equilibrium. On the one hand, modernity is characterized by the increasing rationalization of our lives through science, technology, and the other instruments of modernization. These increasingly regulate and discipline the social body, as the modern project becomes a set of objectives to be realized by the state and the needs of capital. In these terms, modernity reverts to Weber's "iron cage." We become imprisoned within a labyrinth of progress, and ourselves become willing participants in the calculated subjugation of our own lives. In Berman's (1970) terms, we willingly give up our "authentic" lives in exchange for the security and discipline of rationalism. Yet, on the other hand, the forces of modernization represent such profound disruptions in our society and culture – precipitating a whole discourse of modernity based on tropes of exile, displacement, and dislocation – that they may indeed offer opportunities to reconstruct ourselves in new and liberating ways. Berman thus sees in modernity the potential to define ourselves in more "authentic" terms, based not on received social conventions but on radically new roles for individuals and

collectives within a rapidly changing society. The struggle for modern subjectivity, then, involves a new sense of freedom to define one's "authenticity"
according to a changing social, political, and economic environment, even as
the forces that made such a liberating move possible at all are constantly
trying to take that freedom away.

Both Berman (1970, 1982) and Giddens (1990) refer to the tremendous
anxiety that this struggle produces. My idea of the "false modern" is meant to
capture the "problem" of modernity, whereby the authentic possibilities of
modern subjectivity are "traded-in" for a more secure alternative. This would
include the misplaced search for authenticity and tradition in other peoples
and places, as a kind of "balast" to the volatility of modernity, but is most
profoundly exemplified in both the normalizing power of the state and its
agenda of national integration and patriotism, and in the disciplining power
of capital and its need to exploit surplus labor power. One important question
that this distinguishing between the possibilities of an authentic subjectivity
and a "surrendering" to the ready-made identities – the subjectivizations – of
the "false modern," involves the degree to which people have a choice in this
matter. This is a question that also addresses the translatability of essentially
"Western" experiences of modernity to the Chinese context. One of the most
significant developments emerging from the theories of Foucault, for
example, has been in the understanding of colonialism and its powers of
representation (Said 1979; Mitchell 1988). Developments in post-colonial
theory, in which questions are being asked about the experience of modernity
in post-colonial societies by scholars within those societies (and we should
include China among them), have revealed how constrained the discursive
realm of modernity can be for people experiencing rapid development and
modernization at the hands of a powerful state and international capital.
Zhang's (1997) analysis, for example, reveals the significant troubles Chinese
intellectuals have had imagining an indigenous Chinese modernity that
doesn't traffic in the kinds of essentialisms typical of the "false modern."

More to the point, however, is the fact that Berman's perspective may over-
state the clear choice modernity offers people: embrace the anxious and
tenuous freedom of authenticity or surrender to the secure confinements of
instrumental rationalism. By turning our attention to rural China in the late
twentieth century (whereas Berman's work emphasizes late eighteenth- and
nineteenth-century Europe), we come face to face with the truly confined
space of opportunity that "authentic" modern subjectivity offers. The lives of
most Guizhou villagers are such that modernity is thought of as something
far away, something perhaps found in the cities, and certainly something intimately linked to the distant yet powerful state. Rural Guizhou remains a
society dominated by the legacies of internal colonialism, and as with colonialism throughout the world, the notion of subjectivization goes a long way
in revealing the ways in which the experience of modernity is largely about
reproducing the powers of the state and of capital.

The previous chapter's case studies, if nothing else, do reveal the very limited opportunities available to villagers for constructing an authentic modern subjectivity in Berman's terms. In this sense, village subjectivities are being fashioned by appropriating and manipulating dominant representations of the state's *minzu shibie* project, its *wenhua fazhan* project, and the tourism industry's "exoticization project." Constrained as these acts of appropriation may be, we must always remain aware, following from Touraine (1995), of this dimension of subjectivity as a necessary part of the modern experience. Indeed, that any degree of subjectivity is present at all in Guizhou's tourist villages should be testament enough to the necessity of keeping the Subject alive in our analyses of modernity and modernization.

What, then, have we seen in these case studies that points out this admittedly constrained yet nevertheless important presence of the Subject?

In Langde, as in all these cases, the objectifying power of the state and the tourism industry is readily apparent. As with Gaozeng and Zhaoxing, the state project of historic and cultural preservation has been a significant factor conditioning the lives of Langde villagers. An "open-air museum" and a "preserved relic village", Langde has become enveloped in the monumental space and time of the state, much like Herzfeld's case of Rethemnos in Crete. Indeed, Langde's "monumentalization" is perhaps even more thorough than that of Rethemnos – the villagers clearly have less room for negotiating a social space out of this monumentalization than do their counterparts in Crete. They are also explicitly expected to "play the part" of the quaint ethnic folk, displaying for metropolitan tourists (the vast majority of whom, remember, are Chinese) a living version of China's (multi)national mosaic. The visits by officials from the NTA and the state cultural bureau offer the clearest evidence of the state's expectations in this regard. Officials came to Langde explicitly for the purpose of impressing upon villagers their responsibilities in upholding the message of the Chinese nation-state, in which heritage and tradition must be preserved in order to construct a sense of continuity, a kind of glue to hold together the increasingly fragmented terrain of modernization. Finally, Langde villagers are also expected to surrender to the better judgment of the local tourism industry (in fact a mere extension of the local state), which seeks to retain the exclusive right to control Langde's tourism development program.

Importantly, however, the state's efforts at standardization and control are met with a certain degree of subversion and, indeed, hostility, on the part of some villagers. What is significant about this, however, is not simply that we may find instances of resistance among villagers, but that their subversion of the state's objectives is achieved via rhetorical manipulation of the state's own discursive categories. Thus, Shaman Chen claimed that Langde should have a more autonomous position *vis-à-vis* the prefectural tourism bureau by referring to the state's own ideology of tradition and authenticity. The Miao of Langde, for Shaman Chen, had been bestowed with the legitimating mantle of authenticity. They were the "most representative" (*zui you daibiaode*), and "most typical" (*zui you dianxingde*) of all Miao villages. The state's culturalist categories of ethnicity – categories that have been developed for the purposes of regulation, integration, and control – have also become reservoirs of legitimacy for the agendas of Langde villagers themselves. While their prospects for achieving autonomy within Guizhou's growing tourism industry remain perhaps marginal, they have nevertheless learned – as did the residents of Rethemnos Old Town – that the state's rhetorical devices can be turned against it.

This tactic is seen perhaps even more clearly in the case of Gaozeng, a village whose fortunes have also become intimately bound up with the state's project of cultural preservation. In this case, however, the situation is reversed. The state has abandoned its desire to turn Gaozeng into a stage of tradition and authenticity, and has instead begun to focus solely on Gaozeng's role as a local growth pole for the modernizing influences of economic development. The most visible signs of this role have been the architectural developments, as new cement buildings representing the rural credit association and the forestry bureau now provide a shocking contrast to the hundreds of wooden *diaojiaolou* houses that make up the village. As far as the state is concerned, Gaozeng's potential for staging the culture of the nation's "folk" has been ruined (*pohuaile*). What was one day a gem of authenticity has become just another developing village in the eyes of the state.

That the mark of authenticity could be offered and then taken away in such a seemingly arbitrary fashion was, for many Gaozeng villagers, both a verification of the state's power over their lives and an opportunity to reclaim some of that power for themselves. They had learned, in other words, that "playing tradition" could not only result in economic benefits through tourism, but that it more importantly bestowed the prestige of heritage upon their village in the eyes of distant metropolitans. Thus the village elders' association manipulated the rhetoric of preservation and tradition in petitioning the state to reclaim some of their former status as a "preserved relic village." In this way they not only sought to subvert the increasingly dominant attitude that their village was *pohuaile* – thus not worthy of preservation – but also used the state's culturalist categories in order to reconstruct a sense of continuity for themselves. This was represented in the efforts to build a new "wind and rain bridge." This would no doubt attract tourists, but more importantly offered an opportunity, in the eyes of the elders' association, to bring the village together as a community. The long-lost bridge was seen not only as the kind of monument that the state valorizes in its construction of a mythic (and touristic) folk culture heritage, but could also become instrumental in the construction of a new social space in the village, a social space carved within the monumental space of the broader nation-state.

In Zhaoxing, villagers have not had to question their legitimacy for carrying the state-sanctioned torch of the authentic traditional folk. Indeed, their role as such has only increased at the expense of Gaozeng. It is understandable, then, that they have taken to defining themselves in the same terms as the state and the tourism industry defines them – as the "most authentic" of

Dong villages. They have appropriated the rhetoric of authenticity much as have the villagers of Langde. Yet in Zhaoxing there is less evidence of overt antagonism between the interests of villagers and the interests of outside tourism developers. Instead, the significant issue here is the way locals have manipulated the rhetoric of authenticity to maintain distinctions between themselves and outlying communities. Indeed, villagers in outlying communities have been active in claiming to be the "more traditional" villages *vis-à-vis* Zhaoxing proper. Thus, state-sanctioned tourism development, in the hands of locals, is producing a hierarchy of authenticity and tradition between Zhaoxing, Jitang, and more distant places. This is occurring not so much out of competition as out of the need of villagers to exercise some control over the process of development – a process in which authenticity itself has become the most valuable currency.

Finally, we come to Chongan. The situation here differs considerably from the previous three cases. Here the issue is not a state preservation project, nor does the state figure prominently in the local conflicts developing over the trajectory of tourism development. Instead, we find an important dynamic that deserves attention, but that has not been as apparent in the other cases: competing appropriations of dominant representations by different local groups for the purpose of constructing different modern subjectivities. The dominant representations, in this case, are those that have governed the frontier interaction between Han Chinese and minority groups such as the Miao and Ge. Tourism development becomes a vehicle through which these representations get reproduced and/or subverted, depending upon one's social position in relation to them. For Jun Mingyu, tourism has offered an opportunity to recapitulate the "civilizing mission" of Chinese culture on the fringes of the empire. Is this an act of authentic modern subjectivity? Insofar as Jun's efforts have been explicitly conducted outside of the institutions of the broader state, I believe it is. Jun's appropriation of the rhetoric of Chinese "civilization in the wilderness" is, more than anything, an act of local autonomy. In a town whose very existence is tied to a frontier legacy of colonial conquest and integration, Jun seeks to reclaim a tenuous link to a "pastness" that subverts the overpowering mark of "backwardness" that is now applied to all of Guizhou. More than anyone in these case studies, in fact, Jun explicitly understands how the past is now a modern invention, and that modern subjectivity can only be achieved by claiming (indeed, by inventing) the past for oneself.

On the other hand, however, we have the village communities that surround Chongan; they also seek to claim a stake in the region's incipient tourism development. They clearly lack the privileged position in laying claim to the past that Jun Mingyu possesses. Yet they nevertheless have positioned themselves in such a ways as to diminish the monopolizing potential of Jun's representations. Whether their alternative plan for developing the Chongan Gorge can be called an expression of modern subjectivity is perhaps arguable, for the extent to which they are deliberately subverting the kinds of representations appropriated by Jun is difficult to say. But it is significant, I believe, that they have essentially brushed away Jun's efforts and gone about approaching the gorge as a straightforward modernization project. In these terms they have acknowledged their own responsibility, as subjects rather than objects, for challenging the dominant forces that have rendered them poor and discriminated against.

The people in these case studies live lives pervaded by contradiction. In their claims of place-identity based on recycled and appropriated notions of tradition and authenticity, they live in a world that has been significantly shaped by what Urry (1995) terms "aesthetic cosmopolitanism" – that quality of modern reflexivity that drives both the tourist and the provider of the tourism experience. As active participants in the construction of the "support apparatus" (that is, tourist attractions) of modern aesthetics, these villagers can be called modern subjects. What are the implications of this claim for our broader understanding of the condition of modernity in China? How do we situate these village experiences within debates about China's "alternative modernity" or the meaning of modernity in a globalizing world?

To answer these questions one simply needs to revisit the argument made in Chapter 1, that tourism remains one of the most powerful forces through which the Chinese state, and Chinese capital, seek to dominant popular narratives of "modern China." Chinese modernity is very much a touristic modernity, from the patriotic importance invested in Shenzhen's "Splendid China" theme park, to the state sanctioning of ethnic tourism as a means of monopolizing the discursive constructions of the Chinese "folk." One simply has to recall President Jiang Zemin's 1997 visit to the United States to understand the grip that tourism has on China's discursive imaginings. Professing a desire to "learn more about American history," Jiang chose not a trip to the Library of Congress, nor a meeting with scholars, but a visit to the colonial heritage theme park of Williamsburg. There he engrossed himself in a deeper understanding of American traditions by driving through the town, admiring the "old architecture," and having a conversation with an actor dressed up as Thomas Jefferson.

The importance invested in tourism by the state, as well as the burgeoning interests of capital throughout East and Southeast Asia, speaks to another, related, answer to the question of Chinese modernity. The state proceeds from the perspective that modern subjectivity is indeed expressed most profoundly in the form of the tourist. The prospects for a rational, disciplined, and patriotic modern society in China are very much being laid on the doorstep of the tourism industry. "Modern Chinese" are encouraged to travel, to see the sights, the theme parks, the landscape of the nation to which they belong. Nor is this something that has come about only recently. The same argument could be made regarding the mass pilgrimages that took place during the Cultural Revolution, where millions of youth were encouraged to visit the old revolutionary sites around the country, including Mao's birthplace. If tourism is indeed being marshaled in such a way by the state and its modernization project, then we are indeed obliged to question the assumption that the modern Subject is most compellingly found in the form of the tourist. The objectifications of modernity are always resisted, reworked, and manipulated, and in China's case this is most profoundly seen among those who are on the "supply side" of the tourism experience. It is there that we need to look for instances of a more "authentic" modern subjectivity in China.

Villagers thus face the full force of the state's integration and modernization agenda in the form of tourism development. In Guizhou, we have seen this in the various ways the ethnic tourism industry is promoted as a means of "cultural development" – in which development and modernization objectives are coupled with a rhetoric of preservation and heritage. Yet if we proceed from the assumption that we must only look to the tourist for signs of modern subjectivity, then Chinese modernity itself becomes little more than a closed project of national integration, standardization, and social disciplining. It may be marked as "alternative" by state and capitalist elites seeking to differentiate China in the global marketplace of goods and ideas, but it remains a triumph of "false modernity." Focusing, instead, on the experience of villagers themselves, as suppliers of the tourism experience, leaves the question of modernity in China an open one. This is necessary, I believe, in order to account for Chinese modernity as an on-going project subject to a truly complex and confusing range of interpretations, meanings, and manipulations throughout the country. That, ultimately, is the broader argument being made here. It is not enough, in other words, to claim an "alternative modernity" in China, for the discourse of alternative modernity has come to be dominated by the state and capitalist elites. In its dominant form, Chinese alternative modernity remains a false modernity. One must, instead, speak of the struggles for an authentic modern subjectivity that are carried out in multiple places, where local histories and geographies articulate with the broader forces bearing down upon them. The terrain of these struggles is not the global space of transnational capital, nor the national space of the state. Rather, it is found in the myriad landscape of places, where people confront the forces of modernization and turn them into something meaningful.

Glossary

Acronyms

CITS	China International Travel Service
CPC	Communist Party of China
CTS	China Travel Service
FEC	Foreign Exchange Certificates
FYP	Five-Year Plan
GMP	Gross Material Product
GTB	Guizhou Tourism Bureau
HTA	Huangguoshu Tourism Administration
LTA	Longgong Tourism Administration
NMP	Net Material Product
NTA	National Tourism Administration
OTC	Overseas Travel Company
QTB	Qiandongnan Tourism Bureau
RMB	*Renminbi* ("People's Currency")
SEZ	Special Economic Zone

Chinese terms

Diaojiaolou Three-story "post–pile" houses built of wood in the Miao and Dong villages of Qiandongnan

Difang tese "Local specialties" or "local color"

Fengyu qiao or **Hua qiao** "Wind and rain bridge" or "flower bridge": covered bridges built by the Dong in Qiandongnan, and parts of Hunan and Guangxi

Gai tu gui liu Ming and Qing (1368–1911) policy of implementing direct imperial administration of *tusi* lands along China's frontiers

Jiedaifei "Reception fee" paid to ethnic tourist villages for entertaining tourists

Jietuansi Class B travel agencies licensed to arrange, but not host, travel for foreigners

Lüyou tatai, jingmao changxi "Trade performing on a stage built by tourism"

Lüyoure "Tourism fever"

Miaoguan "Miao officials" invested with official rank during the implementation of *gai tu gui liu* in late-imperial Guizhou

Miaojiang "Miao borderlands": the popular term for most of Southeastern Guizhou (Qiandongnan) during late-imperial times

Miaoling A major mountain range stretching across Qiandongnan, forming the watershed divide between the Changjiang and Zhujiang drainage basins

Minwei *Minzu* affairs commission

Minzu "Ethnic group" or "nationality"

Minzu shibie "Ethnic identification"

San xian "Third line" of defense industrialization during the Maoist era

Shaoshu minzu "Minority *minzu*"

Tun tian Military–agricultural colonies established along China's frontiers as early as the Han Dynasty

Tusi "Native chieftains": China's policy initiated during the Han Dynasty of investing frontier elites with hereditary rank and political autonomy in exchange for tribute and maintaining frontier stability

Wenhua "Civilization" or "education" but most commonly translated as "culture"

Wenhua fazhan "Cultural development"

Wenhuabu Ministry of Culture

Wenhuaju Cultural Bureau

Wenwu baohu danwei "Preserved cultural relic": a preservation site recognized by the *wenwuchu*

Wenwuchu Cultural Relics Department of the Cultural Bureau

Xiang Rural township

Zhen Town

Zhutuansi Class A travel agencies licensed to host foreign tourists and receive foreign exchange

Notes

Introduction

1 See, for example, Chen *et al.* (in press), Davis *et al.* (1995), and Guldin (1997).
2 The link between authenticity and modernity here is inspired by Berman (1970).
3 This scenario is, for example, proposed in Wang and Bai (1991).
4 See, for example, the critiques by Berman (1992: 44–5) and MacCannell (1989: ix–xvi).

1 Tourism and modernity

1 According to the "Project Miniature Protest" entered to the National Planning Development Board by the "Economizing Movement" which had formed to protest Mini, the 500 million rupiah project (US $25 million in 1971) used funds which could be put to better use on either 52 small industries or 7 large university campuses, each the size of the prestigious Gaja Mada University (Pemberton 1994: 243).
2 *Minzu* may be translated as either "nationality" or "ethnic group," but has no exact equivalent in English. Throughout this book I have chosen to follow a growing convention among those studying ethnicity in China and leave the term untranslated.

3 Colonizing a "barren and profitless" place

1 This claim assumes an approach to ethnicity based not on cultural or primordial characteristics, but on ethnicity as a social construction conditioned by power relations, a mark of discrimination as well as a strategy of identity formation. (See Kammerer 1988; Keyes 1979; Okamura 1981; and Waters 1990.)
2 Ho (1959: 258) estimates a population of 5.2 million in 1786 and 10.5 million in 1947. Chen *et al.* (1993: 38) give significantly lower population figures than Lee, probably based on official records which were notoriously underestimated: 300,000 in 1578, 509,400 in 1597, and 1.64 million in 1727. Chen (1989: 10) offers yet another set of figures: 510,000 in 1550, 1.4 million in 1732, and 5.4 million in 1840.
3 Chen *et al.* (1993: 38) give the following figures for land under cultivation in Guizhou during this time: 34,431 ha in 1578, 121,327 ha in 1597, and 208,304 ha in 1727.
4 It is unknown how many died during these rebellions in Guizhou, but according to figures in Zhou *et al.* (1987: 17) the total population of Guizhou dropped from 5.44 million in 1851 to 4.49 million in 1878.

5 Stalin's four criteria for nationality identification were: "common language, common territory, common economic life, and a typical cast of mind manifested in a common culture" (Heberer 1989: 30).

6 In 1995 agriculture's share of fixed capital investments in Guizhou had risen to 6 per cent. (See GTN 1993: 99–100; GN 1996: 60.)

7 GTN (1993: 100). Guizhou ranks fifth in the country in coal reserves, second in aluminum resources, and third in manganese reserves. It also ranks among the top five provinces in hydroelectric potential (GN 1996: 379).

8 In 1995, for example, provincial revenues only amounted to 45 per cent of expenditures (GN 1996: 60).

9 Figures based on tables in *China Statistical Yearbook, 1995*. Reprinted in *Provincial China* 1996, 1: 38, 52.

10 Indeed, since the 1984 lending deregulation banks in Guizhou have been lending most of their capital to projects beyond the province rather than finance local development. In 1984, "Hard put to find qualified borrowers locally, the Bank of Guizhou directed 700 million *yuan* out of the province in loans, an amount equivalent to 80 per cent of that year's total financial revenue for the province. The bank's action was tantamount to allowing the entire sum of central government subsidies to flow out of the region." (Wang and Bai 1991: 71).

11 Grain subsidies in 1985, for example, amounted to 17 per cent of total grain consumed in the province (GS 1993: 279).

12 It should be noted that much of this gap is explained in terms of a disparity between urban and rural Guizhou in general, but is magnified when isolating for regions in which minority populations predominate.

13 Net Material Product (*Guomin Shouru*) is the sum of net output value of agriculture, industry, construction, transport, and commerce, obtained by deducting the value of the material consumption of those sectors from the Gross Material Product (*Shehui Zongchanzhi*). The disadvantage of using this indicator is that it excludes non-material production sectors such as services, education, public health, military, and government administration.

14 The poverty line was initially based on an administrative village (*xiang*) average per capita income of less than RMB 120. In 1986, in order to cast a wider net of government assistance, the poverty line was revised to a county (*xian*) average of less than RMB 150 (RMB 200 in minority regions). Authorities in Guizhou indicate that since 1993 the official poverty line in minority regions has increased to the equivalent of RMB 300 per capita annual income.

15 See also GS 1993: 115–19. There is also less redistribution of grain from surplus regions to grain-poor regions within Guizhou. This is because of reforms meant to encourage "agricultural growth poles" in regions suitable for agricultural accumulation. These regions have less of their grain expropriated to poor regions, so that surplus can be invested in economic crops and rural industries.

16 Figures from *China Statistical Yearbook, 1995*. Reprinted in *Provincial China* 1996,1: 48–9.

17 See Chan (1994: 97–114) for a summary of the many ways urban residents have been subsidized by the Chinese state.

18 Interview with anonymous Tourism Bureau official (Guiyang, 10/28/96).

4 False modern triumphant

1 Although as a noun, *minzu* includes the Han, it appears that when used as an adjective the term rarely, if ever, refers to the Han. Just as "ethnic" is rarely thought of as applying to dominant racial groups (such as white Caucasians in the United States), *minzu* is often assumed to simply refer to minority groups.

That, at least, appeared to be the case at this conference. *Minzu* is a less exclusive term than "minority *minzu*," but the issues being discussed dealt quite exclusively with those concerning minority groups.

2   Tourists who made these comments were mostly domestic Chinese. Few of the foreigners present questioned whether what they were seeing was "authentic." For them, it would be difficult to imagine places even more remote than Shidong, with cultures even more "exotic."

3   This pattern has been described in other developing world situations in terms of "articulation of modes of production." Citing research by Wolpe, Hall provides the following statement which resonates strikingly with the situation in Guizhou:

> In South Africa, the tendency of capital accumulation to dissolve other modes is cross-cut and blocked by the counter-acting tendencies to conserve the non-capitalist economies – on the basis that the latter are articulated in a subordinate position to the former. Where capitalism develops by means, in part, of its articulation with non-capitalist modes, "the mode of political domination and the content of legitimating ideologies assume racial, ethnic and cultural forms and for the same reasons as in the case of imperialism . . . political domination takes on a colonial form." [Wolpe] adds: "The conservation of non-capitalist modes of production necessarily requires the development of ideologies and political policies which revolve around the segregation and preservation and control of African 'tribal' societies" – that is, the relation assumes the forms of ideologies constructed around ethnic, racial, national, and cultural ideological elements.
>
> (Hall 1979: 322)

My intent here, however, is not so much to present a theoretical argument about the nature of capitalist expansion than to simply point out the similarities between modernization in Guizhou and neo-colonial patterns of development in other parts of the world.

4   Contract producers earned RMB 3.5 per piece, with each piece selling for RMB 35. Working 12 hours non-stop, a woman could produce two pieces.

5   International arrivals to China are officially arranged into three categories: *waiguo* (foreign), *tongbao*, (compatriot), and *huaqiao* (overseas Chinese). *Huaqiao* is a generally insignificant category, applying only to citizens of the PRC who reside abroad, rather than people of Chinese descent who are citizens of other countries. *Tongbao* refers to those who the PRC considers citizens of China but happen to live in territory controlled by other governments, namely Taiwan, Hong Kong, and Macau. Foreigners make up the rest. The term "international tourists" is used throughout this chapter to refer to the aggregate of all three groups: foreigners, compatriots, and overseas citizens of the PRC.

6   By 1993 promoting Guizhou as an authentic breath of fresh air for modern tourists had become quite popular among tourism planners in general. The following piece of promotional literature is illustrative:

> Guizhou is both new and ancient. Development has started late here. Guizhou has been little affected by the pollution of modern industry, nor has it been assaulted (*chongji*) by modern civilization. Nature is still pristine here, and people still preserve their traditional cultures. There has been very little change here, little cultural corruption (*wenhua xunran*) from the outside. The moun-

tains are green, the water clear. And because they're spread out all over, one can see *minzu* customs just about anywhere.

Guizhou's environment gives people a sense of returning to nature (*huigui daziran*). This is something the people of the developed countries long for (*mengmei yiqiu*). And Guizhou's minorities inspire people to value the preservation of living culture (*huo wenhua*). In some parts of the world, all people have is staged culture (*wutai wenhua*). But in Guizhou, tourists can enter the villages and houses of the minorities, share their lives, understand them.

(Deng 1993: 8–9)

7 Five criteria must be met before a village can be put on the QTB's list: (1) Transportation must be convenient. The village must not be more than 35 kilometers from a hotel and tourists should not have to walk more than 2 kilometers to get there. (2) The village must have distinctive architecture or other cultural features which give it value as a tourist resource; the surrounding landscape must be picturesque. (3) The village must be prepared to receive tourists at any time. (4) The village must be recognized as a local festival site; it must serve as a central gathering point and be recognized locally as a center of cultural and social exchange. (5) Local leadership must be in favor of tourism development.

8 In Langde, an elaborate system of work points was devised to determine the distribution of the *jiedaifei* ("reception fee") to villagers. Different tasks earned different points and villagers kept points recorded in notebooks which were redeemed for cash from the village collective at the end of each month.

9 OTC paid Heitu and Changlinggang a *jiedaifei* of RMB 10 per tourist plus a RMB 60 *huodongfei* ("activity fee") for up to ten tourists, with an additional RMB 10 per tourist beyond that. According to the contract between OTC and Qingzhen municipality, where the villages are located, 20 per cent of the *jiedaifei* ("reception fee") went to the municipal *minwei* office, which played an active role in establishing the villages as tourist sites.

10 This is based on the internal price list from the only agency that was willing to reveal the actual amounts it paid for services in relation to the fees it charged foreign tourists. For example, a group of ten foreign tourists visiting an ethnic village for a day would pay RMB 1,500 in service fees to the travel agency (110 per person "comprehensive service fee" plus a 35 per person "ethnic activity fee"). According to local *jiedaifei* ("reception fee") arrangements, Langde would get 20 per cent (RMB 300) and Changlinggang 14.5 per cent (RMB 160). For a group of 20 foreigners, the percentages would be 10 per cent and 5.3 per cent respectively. For a group of 20 Chinese tourists, the percentages would be 18.8 per cent and 10 per cent respectively.

11 Given the high rates of inflation sustained throughout the mid- to late-1980s, actual increases in village incomes were considerably less than the official figures would indicate.

12 Compensation policies and rates for land vary considerably throughout China. In Longtan in the mid-1980s, I was told, villagers were paid RMB 2,000 per *mu* of Class A paddy, and 480 per *mu* of Class B and C slope-land. Huashishao, near Huangguoshu falls, was paid only RMB 700 per *mu* of Class A paddy in 1980, and 1,100 in 1984. Huashishao's villagers felt cheated by their low rate of compensation, and claimed that another village in the region had been paid RMB 9,000 per *mu* for land which was flooded for a reservoir. I was unable, however, to verify this claim.

5 Reclaiming the tourist landscape

1 At the end of 1996, Langde's souvenir shop had still not been built. The problem, apparently, was not so much lack of capital (the village's advocate from Beijing was providing most of the financing), but conflicts with the county tourism bureau, the prefectural cultural bureau and the QTB. Each of these higher entities had its own reasons: the county had its own plans to turn Langde into some kind of "vacation theme park" and was waiting until it had enough capital; the cultural bureau wanted to maintain Langde's preserved authenticity; and the QTB fell somewhere in between, seeking to maintain as much control as possible over developments in ethnic tourist villages, since it was felt that villagers did not understand how to create a tourist attraction.

2 This role was also highlighted by the fact that Shaman Chen owned the only pool table in the village, which he allowed other villagers to use freely. His "pool hall" became a very popular socializing spot for most of the young males in the village.

3 This is not exactly true. While Langde villagers provided the labor for these projects, Langde had received some RMB 459,000 in investments since 1984, most of which came from the QTB, the *minwei*, and the cultural bureau.

4 This figure is based on aggregate county data, provided in GX (1992).

5 This video was in fact quite revealing in terms of the ideals of *wenhua fazhan* discussed in the previous chapter. The film followed a trajectory of country-woman-ancient-traditional to city-man-contemporary-modern. Village women were first shown performing their "timeless" craft, but later the video's perspective broadened to the whole world by including all the places and forms to which batik had implicitly diffused from Chong'an. The last half of the video was instructional, featuring a very modern man with a shirt and tie giving step-by-step in-your-own-home instructions for making batik. The video ended with the comment that even though modern life isn't the same as traditional life, we can still learn from this ancient craft and apply it to our lives in new and different ways.

6 Tang Yin (1470–1524) was a Suzhou native and a leader in the Wu School of Chinese landscape painting. A hard-drinking eccentric, Tang had been educated for an official career and had even been placed first in the Jiangsu provincial exam in 1498. But when a cheating scandal prevented him from sitting for the highest exam in Beijing, he returned to Suzhou and took up painting as a means of securing respect and social status in society. See Cahill (1978: 193–200) and Clapp (1991).

Bibliography

Adams, K. (1990) "Cultural commoditization in Tana Toraja, Indonesia," *Cultural Survival* 14, 1: 31–4.
Agnew, J. (1989) "The devaluation of place in social science," in J. Agnew and J. Duncan (eds), *The Power of Place: Bringing Together Sociological and Geographical Imaginations*, Boston: Unwin Hyman, pp. 9–29.
Anagnost, A. (1993) "The nationscape: movement in the field of vision," *positions* 1, 3: 585–606.
Anderson, B. (1983) *Imagined Communities: Reflections on the Origin and Spread of Nationalism*, London: Verso.
Anshun Tourism Bureau (1993) *Anshunshi Lüyou Guihua* [Anshun Tourism Plan], Anshun: Anshun Tourism Bureau.
Appadurai, A. (1986) "Introduction: commodities and the politics of value," in A. Appadurai (ed.), *The Social Life of Things: Commodities in Cultural Perspective*, Cambridge: Cambridge University Press, pp. 3–63.
—— (1990) "Disjuncture and difference in the global cultural economy," *Public Culture* 2, 2: 1–24.
Ashworth, G. (1994) "From history to heritage – from heritage to identity: in search of concepts and models," in G. Ashworth and P. Larkham (eds), *Building a New Heritage: Tourism, Culture and Identity in the New Europe*, London: Routledge, pp. 13–30.
Ashworth, G. and Larkham, P. (1994) "A heritage for Europe: the need, the task, the contribution," in G. Ashworth and P. Larkham (eds), *Building a New Heritage: Tourism, Culture and Identity in the New Europe*, London: Routledge, pp. 1–12.
Bandy, J. (1996) "Managing the other of nature: sustainability, spectacle, and global regimes of capital in ecotourism," *Public Culture* 8, 3: 539–66.
Bao, J. (1995) "Zhuti Gongyuan de Fazhan jiqi Yingxiang Yanjiu: Yi Shenzhen Shi Wei Li [The development and influence of theme parks: a case-study of Shenzhen]," unpublished PhD dissertation, Zhongshan University, Guangzhou.
Berger, M. (1996) "Yellow mythologies: the East Asian miracle and post-cold war capitalism," *positions* 4, 1: 90–126.
Berman, M. (1970) *The Politics of Authenticity: Radical Individualism and the Emergence of Modern Society*, New York: Atheneum.
—— (1982) *All That Is Solid Melts Into Air: The Experience of Modernity*, New York: Simon & Schuster.
—— (1992) "Why modernism still matters," in J. Friedman and S. Lash (eds), *Modernity and Identity*, Oxford: Blackwell, pp. 33–58.

Britton, S. (1991) "Tourism, capital, and place; towards a critical geography of tourism," *Environment and Planning D: Society and Space* 9: 451–78.

Burgess, J. and Gold, J.R. (1985) "Place, the media, and popular culture," in J. Burgess and J.R. Gold (eds), *Geography, the Media, and Popular Culture*, London: Croom Helm, pp. 1–32.

Cahill, J. (1978) *Parting at the Shore: Chinese Painting of the Early and Middle Ming Dynasty, 1368–1580*, New York: Weatherhill.

Chan, K.W. (1994) *Cities with Invisible Walls: Reinterpreting Urbanization in Post-1949 China*, Hong Kong: Oxford University Press.

Chayanov, A.V. (1966) *The Theory of the Peasant Economy*, D. Thorner, B. Kerblay, and R. Smith (eds), Homewood, IL: RD Irwin.

Chen, K. (ed.) (1989) *Guizhou Sheng Nongcun Jingji Quhua* [Agricultural Economic Plan for Guizhou Province], Guiyang: Renmin.

Chen, N., Clark, C., Corneau, V., Gottschang, S. and Jeffery, L. (eds) (in press) *Ethnographies of the Urban in Late Twentieth Century China*, Durham, NC: Duke University Press.

Chen, Y. and Wang, J. (1990) "Guizhou jingji diyu fazhan zhanlue qutan [Preliminary inquiry into development strategies for Guizhou's economic regions]," *Guizhou Shifan Daxue Xuebao* [Journal of Guizhou Normal University] 63, 2: 1–6.

Chen, Y., Kuang, F. and Wang, J. (eds) (1993) *Guizhou Sheng Jingji Dili* [Economic Geography of Guizhou Province], Beijing: Xinhua.

Cheung, S. (1994) "Representation and negotiation of Ge identities in southeast Guizhou," paper delivered at the Annual Symposium in Chinese Studies, Berkeley, CA

Clapp, A. (1991) *The Painting of Tang Yin*, Chicago: University of Chicago Press.

Clark, H. (1993) "Sites of resistance: place, 'race,' and gender as sources of empowerment," in P. Jackson and J. Penrose (eds), *Constructions of Race, Place, and Nation*, London: UCL Press, pp. 121–42.

Clarke, S.R. (1907) "The province of Kweichow," in M. Broomhall (ed.), *The Chinese Empire: A General and Missionary Survey*. London: Morgan & Scott, pp. 251–70.

—— (1911) *Among the Tribes in South-West China*, London: Morgan & Scott.

Connell, J. (1993) "Bali revisited: death, rejuvenation, and the tourist cycle," *Environment and Planning D: Society and Space* 11: 641–61.

Conner, W. (1984) *The National Question in Marxist–Leninist Theory and Strategy*, Princeton, NJ: Princeton University Press.

Cresswell, T. (1996) *In Place/Out of Place*, Minneapolis: University of Minnesota Press.

Crick, M. (1989) "Representations of international tourism in the social science: sun, sex, sights, savings, and servility," *Annual Review of Anthropology* 18: 307–44.

Croll, E. (1994) *From Heaven to Earth: Images and Experiences of Development in China*, London: Routledge.

Culler, J. (1981) "Semiotics of tourism," *American Journal of Semiotics* 1, 1–2: 127–40.

Cumings, B. (1993) "Rimspeak," in A. Dirlik (ed.), *What is in a Rim? Critical Perspectives on the Pacific Region Idea*, Boulder, CO: Westview, pp. 29–47.

Davis, D., Kraus, R., Naughton, B. and Perry, E. (eds) (1995) *Urban Spaces in Contemporary China: The Potential for Autonomy and Community in Post-Mao China*, Cambridge: Cambridge University Press.

Deng, Z. (1993) "Shanguo 'tian bao,' de shuguang: guanyu Guizhou fazhan lüyouye yu kaifa ziyuan zhi yantao [Dawn of a mountain kingdom paradise: a study of exploiting resources and developing Guizhou's tourism industry]," paper presented at the Mainland-Taiwan Tourism Conference, Taibei.

Diamond, N. (1988) "The Miao and poison: interactions along China's southwestern frontier," *Ethnology* 27, 1: 1–25.

—— (1995) "Defining the Miao: Ming, Qing, and contemporary views," in S. Harrell (ed.), *Cultural Encounters on China's Ethnic Frontiers*, Seattle: University of Washington Press, pp. 92–116.

Dirks, N. (ed.). (1992) *Colonialism and Culture*, Ann Arbor: University of Michigan Press.

Dirlik, A. (1997) "Critical reflections on 'Chinese Capitalism,' as paradigm," *Identities* 3, 3: 303–30.

Dreyer, J.T. (1976) *China's Forty Millions: Minority Nationalities and National Integration in the People's Republic of China*, Cambridge, MA: Harvard University Press.

Eagleton, T. (1981) *Walter Benjamin, or Towards a Revolutionary Criticism*, London: Verso.

Eco, U. (1986) *Travels in Hyperreality*, New York: Harcourt, Brace, Jovanovich.

Edmonds, R.L. (1994) *Patterns of China's Lost Harmony: A Survey of the Country's Environmental Degradation and Protection*, London: Routledge.

Eldridge, J. and Eldridge (1994) *Raymond Williams: Making Connections*, London: Routledge.

Engels, F. (1884) *The Origin of the Family, Private Property, and the State*, London: Lawrence & Wishart.

Entrikin, J. N. (1991) *The Betweenness of Place: Towards a Geography of Modernity*, Baltimore: Johns Hopkins University Press.

Exley, H.J. (1994) *Proposal for Far Village* (unpublished manuscript).

Fei, X. (1981) *Toward a People's Anthropology*. Beijing: New World Press.

Feifer, M. (1985) *Going Places: Tourism in History*, New York: Stein & Day.

Ferdinand, P. (1989) "The economic and financial dimension," in D.S.G. Goodman (ed.), *China's Regional Development*, London: Routledge, pp. 38–56.

Fink, K. J. (1996) "Review essay – Goethe studies in North America," *Eighteenth-Century Life* 20, 1: 93–100.

Foucault, M. (1977) *Discipline and Punish: The Birth of the Prison* (trans. A. Sheridan), London: Allen Lane.

Frobel, F., Heinrichs, J. and Kreye, O. (1980) *The New International Division of Labor*, Cambridge: Cambridge University Press.

Giddens, A. (1990) *The Consequences of Modernity*, Stanford, CA: Stanford University Press.

GN (*Guizhou Nianjian* [Guizhou Yearbook]) (1996) Guiyang: Renmin.

Goethe, J.W. (1983) *Collected Works, Vol. 1*, V. Lange *et al.* (eds), New York: Suhrkamp.

Goodman, D.S.G. (1983) "Guizhou and the People's Republic of China: the development of an internal colony," in D. Drakakis-Smith and S. Williams (eds), *Internal Colonialism: Essays Around a Theme*, London: Institute of British Geographers, Developing Areas Research Group, Monograph No. 3, pp. 107–24.

—— (1986) *Centre and Province in the PRC; Sichuan and Guizhou, 1955–1965*, Cambridge: Cambridge University Press.

Graburn, N. (1978) "Tourism: the sacred journey," in V. Smith (ed.), *Hosts and Guest: The Anthropology of Tourism*, Oxford: Blackwell, pp. 17–31.

—— (1983) "The anthropology of tourism," *Annals of Tourism Research* 10: 9–33.

Gramsci, A. (1971) *Selections from the Prison Notebooks*, New York, International.

Greenwood, D. (1972) "Tourism as an agent of change: a Spanish Basque case," *Ethnology* 11: 80–91.

—— (1977) "Culture by the pound: an anthropological perspective on tourism as cultural commoditization," in V. Smith (ed.), *Hosts and Guests*, Philadelphia: University of Pennsylvania Press, pp. 129–38.

Gregory, D. (1995) "Imaginative geographies," *Progress in Human Geography* 19, 4: 447–85.

GS (*Guizhou Shengqing* [Guizhou Provincial Gazetteer]) (1993) Guiyang: Renmin.

GTN (*Guizhou Tongji Nianjian* [Guizhou Statistical Yearbook]) (1993) Beijing: Guojia Tongjiju.

Guizhou Sheng Guotu Zongti Guihua [Guizhou Provincial Comprehensive Development Plan] (1992) Beijing: Zhongguo Jihua Weiyuanhui.

Guizhou Sheng Minzu Wenhua Xuehui [Guizhou Provincial *Minzu* Cultural Studies Association] (1991) *Zouxiang Shijie Dachao* [Crossing the Great Bridge to the World], Guiyang: Minzu.

Guldin, G.E. (ed.) (1997) *Farewell to Peasant China: Rural Urbanization and Social Change in the Late Twentieth Century*, Armonk, NY: M.E. Sharpe.

Guo, L. (1993) personal interview (Beijing: 9 November 1993).

GX (*Guizhou Xianqing* [Guizhou County Gazetteer]) (1992) Beijing: Zhongguo Tongji.

Hall, S. (1979) "Race, articulation and societies structured in dominance," in *Sociological Theories: Race and Colonialism*, Paris: UNESCO, pp. 305–45.

Harrell, S. (1990) "Ethnicity, local interests, and the state: Yi communities in southwest China," *Comparative Studies of Society and History* 32, 3: 515–45.

Harrell, S. (ed.) (1995) *Cultural Encounters on China's Ethnic Frontiers*, Seattle: University of Washington Press.

Harvey, D. (1989) *The Condition of Postmodernity*, Oxford: Blackwell.

—— (1995) "Militant particularism and global ambition: the conceptual politics of place, space, and environment in the work of Raymond Williams," *Social Text* 42: 69–98.

Hawkes, D. (1985) "Chu Ci (Songs of the South)," in D. Hawkes (ed. and trans.), *Chu Ci (Songs of the South)*, London: Penguin.

Heberer, T. (1989) *China and its National Minorities: Autonomy or Assimilation?*, Armonk, NY: M.E. Sharpe.

Hendrischke, H. (1997) "Guangxi Zhuang Autonomous Region: towards Southwest China and Southeast Asia," in D.S.G. Goodman (ed.), *China's Provinces in Reform: Class, Community, and Political Culture*, London: Routledge, pp. 17–47.

Heng, G. and Devan, J. (1995) "State fatherhood: the politics of nationalism, sexuality, and race in Singapore," in A. Ong and M. Peletz (eds), *Bewitching Women, Pious Men: Gender and Body Politics in Southeast Asia*, Berkeley: University of California Press, pp. 195–215.

Herzfeld, M. (1991) *A Place in History: Social and Monumental Time in a Cretan Town*, Princeton, NJ: Princeton University Press.

Hill, R.D. (1993) "People, land, and an equilibrium trap: Guizhou, China," *Pacific Viewpoint* 34, 1: 1–24.

Hitchcock, M., King, V. and Parnwell, M. (eds) (1993) *Tourism in South-East Asia*, London: Routledge.

Ho, P. (1959) *Studies on the Population of China, 1368–1953*, Cambridge, MA: Harvard University Press.

Hobsbawm, E. (1983) "Introduction: inventing traditions," in E. Hobsbawm and T. Ranger (eds), *The Invention of Tradition*, Cambridge: Cambridge University Press, pp. 1–14.

Horne, D. (1984) *The Great Museum: The Re-presentation of History*, London: Pluto.

—— (1992) *The Intelligent Tourist*, McMahons Point, NSW: Margaret Gee.

Hosie, A. (1890) *Three Years in Western China: A Narrative of Three Journeys in Ssu-ch'uan, Kuei-chow, and Yun-nan*, London: George Philip.

—— (1914) *On the Trail of the Opium Poppy: A Narrative of Travel in the Chief Opium-producing Provinces of China*, London: George Philip.

Hsieh, S. (1995) "On the dynamics of Tai/Dai-Lue ethnicity: an ethnohistorical analysis," in S. Harrell (ed.), *Cultural Encounters on China's Frontiers*, Seattle: University of Washington Press, pp. 301–28.

Hu, S. (1997) "Confucianism and Western democracy," *Journal of Contemporary China* 6, 15: 347–63.

Huang, B. (1991) "Lun Guizhou minzu jingji 'cheng zhang dian,' de xingcheng [On the formation of 'growth poles,' in Guizhou's *minzu* economy]," in *Guizhou Sheng Shaoshu Minzu Jingji Yanjiu* [Economic Research on Guizhou's Minority Minzu], Guiyang: Renmin, pp. 69–76.

Huang, P.C.C. (1990) *The Peasant Family and Rural Development in the Yangzi Delta, 1350–1988*, Stanford, CA: Stanford University Press.

Huangping Xianzhi [Huangping County Gazetteer] (1992) Guiyang: Renmin.

Iyer, P. (1988) *Video Night in Kathmandu*, New York: Vintage.

Jameson, F. (1984) "Postmodernism, or the cultural logic of late capitalism," *New Left Review* 146: 53–92.

Jenks, R. D. (1994) *Insurgency and Social Disorder in Guizhou: The "Miao," Rebellion, 1854–1873*, Honolulu: University of Hawaii Press.

Jiang, Y. (1985) "Cong Guizhou minzu shibie gongzuo tanqi [Discussion on the basis of Guizhou's ethnic identification work]," *Minzu Yanjiu Jikan* [Nationalities Research Quarterly] 2: 303–18.

Johnson, M. (1994) "Making time: historic preservation and the space of nationality," *positions* 2, 2: 177–249.

Kammerer, C.A. (1988) "Territorial imperatives: Akha ethnic identity and Thailand's national integration," in R. Guidieri *et al.* (eds), *Ethnicities and Nations*, Austin: University of Texas Press, pp. 259–91.

Kaplan, C. (1996) *Questions of Travel: Postmodern Discourses of Displacement*, Durham, NC: Duke University Press.

Keyes, C. (ed.) (1979) *Ethnic Adaptation and Identity: The Karen on the Thai Frontier with Burma*, Philadelphia: ISHI Press.

King, V. (1993) "Tourism and culture in Malaysia," in M. Hitchcock *et al.* (eds), *Tourism in South-East Asia*, London: Routledge, pp. 99–116.

Kirkby, R. and Cannon, T. (1989) "Introduction," in D.S.G. Goodman (ed.), *China's Regional Development*, London: Routledge, pp. 1–19.

Knox, P. and Agnew, J. (1994) *Geography of the World Economy*, 2nd Edition, London: Edward Arnold.

Kornai, J. (1986) *Contradictions and Dilemmas: Studies on the Socialist Economy and Society*, Cambridge, MA: MIT Press.

Lange, V. (1968) "Introduction," in V. Lange (ed.), *Goethe: A Collection of Critical Essays*, Englewood Cliffs, NJ: Prentice Hall, pp. 1–9.

Lardy, N. (1978) *Economic Growth and Distribution in China*, Cambridge: Cambridge University Press.

Lash, S. and J. Friedman. (1992) "Introduction: subjectivity and modernity's Other," in S. Lash and J. Friedman (eds), *Modernity and Identity*, Oxford: Blackwell, pp. 1–30.

Lea, J. (1988) *Tourism and Development in the Third World*, London: Routledge.

Lee, J. (1982) "Food supply and population growth in southwest China," *Journal of Asian Studies* 41, 4: 711–46.

Lefebvre, H. (1991) *The Production of Space* (trans. D. Nicholson-Smith), Oxford: Blackwell.

Lei, G. (1992) "Shuizu wenhua yu xiandaihua," *Guizhou Minzu Yanjiu* [Guizhou *Minzu* Research] 1: 33–6.

Leishan Tourism Bureau (1996) Bureau director, personal interview (Leishan, 1 Novermber 1996).

Leung, H.C.K. and Chan, K.W. (1986) "Chinese regional development policies: a comparative reassessment," paper delivered at the Annual Meeting of the Canadian Asian Studies Association, Winnepeg, Canada.

Li, R. (1991) "Guizhou shaoshu minzu zizhi difang jingji shehui fazhan qingkuan cunzai wenti ji jinhou fazhan de jianyi [Current conditions, remaining problems, and suggestions for future development in the socio-economic development of Guizhou's minority nationality autonomous regions]," in *Guizhou Sheng Shaoshu Minzu Jingji Yanjiu* [Economic Research on Guizhou's Minority Nationalities], Guiyang: Minzu, pp. 1–9.

Liang, F. (1993) "Guizhou's ordinance industry turns civil," *Beijing Review* (October 11–17): 12–15.

Lin, J. (1992) "Qingchao qianqi wanshan Guizhou sheng jianzhi, kaipi 'Miaojiang,' jiqi yingxiang [Influences of the Qing's early perfection in integrating and opening the 'Miao borderlands,']," *Guizhou Minzu Yanjiu* [Guizhou *Minzu* Research] 4: 50–7.

Lin, Y. (1941) "The Miao-Man peoples of Kweichow," *Harvard Journal of Asiatic Studies* 5, 3: 261–344.

Liu, X. (1994) *Guizhou Luyou Puluren* [Pioneers of Guizhou tourism], Beijing: Zhongguo Luyou.

Longhurst, B. (1991) "Raymond Williams and local cultures," *Environment and Planning A* 23, 2: 229–38.

Lowenthal, D. (1985) *The Past is a Foreign Country*, Cambridge: Cambridge University Press.

Lukács, G. (1968) *Goethe and his Age* (trans. R. Anchor), London: Merlin.

—— (1972) *Studies in European Realism: A Sociological Survey of the Writings of Balzac, Stendhal, Zola, Tolstoy, Gorki, and Others* (trans. E. Bone), London: Merlin.

MacCannell, D. (1989) *The Tourist: A New Theory of the Leisure Class*, Rev. Edition, New York: Schocken.

Massey, D. (1992) "A place called home?," *New Formations* 17: 3–17.

—— (1993) "Power geometry and a progressive sense of place," in J. Bird, B. Curtis, T. Putnam, G. Robertson and L. Tickner (eds), *Mapping the Futures: Local Cultures, Global Change*, London: Routledge, pp. 59–69.

Michaud, J. (1993) "Tourism as catalyst of economic and political change; the case of highland minorities in Ladakh (India) and northern Thailand," *Internationales Asienforum* 24, 1: 21–43.

Mitchell, T. (1988) *Colonizing Egypt*, Cambridge: Cambridge University Press.

Morgan, L.H. (1877) *Ancient Society*, Cambridge, MA: Harvard University Press.

Naisbitt, J. (1995) *Megatrends Asia: The Eight Asian Megatrends that are Changing the World*, London: Nicholas Brealy.

Nash, D. (1984) "The ritualization of tourism: comment on Graburn's 'The anthropology of tourism'," *Annals of Tourism Research* 11: 503–7.

Naughton, B. (1988) "The third front: defense industrialization in the Chinese interior," *China Quarterly* 115: 351–86.

Oakes, T. (1995) "Shen Congwen's literary regionalism and the gendered landscape of Chinese modernity," *Geografiska Annaler B*, 77, 2: 93–107.

Okamura, J. (1981) "Situational ethnicity," *Ethnic and Racial Studies* 4, 4: 452–64.

Ong, A. (1996) "Anthropology, China, modernities: the geopolitics of cultural knowledge," in H. Moore (ed.), *The Future of Anthropological Knowledge*, London: Routledge, pp. 60–92.

—— (1997) "Chinese modernities: narratives of nation and of capitalism," in A. Ong and D. Nonini (eds), *Ungrounded Empires: The Cultural Politics of Chinese Transnationalism*, London: Routledge, pp. 171–202.

Oppermann, M. (1992) "International tourism and regional development in Malaysia," *Tijdschrift voor Econ. en Soc. Geografie* 83, 3: 226–33.

Oudiette, V. (1990) "International tourism in China," *Annals of Tourism Research* 17: 123–32.

Palmer, C. (1994) "Tourism and colonialism; the experience of the Bahamas," *Annals of Tourism Research* 21, 4: 792–811.

Pemberton, J. (1994) "Recollections from 'Beautiful Indonesia' (somewhere beyond the postmodern)," *Public Culture* 6(2): 241–62.

Perkins, D. (1969) *Agricultural Development in China, 1368–1968*, Chicago: Aldine.

Picard, M. (1993) "Cultural tourism in Bali; national integration and regional differentiation," in M. Hitchcock, V. King and M. Parnwell (eds), *Tourism in South-East Asia*, London: Routledge, pp. 71–98.

Popper, K. (1962) *Conjectures and Refutations*, London: Routledge.

Pred, A. and M. Watts. (1992) *Reworking Modernity: Capitalisms and Symbolic Discontent*, New Brunswick, NJ: Rutgers University Press.

Qiandongnan Miaozu Dongzu Zizhizhou Gaikuang [Summary of Qiandongnan Miao and Dong Autonomous Prefecture] (1986) Guiyang: Renmin.

Rabbetts, J. (1989) *From Hardy to Faulkner: Wessex to Yoknapatawpha*, New York: St Martin's Press.

Rabinow, P. (1989) *French Modern: Norms and Forms of the Social Environment*, Cambridge, MA: MIT Press.

Ran, M. (1991) "Guizhou sheng shaoshu minzu pinkun diqu jingji kaifa de xianzhuang, zhiyue yinsu yu duice [Economic development in Guizhou's impoverished minority *minzu*regions: present situation, causal factors, and countermeasures]," in *Kaifa Da Xinan; Guizhou Guangxi Xizang Juan*[Exploit the Great Southwest; Guizhou, Guangxi, Tibet Edition], Beijing: Xuefan, pp. 218–32.

Relph, E. (1976) *Place and Placelessness*, London: Pion.

Rofel, L. (1992) "Rethinking modernity: space and factory discipline in China," *Cultural Anthropology* 7, 1: 93–114.

Rose, G. (1993) *Feminism and Geography*, Cambridge: Polity Press.

—— (1994) "The cultural politics of place: local representation and oppositional discourse in two films," *Transactions of the Institute of British Geographers* 19: 46–60.

Said, E. (1979) *Orientalism*, New York: Vintage.

—— (1993) *Culture and Imperialism*, New York: Vintage.

Salisbury, H. (1985) *The Long March: The Untold Story*, New York: Harper & Row.

Schattschneider, E. (1996) "The labor of mountains," *Positions* 4, 1: 1–31.

Schein, L. (1989) "The dynamics of cultural revival among the Miao in Guizhou," in C. Chao and N. Tapp (eds), *Ethnicity and Ethnic Groups in China*, Hong Kong: Univeristy of Hong Kong Press, pp. 199–212.

—— (1993) "Popular Culture and the Production of Difference; the Miao and China," unpublished PhD dissertation, University of California at Berkeley.

Sears, J. (1989) *Sacred Places: American Tourist Attractions in the Nineteenth Century*, Oxford: Oxford University Press.

Shaw, G. and Williams, A. (1994) *Critical Issues in Tourism: A Geographical Perspective*, Oxford: Blackwell.

Shen, C.W. (1934) *Congwen Zizhuan* [Congwen's Autobiography], Shanghai.

——(1982) *Recollections of West Hunan* (trans. G. Yang), Beijing: Panda.

Shen, P. and Cheung, Y. (eds) (1992) *China Folk Culture Villages*, Hong Kong: China Travel Advertising.

Shih, S. (1995) "The trope of 'Mainland China' in Taiwan's media," *positions* 3, 1: 149–83.

Sibley, D. (1995) *Geographies of Exclusion: Society and Difference in the West*, London: Routledge.

Silver, I. (1993) "Marketing authenticity in Third World countries," *Annals of Tourism Research* 20: 302–18.

Sim, S. (1994) *Georg Lukács*, New York: Harvester Wheatsheaf.

Siu, H. (1989) *Agents and Victims in South China: Accomplices in Rural Revolution*, New Haven, CT: Yale University Press.

Skinner, G. W. (ed.) (1977) *The City in Late Imperial China*, Stanford, CA: Stanford University Press.

—— (1985) "The structure of Chinese history," *Journal of Asian Studies* 44, 2: 271–92.

Smith, D. (1989) "Relating to Wales," in T. Eagleton (ed.), *Raymond Williams: Critical Perspectives*, Cambridge: Polity Press, pp. 34–53.

Soja, E. (1989) *Postmodern Geographies: The Reassertion of Space in Critical Social Theory*, London: Verso.

Solinger, D. (1977) *Regional Government and Political Integration in Southwest China, 1949–1954*, Berkeley: University of California Press.

Spence, J. D. (1981) *The Gate of Heavenly Peace: The Chinese and their Revolution, 1895–1980*, New York: Penguin.

Spencer, J. R. (1940) "Kueichou: an internal Chinese colony," *Pacific Affairs* 13: 162–72.

Stevens, S. (1991) "Sherpas, tourism, and cultural change in Nepal's Mt. Everest region," *Journal of Cultural Geography* 12, 1: 39–58.

Sun, J. (1994) Guizhou Tourism Bureau Director of Promotion and Marketing, personal interview (Guiyang, 1 August 1994).

Taijiang *Minwei* (1996) Taijiang *Minzu* Affairs Commission Director, personal interview (Taijiang, 4 November 1996).

Tang, W. (1991) *Regional Uneven Development in China, with Special Reference to the Period between 1978 and 1988*, Hong Kong: Chinese University of Hong Kong, Department of Geography Occasional Paper No. 110.

Touraine, A. (1995) *Critique of Modernity* (trans. D. Macey), Oxford: Blackwell.

Turnbridge, J. (1994) "Whose heritage? Global problem, European nightmare," in G. Ashworth and P. Larkham (eds), *Building a New Heritage: Tourism, Culture and Identity in the New Europe*, London: Routledge, pp. 123–34.

Turner, L. and J. Ash. (1975) *The Golden Hordes: International Tourism and the Pleasure Periphery*, London: Constable.

Unger, J. (1994) "'Rich man, poor man': the making of new classes in the countryside," in D.S.G. Goodman and B. Hooper (eds), *China's Quiet Revolution: New Interactions between State and Society*, Melbourne: Longman Cheshire, pp. 43–63.

Urry, J. (1990) *The Tourist Gaze: Leisure and Travel in Contemporary Societies*, London: Sage.

—— (1995) *Consuming Places*, London: Routledge.

Van den Berghe, P. (1992) "Tourism and the ethnic division of labor," *Annals of Tourism Research* 19: 234–49.

Van den Berghe, P. and Keyes, C. (1984) "Tourism and re-created ethnicity," *Annals of Tourism Research* 11: 343–52.

Wang, S. (1989) *Dongzu Wenhua Yu Xisu* [Culture and Customs of the Dong], Guiyang: Minzu.

Wang, X. and Bai, N. (1991) *The Poverty of Plenty* (trans. A. Knox), New York: St Martin's Press.

Wang, Y. (1973) *Land Taxation in Imperial China, 1750–1911*, Cambridge, MA: Harvard University Press.

Waters, M. (1990) *Ethnic Options: Choosing Identities in America*, Berkeley: University of California Press.

Whitney, J. (1980) "East Asia," in G. Klee (ed.), *World Systems of Traditional Resource Management*, Silver Spring, MD: V.H. Winston, pp. 101–29.

Widdowson, P. (1989) *Hardy in History: A Study in Literary Sociology*, London: Routledge.

Weins, H. J. (1967) *Han Chinese Expansion in South China*, Hampten, CT: Shoe String Press.

Williams, R. (1960) *Border Country*, London: Hogarth.

—— (1966) *The English Novel: From Dickens to Hardy*, Oxford: Oxford University Press.

—— (1973) *The Country and the City*, Oxford: Oxford University Press.

—— (1977) *Marxism and Literature*, Oxford: Oxford University Press.

Wilson, A. (1994) "The view from the road: recreation and tourism," in S. Norris (ed.), *Discovered Country: Tourism and Survival in the American West*, Albuquerque: Stone Ladder Press, pp. 3–20.

Wilson, D. (1993) "Time and tide in the anthropology of tourism," in M. Hitchcock, V. King, and M. Parnwell (eds), *Tourism in South-East Asia*, London: Routledge, pp. 32–47.

Wilson, R. (1995) "Bloody Mary meets Lois-Ann Yamanaka: imagining Hawaiian locality from *South Pacific* to Bamboo Ridge," *Public Culture* 8, 1: 127–58.

Wong, C. (1991) "Central-local relations in an era of fiscal decline: the paradox of fiscal decentralization in post-Mao China," *China Quarterly* 128: 691–715.

Wong, C. (ed.) (1995) *Financing Local Government in the People's Republic of China* [Draft version], Manila: Asian Development Bank.

Wong, C., Heady C. and Woo, W.T. (1995) *Fiscal Management and Economic Reform in the People's Republic of China*, Hong Kong: Oxford University Press.

Wood, R. (1984) "Ethnic tourism, the state, and cultural change in Southeast Asia," *Annals of Tourism Research*, 11: 353–74.

—— (1993) "Tourism, culture, and the sociology of development," in M. Hitchcock, V. King, and M. Parnwell (eds), *Tourism in South-East Asia*, London: Routledge, pp. 48–70.

—— (1997) "Tourism and the state: ethnic options and constructions of otherness," in M. Picard and R. Wood (eds), *Tourism, Ethnicity, and the State in Asian and Pacific Societies*, Honolulu: University of Hawaii Press, pp. 1–34.

World Bank (1992) *China; Reform and the Role of the Plan in the 1990s*, Washington, DC: The World Bank.

Xu, G. (1996) "Tourism and Local Economic Development in China: Case Studies of Guilin, Suzhou, and Beidaihe," unpublished PhD dissertation, Johannes Gutenberg University.

Yang, G. (1991) *Xian Lüyou Kaifa yu Buju* [Development and Distribution of Tourism Resources in Southwest China], Beijing: Zhongguo Kexueyuan Jishu Chubanshe.

Yang, M. (1997) "Mass media and transnational subjectivity in Shanghai: notes on (re)cosmopolitanism in a Chinese metropolis," in A. Ong and D. Nonini (eds), *Ungrounded Empires: The Cultural Politics of Chinese Transnationalism*, London: Routledge, pp. 287–319.

Ye, S. (1993) "Urban systems and the exploitation of natural resources in Southwestern China," in C. Kok *et al.* (eds), *Arbeiten für Chinaforschung*, Bremen: Zentraldruckerei der Universität Bremen, pp. 125–35.

Yeoh, B.S.A. and P. Teo. (1996) "From Tiger Balm Gardens to Dragon World: philanthropy and profit in the making of Singapore's first cultural theme park," *Geografiska Annaler* 78, 1: 27–42.

Yu, H. (1997) "Shilun Qing dai Yong Zheng shiqi Guizhou de gai tu gui liu [An examination of 'gai tu gui liu' in Guizhou during the Yongzheng period of the Qing]," *Guizhou Minzu Yanjiu* [Guizhou *Minzu* Research], 2: 26–34.

Zhang, N. (1995) "Minzu zizhi difang gaige kaifang shiyanqu de zhengce yanjiu [Policy research on open reform experimental zones in *minzu* autonomous regions]," *Guizhou Minzu Yanjiu* [Guizhou *Minzu* Research] 1: 31–3.

Zhang, S. (1993) "Zhenjian Tiaochu Bashiwan," in *Zhongguo Qiye Yinghao*, Beijing: Qiye Guanli, pp. 23–8.

Zhang, X. (1997) *Chinese Modernism in the Era of Reforms: Cultural Fever, Avant-Garde Fiction, and the New Chinese Cinema*, Durham, NC: Duke University Press.

Zhang, Y. (1995) "An assessment of China's tourism resources," in A. Lew and L. Yu (eds), *Tourism in China*, Boulder, CO: Westview, pp. 41–59.

Zhang, Z. (1966) *The Party and the National Question in China [A Discussion of the National Question in the Chinese Revolution and of Actual Nationalities Policy* (trans. G. Moseley), Cambridge, MA: MIT Press.

Zhou, C., He, C. and Zhang, Y. (eds) (1987) *Guizhou Jindaishi* [A Recent History of Guizhou], Guiyang: Renmin.

ZLN (*Zhongguo Lüyou Nianjian* [China Tourism Yearbook]) (1993) Beijing: National Tourism Administration.

ZTN (*Zhongguo Tongji Nianjian* [China Statistical Yearbook]) (1995) Beijing: Guojia Tongjiju.

Zurick, D. (1992) "Adventure travel and sustainable tourism in the peripheral economy of Nepal," *Annals of the Association of American Geographers* 82, 4: 608–28.

—— (1995) *Errant Journeys; Adventure Travel in a Modern Age*, Austin: University of Texas Press.

Newspapers and Pictorials

China Daily (Beijing)
Guizhou Dushi Wanbao [Guizhou Capital Nightly] (Guiyang)
Guizhou Huabao [Guizhou Pictorial] (Guiyang)
Guizhou Ribao [Guizhou Daily] (Guiyang)
Qiandongnan Bao [Qiandongnan Daily] (Kaili)
Xingdao Ribao [Xingdao Daily] (Hong Kong)

Index

Note: Page numbers in *italics* refer to figures.

Horne, D. 19, 33–4, 133
Hosie, A. 85, 99, 100
Huang, P. 97, 99
Huangguoshu Falls 125, 128–9, 159
Huangguoshu Tourism Administration
   (HTA) 183–4
Huashishao *see* tourist villages
Hubei 109, 214
Hunan 98, 109, 214

Indonesia 35, 36–7, 38–9
industrialization 107–11, 112
Ironbridge, Great Britain 33–4

Jackson, J. 21–2
Jameson, F. 67
Japan 40; tourists in Guizhou *3*, 163,
   169, 199
Jenks, R. 91, 92, 94, 95, 97
Jiang Yongxing 105
Jiang Zemin 124, 228
Jiangsu 112
Jiangxi 214
Johnson, M. 77–80
Jun, M. 216–20, 227–8

Kaili (city) 138, 139, 147, 177, 196, 198,
   207, 212, 222; crafts market 152–3;
   crafts production 150, 155;
   development zones 123; drum tower
   210; employment of village youth
   174, 199; ethnic tourism development
   127, 171, 172; tour guides 208; travel
   agencies 169, 176
Kaplan, C. 19, 24
Keyes, C. 66
Kirkby, R. 107
Korean Folk Village *see* theme parks
Kornai, J. 108
Kunming, Yunnan 88, 110, 165, 180;
   employment of Guizhou youth 174;
   portal for Southeast Asian tourists
   167; vacation resorts 127

Ladakh 132, 134
Langde *see* tourist villages
late capitalism 65
Lee, J. 89, 90
Leishan (county) 116
Lhasa, Tibet 107
Lin, J. 95, 97
Lin, Y. 92, 93
Liupanshui (city) 113

local nationalism 102–3, 105
Longchuanjie (Dragon Boat Festival)
   146–7, 215–16
Longgong *see* Dragon Palace
Longtan *see* tourist villages
Lowenthal, D. 28, 73
Lukács, G. 29

MacCannell, D. 16, 19, 23–4, 27
Malaysia 38, 42
market socialism 52, 121–5, 126
Marx, K. 17, 18, 62, 104, 140
Massey, D. 62–3
Miao *see minzu* groups
Miao borderlands *see Miaojiang*
Miaojiang (Miao borderlands) 95–7, 98,
   170, 172, 174, 193
Michaud, J. 132, 133, 134
minzu ("nationality") 8–9, 53, 103–6,
   192, 193; and Chinese modernity
   135–6, 137–40, 158; clothing fashion
   show 137–8; cultural
   commodification of 148–57; cultural
   preservation 178–80; cultural
   production 140–8; tourism 1–6, 126,
   158, 159–61, 166–7, 168–75, 180–5,
   193–221; *see also minzu* groups
minzu groups 8–9, 53, 103–6, 138, 149,
   155; Bouyei 9, 105, 127, 144, 179;
   Bouyei as tourist attraction 183–5;
   Dong 9, *54*, 105, 127, 137, 139, 143,
   147, 177, 179, 204–5; Dong New Year
   celebration 143; Dong as tourist
   attraction 49, 206–13; Ge 105, 214;
   Ge crafts 216–18; Ge and tourism
   development 220–1; Ge as tourist
   attraction 217; Gelao 105; Miao 9,
   55, 91–3, 95–7, 104–6, 137, 138–9,
   171, 193–204, 212, 214, 216, 220, 225,
   227; Miao crafts 149–57; Miao
   festivals 145–8, 215–16; Miao, land
   alienation among 91, 92, 97; Miao,
   poverty of 86, 97, 98, 101, 106; Miao
   "raw" and "cooked" 95; Miao
   rebellion 86, 91, 95, 96–7, 194, 196;
   Miao as tourist attraction 1–6, 49,
   126, 127, 144, 159, 169, 171, 173–4,
   179–83, 197–204, 217; Yi 127
minzu shibie see ethnic identification
   project
modernity 7, 13–20; "alternative" 40–5,
   48, 56; Chinese 45–7, 52–3, 56–7, 139,
   228–9; "false" vs "authentic" 7,
   10–11, 76, 223–4, 229; and place